A New Old Damascus

Indiana Series in Middle East Studies

Mark Tessler, general editor

Indiana University Press • Bloomington and Indianapolis

A NEW OLD DAMASCUS

Authenticity and Distinction in Urban Syria

Christa Salamandra

This book is a publication of
Indiana University Press
601 North Morton Street
Bloomington, IN 47404-3797 USA

http://iupress.indiana.edu
Telephone orders   800-842-6796
Fax orders   812-855-7931
Orders by e-mail   iuporder@indiana.edu

The paper used in this publication meets the minimum
requirements of American National Standard for Information
Sciences—Permanence of Paper for Printed Library Materials,
ANSI Z39.48-1984.

Manufactured in the United States of America

Library of Congress Cataloging-in-Publication Data

Salamandra, Christa.
  A new old Damascus : authenticity and distinction in urban Syria /
Christa Salamandra.
     p. cm. — (Indiana series in Middle East studies)
  Includes bibliographical references and index.
  ISBN 0-253-34467-0 (cloth : alk. paper) — ISBN 0-253-21722-9
(pbk. : alk. paper)
  1. Ethnology—Syria—Damascus. 2. Social structure—Syria—
Damascus. 3. Group identity—Syria—Damascus. 4. Damascus
(Syria)—Social life and customs. 5. Damascus (Syria)—Religious life
and customs. I. Title. II. Series.
  GN625.S95S35 2004
  305.8'0095691'44—dc22

                          2004009433

1 2 3 4 5 09 08 07 06 05 04

To my parents

Jack and Elizabeth Salamandra,
and in memory of my sister Bethann.

Contents

Acknowledgments

This book is drawn from research conducted in Damascus for twenty-four months, from 1992 to 1994, with a monthlong return visit in February–March 1996. Fieldwork was supported by grants from the Social Science Research Council and the Linacre House Trust, and sponsored by the Syrian Directorate of Antiquities.

To adequately thank all the individuals who helped would require at least a name for every page. In Damascus, special thanks go to Iman Abdul Rahim for intellectual input and enduring friendship. Rebecca Foote, Hana Nahas, Mary Tahan, Steven Tamari, and Elizabeth Thompson provided numerous contacts during the initial stage of fieldwork. The many Syrians who lent their time and energy I must thank anonymously, but their patience and generosity warrant more acknowledgment than a mere ethnography can pay.

My deepest gratitude goes to Paul Dresch, whose breadth of vision and feel for ethnography sustained me through each stage of fieldwork and writing. Many others read and commented on various sections of the manuscript: Mukulika Banerjee, Morgan Clarke, Roberta Dougherty, Dale Eickelman, Annie Hudson, Pratima Mitchell, David Odo, James Piscatori, Diane Scheinman, Ken Seigneurie, Jonathan Shannon, Andrew Shryock, Fawwaz Traboulsi. Marlin Dick, who shares my sensitivity to Damascene dialect, helped with transliteration. Walter Armbrust's tireless, sensitive engagement warrants special mention. Thanks also to Rebecca Tolen, my editor at Indiana University Press, for careful reading and helpful advice, and to John Mulvihill for his thorough copyediting.

My Lebanese American University colleagues, especially Sami Baroudi, created an ideal environment for the final stages of writing. Mona Khalaf and the research staff at the Institute for Women's Studies in the Arab World offered valuable comments and suggestions on my gender material. Social Science and Education Division research assistants Layal Abu Darwich, Mohammed Ayoub, and Jean-Paul Chamie helped with numerous last-minute queries. LAU graphic arts student Yasmina Take Arslan designed the map of elite Damascus.

For friendship and unflagging support across time and space, I must thank Gail Baker, Jane De George, Samer El-Karanshawy,

Gwenda Foord, Cristina Mansfield, Francisca Mutapi, Marcus Parker-Rhodes, Faujja Singh, and Lynne Townley.

Much of the credit for the virtues of this book, but none of the blame for its faults, goes to these individuals and many others who helped along the way.

Note on Transliteration

This book transliterates Arabic words by slightly amending the International Journal of Middle Eastern Studies system for formal Arabic. Certain cumbersome diacritical marks are omitted, though the hamza and ain are retained. Slight adjustments have been made for prepositions connected to nouns (*fil-bayt* rather than *fi-l-bayt*).

For strictly colloquial words, I have used a separate system. When the word in question involves no significant difference in pronunciation between the colloquial and the standard (for example, *ahl al-rif*), the standard, formal transliteration scheme is used. However, I have not taken colloquial words and tried to fit them into a straitjacket of formal Arabic. As a general rule, I have transliterated most words as they are pronounced in Damascene colloquial Arabic. For instance, the *ta marbuta* is rendered "eh" rather than the more usual "a" or "ah."). Nonetheless, I have retained the letter *qaf,* as is standard practice in colloquial transliteration.

A New Old Damascus

Introduction
A Return to the Old

Damascus measures time not by days and
months and years, but by the Empires she
has seen rise and prosper and crumble to
ruin. She is a type of immortality. . . .
Damascus has seen all that has ever
occurred on earth, and still she lives.
She has looked on the dry bones of a
thousand empires, and will see the tombs
of a thousand more before she dies.
Although another claims the name, old
Damascus is by right, the Eternal City.
—**Mark Twain,** *The Innocents Abroad*

If you enter the Old City of Damascus at Bab Sharqi (the Eastern
Gate), walk a few yards along a Street Called Straight, and turn
down the first narrow alley on your right, you will find, jutting out
from among the inward-looking Arab-style houses of this quiet residential quarter, a sign advertising "Le Piano Bar." Enter through the
carved wooden door, walk along the tile-covered foyer, under the
songbird's cage, past a display case strung with chunky silver neck-
laces, and step up a stone platform to the raised dining room. Here
well-heeled Syrians sit at closely spaced tables, drinking *arak*[1] and
Black Label whiskey, and eating grilled chicken or spaghetti. The
walls around them are decorated, each in a different style. One features a collection of Dutch porcelain plates set into plaster. In another, strips of colored marble hold a series of mosaic-lined, glass-
covered cases displaying wind instruments. A third wall features two

floral wrought-iron gated windows draped in a locally produced striped fabric. Wrought-iron musical notes dance on the last. At the front of the long, arch-divided room is a huge mother-of-pearl-framed mirror. Set into the top of the mirror is a digital billboard across which Le Piano Bar's menu and opening hours float repeatedly. Patrons listen politely as the proprietor sings "My Way" and other Frank Sinatra favorites to a karaoke backing tape. When he finishes, video screens tucked into corners feature Elton John song sing-alongs. Some nights a pianist and clarinetist play Russian songs as patrons clack wooden castanets.

On the surface, Le Piano Bar appears as kitsch, as a complete loss of aesthetic confidence. With its ironic iconography drawing on past and present, near and far, local and global, this establishment provides a point of access into the experience of late-twentieth-century modernity in Syria, reflecting its disjunctures and contradictions, fragmentations and paradoxes. It forms part of a complex system in which social distinction is negotiated through an idiom of local public culture. Neither kitsch nor cultural imperialism, Le Piano Bar operates as a system of signs whose decoding reveals a cosmopolitanism that values the local alongside the global. It is among the most colorful of a range of new cultural forms invoking Old Damascus. Restaurants, cafés, television programs, nostalgic memoirs, art exhibits, and social gatherings all attempt to reproduce tradition through the terms of a newer, wider world. They are also highly contentious constructs which often operate as idioms of exclusion, distinguishing an old urban elite from powerful new rivals.

Le Piano Bar and other cultural forms recreating tradition are relatively new to Syria. Selective consumption of these forms has become a mode of identity construction: Damascenes and others state their social position through what they buy, eat, wear, and do in their leisure hours. As Pierre Bourdieu has shown, consumption preferences are not matters of individual taste; they are significant indicators of social status (1984). I argue that even when consumption patterns are similar, the ways in which various groups talk about consuming are not. In Damascus, it is not just consumption of various representations of the Old City that distinguishes group from group, it is the ways in which consumption is discussed and debated. Many Syrians watch serial dramas set in Old Damascus, and visit Old City theme restaurants, but the significance of these practices differs according to the consumer's social position and identity.

Much of this identity construction through consumption is taking place in and around new public arenas. Here the concept of public culture, as developed by the pioneering journal of the same name, provides a useful framework. Studies of public culture are concerned with the local production and reception of transnational cultural forms, often in urban non-Western contexts. As Carol Breckenridge and Arjun Appadurai note, "much of the non-Western world has now adopted forms of technological representation, consumption and commodification which are harnessed to the idiosyncrasies of their own traditions, and to the ways in which indigenous elites reconstruct these traditions" (1988: 1). I would add that what is occurring in Damascus is not merely a synthesis of local tradition with Western form, but the very construction of the local. Damascenes are producing and reproducing—and marketing—a sense of Damasceneness: a rich "authenticity" as they see it, a bogus elitism to the newcomers who share the city with them. In the Old City itself, whose largely poor, migrant inhabitants are confined to ways of life rather than lifestyles, gentrified and commodified reinventions of tradition offer elite Damascenes a mode of self-definition and group differentiation. The present work explores processes of elite identity construction among Damascenes, and the reactions to them of other groups living in the city.[2]

Throughout the 1980s and 1990s, elite Damascenes produced and consumed a "return to the old" (*ʿawda lil-qadim*).[3] Whereas elite culture of the previous three generations strove to "imitate the West," as one informant put it, that of the early 1980s onward featured references to putatively "authentic" Damascene "customs and traditions" (*ʿadat wa taqalid*). The city's old leading families, who decades earlier left the Old City for the modern neighborhoods beyond its walls, are revisiting Old Damascus in the form of new leisure and consumptive practices. New additions to elaborate hotel weddings, a central focus of Damascene elite social life and competitive display, illustrate this phenomenon.[4] According to a Damascene informant:

> Elite weddings of the 1970s used to imitate Western church weddings. But now [1992] you'll find that the more noble the Old Damascene family, the more the wedding—even though held at the Sheraton—will resemble one held in the Old City quarter of al-Maydan in the 1950s. They started having men wearing swords and shields, and the old-fashioned bridal procession (*zaffeh*) with traditional musicians. This has happened recently, in the past five years.[5]

Cultural forms and practices such as weddings increasingly make reference to "Old Damascus." In Syrian usage, the term "Old Damascus" refers to a number of interrelated phenomena. Most tangibly, it connotes the physical space of the Old City itself, past and present. Parts of Old Damascus have been torn down to make way for concrete high-rises and modern boulevards, but many quarters remain standing, including those inside the Old City walls. Old Damascus also refers to a lifestyle associated with the city as it was—or supposedly was—before the major social, political, and economic transformations that began in the early 1960s. Lastly, Old Damascus is an image of the past commodified in the form of restaurants, cafés, television programs and advertisements, social events, art and photography exhibits, and books. All these aspects converge into an arena of social contestation and identity construction among contemporary Damascus dwellers.

The Damascene "return to the old" is a quintessentially modern phenomenon. It is no less authentic a facet of Syrian society than any other. I am not concerned with the degree to which my upper-middle-class or intellectual informants represent an authentic Syrian prototype. Both marginal (Arab, Third World, and relatively isolated) and central (urban, educated, cosmopolitan, and relatively well-off), they represent an experience of non-Western modernity, with all its contradictions and complexities. "Authenticity" in this context is a Syrian construct—a field of contestation rather than an essence. The debate over what constitutes authenticity forms the subject of the pages to come.

Fieldwork in Damascus

Fieldwork was not my first in-depth experience of Syria. In 1987, I spent a year in Damascus studying Arabic through a Fulbright grant just after I had completed a bachelor's degree in Near Eastern languages and literatures. The first semester I lived in student dormitories, experiencing intimate day-to-day interaction with Syrian women students from a variety of backgrounds. For the second half of the year I moved to the Old City, renting a ground-floor room in a house in the quarter of Bab Tuma (St. Thomas Gate), with recent migrants from the Hawran region of southern Syria, a lower-middle-class family in the process of adjusting to urban life.

For most citizens of Damascus, material conditions were dismal. Long daily power cuts afflicted the many who could not afford private generators. Domestic industry—now booming—was then minimal, and importation limited. Frequent attempts to stem the flow of smuggling from Lebanon and Jordan sparked severe shortages in basic commodities like rice, tea, sugar, heating oil, and cooking gas. The resourcefulness of all Syrians was mobilized, stretching patronage relationships and familial obligations to the limit.

With its clean-swept streets and meager, hidden nightlife, Damascus presented a tidy but frugal facade. Public culture was much less developed than it is now, with only a handful of hotels and restaurants. Officialdom frowned on conspicuous public displays of consumption, even limiting the depiction of luxury foods on state-controlled television. Yet amid this bleak cityscape, in which many were forced to spend much of their time foraging for life's necessities, there were hints of a very different lifestyle. One afternoon I went to change currency at the Sheraton Hotel, a venue far removed from both my student lifestyle and my working-class background. I saw there a group of seven or eight women lounging on the lobby's plush leather chairs, waiting to dine at the hotel's French-style restaurant. I sat for a few minutes, mesmerized, watching from behind a large potted plant. The image of these lavishly dressed, expensively coiffed "ladies who lunch," and its contrast with most of what lay outside that hotel haunted me. When I returned to Syria for fieldwork in the autumn of 1992, I planned to focus my research on public culture and social distinction among the elite, a group largely missing from the ethnography of the Middle East. I was to discover a burgeoning new public arena of leisure sites in which old and new classes displayed status and wealth.

Damascus did not prove the easiest of field sites. My relative youth and gender facilitated certain relations and in some cases may have eased suspicions; it also produced tensions that were not easily overcome. Patriarchal structures in elite, urban Syria pitted women against women, and a foreign woman entering this field had to cope with intensely competitive social and professional interactions. Another obstacle is the general assumption, shared by Syrians of all social and religious groups, that foreign researchers are spies. Such suspicion is a common fieldwork hazard in much of the Arab Middle East.[6] As one informant bellowed at me repeatedly, "Your question is CIA, not academic." Another mentioned the reaction of her fellow Syrians when they learned she worked with foreign scholars: "People said, 'Don't you know all these foreigners are spies? How can you bring X to the Arab Club, what if she's a spy?' and I said, 'What if she is a spy, she is asking only very general questions.' But still, people are very suspicious of foreigners, and this is from a political point of view."

Likewise, a Syrian friend argued that, even if we foreign researchers do not see ourselves as spies, our funding bodies have links

to Western intelligence services, who then make use of our published work. Even as I cited the masses of scholarship produced each
year, the relative obscurity of ethnography within this body, and the
minuteness of its audience, I could not convince him that I was anything other than a colonial ethnographer hired to help subdue the
natives.

Anthropology itself is new to Syria, and few anthropologists
have worked on Damascus. There are no Syrian anthropologists and
no department of anthropology in any Syrian university. Nor was
ethnography a concept familiar to any other discipline; Damascus
University's sociology department privileges quantitative approaches. Given the lack of indigenous anthropological scholarship, my
highly educated informants had difficulty understanding ethnographic research and were sometimes perplexed at my choice to
speak to them rather than rely solely on classical historical sources
on the city.

Compounding this unfamiliarity with ethnographic practice was
my focus on popular culture. Given the relative novelty and marginality of popular cultural forms as objects of social scientific inquiry,
the Syrians' incredulity toward my study was hardly surprising. Popular culture appeared an odd, unusually difficult object of investiga-
tion to Syrians, given the strong bias in Arab culture toward the classical over the vernacular (see chapter 6). This distinction, linked to
the wide diglossia of the Arabic language, is even more pronounced
in Syria than it is in Egypt or the Arabian Gulf countries, where colloquial forms are given socially valued literary expression.[7] A scholarly interest in restaurants and television programs struck Syrians as
very strange, as indeed it has some of my Oxford colleagues.[8]

Yet the Damascene case underscores the salience of popular culture. While my informants suggested I read Muhammad Kurd 'Ali
and other scholars of Damascus, what they spoke of in everyday discussions of the city were its representations in the popular media. To
ignore the significance of such material is to consign places like Syria
to archaic stereotypes of non-modernity. Even among the small-
scale, non-literate groups who form a more traditional subject of anthropological inquiry, popular culture has become an increasingly
meaningful aspect of the everyday social world.[9]

Another important element in contemporary academic perceptions of Syrian life is the structure and influence of the Syrian state,
with its strong and sometimes ruthless security apparatus. My work
underplays this aspect of Syria, which is often overblown in both
politically oriented scholarship and in the Western media and popu-

lar imagination. To the casual visitor the overwhelming icono-
graphic images of the president and presence of armed guards on
the streets of Damascus may suggest a more intrusive police state
than actually exists. I never experienced any hint of harassment, although I conducted research openly, often taking notes and holding
interviews in public spaces such as the Cham Palace Hotel's Café
Bresil, or the Lanterna Restaurant.[10] Syrian officials, on the rare occasions I had dealings with them, were always helpful and supportive. Nor to my knowledge were any Syrians involved with my research compromised. Nevertheless, I remained acutely aware that
my topic ventured into the sensitive terrain of class, religious, and
regional distinctions anathema to Baʿthist ideology and suggestive of
political critique. I am grateful to the many Syrians who generously
spoke to me, despite any self-censorship their instincts might have
suggested.

Elite Identities

Understanding the Old Damascus phenomenon requires familiarity with the social configuration of contemporary Syria, a country
which presents a complex array of crosscutting, overlapping, and often interdependent religious, class, regional, and ethnic identities.
The Syrian socialscape remains largely shrouded in scholarly silence,
as both foreign and local researchers avoid contemporary—and
therefore politically sensitive—topics in this near police state. A lack
of reliable statistics compounds the problem. Given the shortage of
anthropological and sociological studies, and the pre-1960 focus of
most historians, it is work on politics and political economy that has
come to shape Western understandings of contemporary Syrian society. Most of this material centers on the history of the Arab Socialist Baʿth (Renaissance) Party and its almost forty-year control of the
Syrian polity. That the rise of the Baʿth continues to fascinate political analysts is unsurprising, for it is a "rags to riches" story of impoverished peasants from a stigmatized religious sect wresting political
control from an urban elite of "notable" families who had dominated
local political and social life for decades, if not centuries.[11]

It is difficult to overemphasize the degree to which the Damascene elite families dominated the Syrian polity and society before
the Baʿth era. Writing of mass political mobilization in the 1920s,
James Gelvin stresses the reluctance of "the enlightened" (*al-mu-
tanawwirun*) Damascenes to expand the nationalist movement beyond their own narrow circle (1998: 63–65). The Syrian nationalist
movement was largely composed of the Damascene elite, who "never

negotiated with the population about ideology or program, . . . never synthesized a political discourse that was compelling to non-elites, and . . . never established bonds with the population comparable to those established between nationalist elites and their future compatriots in other areas of the world" (ibid.: 35).

The position and status of the city's leading families remained stable during the first half of the twentieth century, despite the widespread social and economic changes wrought by war, famine, and colonialism. The first blow to this monopoly came with the attempted unification with Egypt and the implementation of Nassarite socialist policies (1958–61). With the consolidation of the Ba'th Party government in 1963, political power shifted to a largely non-Damascene and non-urban military elite which became even more powerful after the perceived successes of the 1973 war. During early years of Ba'thist rule, Damascenes were systematically displaced from key positions in the military, the government, and the party. Today they occupy no key positions in any of the various security forces that most political analysts believe hold the reins of power in Syria.

In the economic realm, Damascene notables had to vie with and sometimes lost out to new competitors, including the state, as the nationalizations of the mid-1960s undermined the notables' control of commerce and industry. New bureaucratic and party elites emerged as the regime expanded its power base. Former peasants who made fortunes in the Gulf during the oil boom of the 1970s often returned not to their villages but to Damascus and formed part of a class of nouveaux riches with strong links to the regime.

Foremost among the Damascenes' rivals were members of the 'Alawi religious sect. In a stunning reversal of fortunes, this group, once at the very bottom of the social scale, rose to the loftiest heights of political power, and now controls most key positions in the al-Asad government. Considered heretical by the Sunni Muslims who long dominated Syrian cities, the 'Alawi, or Nusayri religious sect, an offshoot of Shi'i Islam, is a syncretic blend of Muslim, Christian, and Judaic beliefs and practices.[12] In the nineteenth century, the 'Alawis of the coastal villages of northern Syria were an oppressed and exploited minority who often worked as sharecroppers and sent their daughters to the cities—Damascus in particular—to work as servants in wealthy households. As part of their "divide and rule" tactics, French Mandate officials recruited large numbers of 'Alawis into their army, thereby exacerbating tensions between rural 'Alawis and urban Sunnis.[13]

The 'Alawis' history, of which both they and their Damascene counterparts are keenly aware, is one of poverty, humiliation, and servitude. Once a pejorative, the term "'Alawi" now suggests the source of political power and repression. 'Alawis and non-'Alawis alike voice it in only the most hushed of tones, or use one of a variety of code terms instead. Categories such as "the foreigners" (al-ghurbatliyyeh), "villagers" (qarawiyyin), "people from the countryside" (ahl al-rif), "peasants" (fellahin), or "minorities" (al-'aqalliyyat) usually refer to 'Alawis in particular. "People of the plain" (ahl al-sahil) always does.

In everyday discussions, Syrians often equate 'Alawi identity with both parvenu gaucheness and undeserved influence. How accurately this perception reflects contemporary realities is difficult to assess. The relationship of sectarian, regional, and class affiliations among Syria's elites is complex and ever shifting. Analysts who have attempted to categorize Syria's class structure—admittedly a mammoth task—have not shown how sectarian and regional affiliations intersect with those of class (Longueness 1979; Perthes 1991; Bahout 1994). No one has analyzed the sectarian or regional composition of the Damascus class structure in the way that Hanna Batatu (1999) has Syria's rural notables, even though these affiliations are significant to Damascus dwellers themselves and are invariably invoked in discussions of power, privilege, or poverty.

Social distinctions of all kinds are increasingly salient, despite—or perhaps because of—the Ba'th Party's official forty-year effort to obliterate them. Central to the Ba'th socialist version of Arab nationalism was the dissolution of divisive class, regional, and religious difference. According to the party's constitution: "The Arab nation constitutes a cultural unit. Any differences existing among its sons are accidental and unimportant. They will disappear with the awakening of the Arab consciousness" (cited in Haim 1962: 233).

The Ba'th project sought to create a sense of nationhood binding a multiplicity of ethnic, regional, religious, and linguistic groups. The modern nation of Syria has little historical resonance. The former entity was both larger—the Ottoman province of Greater Syria—and smaller—individual cities, towns, and villages. Before the Mandate period (1922–1946), city—even quarter—affiliations predominated; Syrians identified themselves as Damascene or Aleppine, and rarely as Ottoman (Thompson 2000: 176). The nationalization process attempted to create national—and beyond this pan-Arab—concepts of connectedness to replace those of locality, religion, and class. This does not mean that Syria became more homogeneous or egalitarian during the nationalist socialist heyday of the 1960s and 1970s. It does mean that public expressions of subnational identities were taboo. Those committed to Arab nationalism believed in its homogenizing policies. Recent assertions of local elite identity by prominent former nationalists testify to the failure of the Baʿth socialist project. As a young woman originally from the city of Homs told me, "I don't remember people mentioning where they were from, or what sect they were when I was at school. Now that's all you hear."

A relative easing of constraints on freedom of expression during the 1990s opened up space for the public expression of difference, as the global demise of socialist ideology weakened its homogenizing principles. Lively debate over formerly taboo subjects began to take place in and around the media and performing arts. After a long period of keeping a deliberately low profile, the Damascene merchant class—sons and daughters of the old urban ruling elite—began to reassert itself. The Damascene elite expresses a local religious, cultural, and class identity long antithetical to Baʿth Party policy and to the current regime, and it does so loudly.

Urban Transformation

The political displacement of the old elite is reflected in a changing urban landscape. Damascus experienced rapid population growth throughout the twentieth century, and much of this increase involved the movement of rural people, ʿAlawis and others, to the city. Old Damascus proponents often date this influx of migrants from the countryside to the rise of the Baʿth Party and ʿAlawi dominance; yet the process actually began during the interwar Mandate period, when the city's population doubled. Some migrants sought economic opportunities in the capital after the famines of World War I decimated Syria's agricultural base. Others came during the 1950s, when new agricultural practices and growing urban job opportunities rendered peasant life increasingly untenable. Capitalist development replaced sharecropping tenure systems with mechanization and wage labor, transforming peasants into a rural proletariat and creating widespread unemployment. In the 1960s, the rise to power of the armed forces brought many peasant families, often ʿAlawis, to new, cheaply built housing on the outskirts of Damascus. One Damascene informant describes the impact of this influx, revealing a mood of alienation shared by many who identify with the old social order:

The people of Damascus have resentment (*istiya*) toward all things not Old Damascene. Damascus now has three million inhabitants, and of these, no more than half a million are of Damascene origin. The rest are from outside; Damascenes call them *ghurbatliyyeh,* the foreigners. The Damascenes are returning to their old customs to distinguish themselves from everything non-Damascene.

Large-scale migrations of peasants to cities, and the profound social and economic changes that result, are global phenomena. What renders the Damascene case distinctive is that these rural migrants are perceived by the displaced political elite to have usurped control of the state. When Damascenes refer to these "outsiders," they often do so in sectarian terms, associating migrants with ʿAlawis. Yet it is important to stress that "ʿAlawi" here connotes not merely a sect, but a range of real and perceived class, cultural, regional, and linguistic characteristics. In heterogeneous settings, social distinctions as lived experience are messier and more complex than even the most rigorous social scientific classification scheme would suggest. James Scott's metallurgic metaphor captures this ambiguity nicely: "the Malay typically experiences the shopkeeper and the rice buyer not only as a creditor and a wholesaler, but also as a person of another race and another religion. Thus the concept of class as it is lived is nearly always an alloy containing base metals; its concrete properties, its uses, are those of the alloy and not of the pure metals it may contain" (1985: 44).

In other words, the social differentiations I am exploring are not those of religion in the narrow sense, but of *habitus,* of orientation to the world, of tastes, attitudes, and perceptions (Bourdieu 1977). Such distinctions are not primordial or static; they are continually reconstructed in accordance with changing circumstances—in some historical contexts emphasized, in others downplayed. For instance, heightened sectarian tensions emerged in nineteenth-century Damascus, when the predominance of Christian merchants among those who benefited from the European incursion into local markets sparked a brief but dramatic surge in anti-Christian violence (Reilly 1996). Allegiances are multiple; as Yahya Sadowski notes, "loyalties to one's confessional group compete or are synthesized with other parochial bonds to family, tribe, or cult, and with more universal ties to class, party, even nation" (1988: 163).

This understanding of social distinction takes us beyond the dichotomy of sectarianism versus other affiliations set out in much of the political science literature. It helps explore the contradiction of

'Alawi dominance of the Syrian polity despite the Ba'th Party's avowedly secular ideology. The 'Alawis are merely the most powerful and most visible embodiment of what Damascenes perceive as "other." Thus what I refer to as "social distinction" cannot properly be reduced to sectarianism. I argue that sectarian references operate as local idiom rather than as analytic categories. The challenge for the analyst is not to avoid the apparent misconceptions built into these categories of distinction, but rather to situate them into analytic frames that help us understand how local idioms work.

In Syria, religious and class distinctions elide with those of region. The town/country tensions French anthropologist Jacques Weulersse found in the 1930s are, as he predicted, increasingly pronounced (1946: 87). So obvious are rural-urban distinctions that even Western journalists cannot ignore them. Charles Glass, for instance, treats the issue in the Damascus section of his Middle East travelogue (1990). The city, some feel, is becoming ruralized: "city people are eating village food," as one Damascene put it. But food often crosses boundaries that people cannot or will not cross (Appadurai 1988: 7). The availability of country food items does not imply growing social acceptance, or cosmopolitan embrace, of those less urban. Damascenes are clear about what they see as the inappropriateness of country people in the city. According to a Damascene industrialist:

> The villagers are not only bringing their families; they're bringing their way of life into the city. They're living a villager's life in the city, and this is having negative effects on the city itself. They are not adapted to city life, and this is bad for the city, especially if it is Damascus.

Negative stereotypes of the rural other are common. A prominent Old Damascus advocate I interviewed stressed the supposed backwardness of rural people, arguing that polygamous peasants—unlike sophisticated urbanites—exploit their women: "[Male] peasants in our society are lazy," he noted. "But the ladies, if you can call them that, rise at 5:00 and do all the work." A sense of embattlement, even a fear of contamination, is palpable and frequently expressed in concerns over exogamy among Damascenes:

> It's becoming more important for Damascenes to marry Damascenes, much more so than it was ten years ago. That way, you'll belong to a part of this country that has prestige, and not just in terms of money. Sometimes it's even easier to tell your friends you're marrying a foreigner, as long as he's a Muslim, than someone from a Syrian village.

Collective insecurity often results from changes in the balance of power between established groups and those perceived as outside either the physical space of the city or the metaphoric space of the elite. When social groups are forced into situations of interdependence, and formerly subordinate "outsiders" compete with established elite "insiders," their new relationship is often expressed through the construction of identity or "we-images" (Mennell 1994: 182–184). A dramatic instance of "we-image" making can be seen in Damascus, where the power balance between an old urban elite and formerly disadvantaged migrants has not merely shifted but, to a certain degree, been reversed.[14] A strong sense of a Damascene "we," expressed and debated in myriad representations of Old Damascus, is a reaction not merely to the numbers of outsiders, but also to the political power these former social inferiors now hold. In this world seemingly turned upside down, the old social hierarchy is continually invoked. As one Damascene observed, "Damascenes live more in the past than in the present because they no longer have power."

The heightened emotion permeating the old Damascus debate reflects more than mere insecurity. Fear, and not fear of the regime alone, is perhaps the dominant characteristic of urban Syrian society. Some scholars of urbanism see fear and anxiety as the counterpoint to the stimulation and excitement of city life. Urban culture must accommodate fear of strangers, and the aggression and paranoia it produces, and balance it with security and stability (Robins 1995: 48–49). In Damascus, fear of strangers combines with fear of the political unknown. Memories of violent political upheavals during the decade after independence—when successive coups d'état rendered life in the capital a nightmare of uncertainty—and the cautionary tale of next-door Lebanon—where years of civil war devastated worldly, cosmopolitan Beirut—create a sense of trepidation. This anxiety became palpable after the death of Hafiz al-Asad's son and heir apparent, Basil; a state of panic over what might happen, should the president succumb to his grief, gripped an urban population at best ambivalent toward the regime. Against this backdrop of anxiety, images of a safer, more confident past have come to dominate the collective imagination of the Damascene elite. In the world they hark back to, the Damascenes knew who they were, and where they stood.

Who Really Rules?

In a context of competing elites, it is difficult to ascertain which group wields which form of power. ʿAlawis, who make up an estimated 11.5 percent of the Syrian population, are over-represented in the upper ranks of the army and the Baʿth Party, and in the president's inner circle. The extent to which "confessional" or "sectarian" linkages characterize the top levels of the al-Asad regime has dominated analyses of the Syrian polity.[15] The plethora of material on this aspect of Syrian society, and the neglect of much else, is striking. Opinions differ as to how much power is concentrated in the hands of al-Asad's co-religionists, or members of his tribe.[16] Yet while estimates vary on the exact composition of the regime, all observers agree that it does not include, to any significant degree, members of the old Damascene elite. The few Sunni Muslims who have played a major role in the regime have not included Damascenes.

While the Damascenes have been exiled from the upper ranks of the political elite, they are far from disenfranchised. They retain other forms of power. Indeed, determinations of who actually dominates social and economic life in Syria depend on how and by whom dominance is defined. For the Old Damascus supporters, it is the barbarians from the countryside, particularly the ʿAlawis who destroyed the older, Damascene-controlled forms of commerce by applying socialist policies, yet have themselves made fortunes by licensing legal trade and controlling smuggling. Damascenes believe the al-Asad regime has sought to obliterate Sunni (Damascene) economic, social, and religious life. After a Sufi ceremony on the Night of Power,[17] during which this ethnographer was treated to a display of local Sunni culture, a Damascene television director described the government's position: "There used to be a lot more ceremonies like this one, but the government did away with them. They try to destroy everything Sunni. What I like about you, is that you really respected this ceremony. You don't see it as evidence of backwardness. This government thinks all people need is to eat and go to the toilet."

But just what is a Damascene; more specifically, who are the old elite families? It is not clear how deep a family's roots in the city must be and how prominent a family must have been to merit a place among the notables. The concept of the urban notable, *bint* or *ibn ʿaʾileh,* is somewhat ambiguous. Certainly, a series of well-known names are always included in this category, but it is sometimes more loosely applied. Even more problematic is the question of where the old elite families are now, and what their relationship is to what in later chapters I call the Old Damascus movement. Many old elites have married into the new monied classes. Others left Syria decades ago with the advent of Baʿth Party rule. Some who now identify with old elite culture lack notable pedigree.[18]

The answer to who can legitimately claim Old Damascene status may seem obvious, but a "social register" approach is ultimately un-helpful. What is sociologically significant is not so much the validity of status claims but how these claims are used in urban identity con-tests, among social rivals, when identification with the "customs and traditions" of a bygone social and political order form an idiom of cri-tique, even resistance. Authenticity becomes a tactic (Clifford 1988: 11–12).

Authenticity

The growing interest in Old Damascus is a local expression of a global modernity, drawing on notions of native authenticity derived from a transnational marketplace of commodities and ideas. Au-thenticity, the notion that some cultural forms are more "real" or valid than others, developed within a specific social and historical context. Anthropological discussions are apt to link the origins of au-thenticity to social transformations in early modern Europe. With the demise of the divinely ordained social hierarchies of the Middle Ages, we are told, social positions became social roles, as the feudal worldview gave way to notions of society in which individuals were no longer defined solely by social rank. These new social roles came to be distinguished from inner, essential, or "authentic" selves. Hence the modern concern with authenticity (Handler 1986: 2–3). Au-thenticity, according to Richard Handler, is culturally specific:

> I take "authenticity" to be a construct of the modern Western world. That it has been a central, though implicit, idea in much anthropological en-quiry is a function of a Western ontology rather than of anything in the non-Western cultures we study. Our search for authentic cultural experi-ence—for the unspoiled, pristine, genuine, untouched and traditional—says more about us than about others. (ibid.: 2)

To take Handler's analysis a step further, one might argue that "the modern Western world" is itself an academic construct, as is the absolute distinction between ourselves, the anthropologists who share a Western intellectual tradition, and the non-Westerners we study.[19] The Syrian case problematizes such reified dichotomies. Syria is a southwest Asian country which since antiquity has main-tained strong intellectual and cultural linkages with the wider Mediterranean basin. It shares in the cultural and intellectual tradi-tions of Islam, which, while associated with the "Orient," have both drawn on and influenced Western philosophy. Many of my infor-mants were educated in and frequently visit Europe and the United

States. They are aware of and influenced by Western academic notions of authenticity, as well as by more indigenous Islamic concepts (which were in turn informed by cosmopolitan currents). As will be shown in the ethnography that follows, the concern with authenticity is not an anthropologist's Western preoccupation, but rather arises in specific social and cultural contexts which are in part unique and in part shared with a wider world.

Authenticity often involves a sense of timelessness; in Western art markets, "authentic primitive" pieces are those untouched by history and contact with the West (Errington 1998: 71–73). In some contexts, criteria for authenticity shift from product to producer. For instance, legislation in the United States ensures that handicrafts sold as "authentic Navajo jewelry" must be produced by "authentic" Navajos (ibid.: 141). Creations using non-indigenous materials and techniques are authenticated through notions of race or ethnicity (ibid.: 144–145). In a context of heightened identity politics, authenticity becomes a means of controlling representation. As we shall see, Damascenes very often point to the local origins of a culture producer as evidence of a product's authenticity; a non-Damascene screenwriter's research-based depiction of Damascus is dismissed in favor of lived experience. Having the right to speak for an identity is as important as, and indeed often overrides, what is actually said. I therefore seek not to define authenticity, but rather to explore the uses of this concept in the processes of identity construction and social distinction.

The concept of authenticity and the understandings of self and society in which it is embedded emerge as crucial aspects of modernity. The social, cultural, and intellectual condition we think of as modern is said to have its seeds in the Renaissance, its roots in the Enlightenment, and its fruition in the Industrial Revolution in Europe; it was spread to the non-West, a problematic but apparently indispensable category, through processes of colonialism and, later, globalization. Modernity is often understood to involve radical rupture with past ways of thinking and behaving, the inculcation of rationalization, secularization, and new notions of time and space. Modernity is now a global phenomenon, but one that is locally distinct. These local modernities form the focus of a growing number of ethnographies, including my own.

The modern concept of authenticity necessitates a distance from any thing or quality associated with the past, and this distance in turn provides the necessary contrast between "the traditional" and the "modern." However, contradictory as it may seem, in the Arab world, as in the West, the "modern" and the "traditional" are qualities as likely to be fused as they are to be opposed. Arab constructs of modernity are deemed legitimate only if they seem to involve significant continuities with the Arab-Muslim past (Armbrust 2001: 26–27; 1996). In Damascus, claims and counterclaims of authenticity are the hallmark of local modernity. They are understandings of the past that are intrinsically linked to the present, and used in identity contests of a very contemporary sort.

Arab and Middle Eastern Authenticities

In Syria, as elsewhere in the Middle East, modernist notions of authenticity operate alongside and sometimes merge with indigenous understandings. The concept of authenticity, *asala*, has long been an important component of notions of the self and society in Arabic-speaking regions. Derived from the Arabic root A-S-L, *asala*, "authenticity," is related to *asl*, which translates as "origin," "source," "root," and "descent." *Asl* refers to a person's social, genealogical, or geographic origins, or to the place from which his or her roots extend. From the same Arabic root comes the adjective *asli*, "authentic."

Concepts of and calls for authenticity in the modern Arab world often reflect the perceived failures of Enlightenment rationality and modernization projects (Meijer 1989, 1999; Lee 1997; Nieuwenhuijze 1997). Romanticist notions of authenticity were a key feature of Arab nationalist thought. Syrian Baʿth Party founder Michel Aflaq posited an "Arab spirit" (*al-ruh al-ʿarabiyya*), an essential national character, a living history, and a moral imperative free from Western imperialist influences (al-Khalil 1989: 192–209). German Romantic notions of the "folk," an authentic cultural essence based on an "original" language, informed the writings of another Syrian nationalist, Satiʿ al-Husari (Tibi 1997: 125–141). It is telling that these models of "authentic Arab national identity," defined so starkly against the West, were constructed within and from an intellectual climate engendered and dominated by European thought.

In keeping with the strong textual bias in academic study of the Middle East (Said 1978; L. Abu-Lughod 1990: 83), work on authenticity in Middle Eastern contexts has focused primarily on scholarly discourse. Only a handful of studies examine notions of authenticity expressed in popular culture. In Iran, the term *javanmard*, literally "man of integrity," connotes qualities of courage, generosity, honor, modesty, and humility (Adelkhah 1999: 31). Like the authenticity of the European existentialist, that of the *javanmard* allows him to stand back from the everyday social world (ibid.: 43–46). His behavior is both strategic—designed for social effect—and individualistic. He combines conformity to the values of Iranian society with nonconformity, by taking those values to an anti-social extreme (ibid.: 45–46). Heavily imbued with nostalgia, the concept is rarely used in reference to living individuals (ibid.: 31–32). The *javanmard* is a hero of the past, rather than an authentic Iranian of the present.

In contemporary Cairo, identity constructs employ two parallel notions of authenticity, one classicist, involving a synthesis of Western and indigenous high culture, and the other the folkloric *ibn al-balad,* "son of the nation," or "son of the town." These two versions, a "split vernacular" which Walter Armbrust relates to the diglossic split between standard and colloquial forms of Arabic, operate in continual tension (1996: 25). Similar to the Iranian *javanmard,* the term *ibn al-balad* can mean "salt of the earth," or "rough diamond" (Armbrust 1996: 25; Adelkhah 1999: 38). *Ibn al-balad* connotes both a set of attributes and a social group perceived to embody them. A nineteenth-century pejorative, the concept gained social status with the rise of modern Egyptian nationalism (El-Messiri 1978: 37). Egyptians associate *ibn al-balad* with Old City quarters, traditional food and dress, and the values of gallantry (*shahama*), conservatism, cleverness (*fahlawa*), common sense, independence, generosity, masculinity, and joviality (ibid.: 49–55), characteristics also associated with the *zgurt* or *shaykh al-shebab* of Old Damascus. In practice, *ibn al-balad* serves as an idiom, invoked by different social actors in various contexts, opposing the local authentic to the Westernized inauthentic.[20] Its opposite construct is the foreign-influenced *ibn al-zawat,* "son of the upper classes" (ibid.: 7).

The authenticity invoked in Old Damascus discourses is neither that of classic modernist, nor that of the *ibn al-balad*-like *zgurt*. It cannot be claimed by all who inhabit the city. It most closely resembles another Cairene idiom, *ibn nas,* "son of society." Like the *ibn nas,* the Damascene *ibn ʿaʾileh,* "son of a good family," is both authentically local and urban, and solidly upper-middle or upper class. *Ibn ʿaʾileh* identity is a hybrid combining elite and folk attributes. Representations of Old Damascene authenticity, as expressions of *ibn ʿaʾileh* identity, encompass both the "high" of classical Arabic music and poetry and the folkloric of everyday life in the Old City quarter. In elite constructions of Old City authenticity, colloquial songs and proverbs appear as often as their classical counterparts.

In the Middle East generally, calls for authenticity often take the form of Islamist, nationalist, or nativist arguments against Western cultural imperialism, the West's cultural invasion (*al-ghazu al-thaqafi*). By contrast, the Damascus debate centers on a range of perceived differences, of varied approaches to modernity which are only tangentially related to Westernization. It is an issue that pits Westernized elite against Westernized elite, and notions of Western dominance play only in its margins. As a value subject to dispute, authenticity, like so much else in contemporary Syria, is in a constant state of transformation. It now connotes a self-conscious choice between cultural forms presented as genuine and those dismissed as spurious. Both a tactic and a prize in the agonistic contests for symbolic and material power that shape the lives of the Damascene elite, "authentic culture" is the stuff of social distinction in contemporary Syria, and lies at the heart of arguments over who is perceived to rule, who once ruled, and who no longer rules.

Contests

My ethnography departs from the many studies treating consumption and identity construction as modes of resistance to state dominance. This literature often depicts expressive, mediated, and commodified cultural forms as weapons in ongoing struggles against state hegemony. A dichotomy often emerges between a didactic and self-interested state, on one side, and marginalized, disenfranchised, or otherwise non-elite groups of citizens on the other. Michael Herzfeld questions this distinction by opening up the very notion of the "state" as a category. He warns against reifying a "state" among whose ranks number plenty of ordinary folk of the sort anthropologists often write about (1997). His concept of disemia, the interplay between officially sanctioned culture and the various interpretations and expressions of non-state actors, problematizes the state/people dichotomy. For Damascus, it is necessary to shift the focus further from a state that features as but one of many forces shaping identity and culture construction. The binary tensions Herzfeld points to are multifarious in Damascus, and routinely give way to what Andrew Shryock, in his study of contests over national identity in Jordan, calls "contentious multivocality" (1997: 313). From the Damascus case emerges an array of individuals and groups challenging one another over various representations of past and present, of culture and history, that range from bodily adornment and family honor to theme restaurants and television dramas.

I argue that the state is but one of many voices in a cacophony of argumentation. Damascus dwellers' claims and counterclaims to authenticity are aimed at one another as well as at the state. In fact, the Syrian state often attempts to stifle the social divisiveness emerging in identity contests. As will be shown in the case of the television series *Damascene Days* (chapter 4), producers and consumers alike appropriate cultural products seemingly intended as celebrations of national community, and use them as weapons in status wars, outmaneuvering the state's intentions. An ethnography of elite groups, whose symbolic and material power often compares with that of the state, provides a key opportunity to challenge assumptions of state centrality.

This work problematizes a related dichotomy, that between production and consumption, demonstrating that even cultural producers affiliated with the state (as most producers in Syria are, to some degree) often distance themselves from state ideology, or disapprove of state constructs of local and national culture. Syrian elites are both state-sponsored producers and critical consumers. Furthermore, the relatively small social field of elite Damascus enables—indeed necessitates—treating producers as consumers as well.

Disputes occur over national culture in Syria, as elsewhere, but highly localized contests often seem more important to Damascenes, whose one-upmanship is geared toward attaining and maintaining prestige and position at sub-national levels. These locally oriented, agonistic practices have most often been associated with rural men. While urban men are also masters of this combative style, urban women, as guardians of family honor and showpieces of family wealth, are central contestants in status games.[21] Women's prestige contests are a telling variation on themes of social contest that orient debates over how Old Damascus and the Damascenes should be represented. Family prestige and local authenticity are both elusive prizes in a larger culture of competitive consumption and identity politics.

For all these reasons, I am reluctant to present the Old Damascus movement and its detractors as exemplars of resistance against the state. Instead, I treat contestation itself as a central mode of sociability, as Campbell (1964) and Herzfeld (1985) have shown for rural Greece, Gilsenan in a Lebanese village (1996), Meneley in a Yemeni town (1996), and Shryock and Howell among urbanized tribal elites in Jordan (2001). Agonistic competition, so prominent in these diverse settings, is a form of social engagement that contemporary Damascenes enact in patterns of consumption and in new arenas of public culture. For example, debates over representations of Old Damascus and arguments over how to judge beauty contests form part of the same poetics of contestation, argumentation, and accusation.

The salience of agonistic competition among the elites of Damascus suggests an older European anthropology that explored cultural similarities among Mediterranean lands.[22] This line of inquiry has fallen out of fashion, perhaps due to a preoccupation with Islam in studies of the Middle East and to reservations over unifying concepts of region.[23] I am not positing a unified Mediterranean culture, but rather advocating a comparative approach tracing linkages, continuities, and convergences. The primacy of contestation as a mode of sociability in Damascus points to parallels with other Levantine societies and with those of the northern Mediterranean. Exploring such linkages both illuminates the practice itself and avoids the perils of particularization.[24] If, in a public culture of restaurants, hotels, and media, one observes the modes of contestation found by ethnographers of Greece and the Levant in households and village cafés, then these parallels warrant exploration.

Consumption Takes Hold

Arguments over Old Damascus occur as economic liberalization renders material wealth an increasingly important measure of status in Syria. Areas of the city are heavily marked in this way, as a house in an elite district is the clearest and most unmistakable mark of social prestige (see chapter 1). People speak wistfully of a time when education and family background were more important. According to a young writer from the northern Syrian city of Aleppo, "It used to matter, who you were and what you did, but now all that matters is consumption."

Ironically, this alleged privileging of economic capital above all else is in part a result of the Ba'th Party's socialist policies. The authority of the old elite families was linked to a combination of political and economic dominance, access to the West in the form of travel, education, and consumer goods, and an urbane, cultivated lifestyle of sophisticated discourse, refined manners, and attention to matters of taste. It was sometimes connected to religious learning. A shift has occurred in the understanding of what is considered elite. A culture of consumption of the modern sort has arisen in place of older forms of social distinction, as state control of licensing channeled access to resources into the hands of new elites. In the socialist heydays of the 1970s and 1980s, hard-to-come-by prestige commodities, such as fashionable European clothing, loudly signaled those with connections. The economic liberalization, or *infitah* (opening), from the late 1980s onward expanded practices of competitive consumption, and invigorated a new regionally and religiously mixed middle class (*al-tabaqa al-jadida*) for whom Damascene identity no longer served as a key elite marker. The pace of these developments traumatized the old urban elite. In the words of one old family Damascene:

> From the 1960s onward, Damascene society was shaken by the emergence of a new bourgeoisie that exploited its links with the regime, and profited from a gray area between public and private. People who ten years ago wore plastic sandals (*shahata*) and rags now boast of their involvement in international business deals worth millions. Damascene society has been shaken to the core, and *ibn ʿaʾileh* appears a mere atom next to the new monied person. Expressions like *ibn ʿaʾileh* that used to have a social and economic base no longer have the same meaning.

It is also ironic that nostalgia for Old Damascus, the yearning for a time before money mattered above all else, is finding expression in commodified form. This study explores the debates surrounding the commodification and consumption of Old Damascus as both a physical space and imagined idea. It focuses on processes of identity construction through practices of consumption among an urban Arab elite, a topic long neglected in anthropological literature.[25] I argue that agonistic competition is a key mode of sociability among elite Syrians, and that both the city itself and the public cultural forms invoking it form nodes around which much of this contestation occurs. Early in my fieldwork, it became apparent to me that Damascus and Damasceneness form a nexus linking local discussions of class and sect, tradition and modernity, culture and politics, identity and otherness. Individuals and groups vie for social prestige and moral authority using a language of sectarian-regional distinction. Discourses of Damasceneness operate as points of identification, and as idioms of social and political critique. Such critique often takes place through agonistic criticism, a mode of sociability I have dubbed a "poetics of accusation."

In the ensuing chapters I focus on various realms in which Damascus, both as space and as metaphor, features both as a theme for commodity production and as a site of cultural, social, and political contestation. Chapter 1 sketches the layout of the city, illustrating the inscription of social difference in physical space. I map out an urban geography of distinction in which neighborhoods operate as symbolic reference points, marking residents' class, sectarian, and regional identities. Chapter 2 begins to examine the identity contests occurring within this cityscape, focusing on how sectarian, regional, and class identities are (re)produced and expressed through marriage patterns and leisure practices among women. Through competitive consumption and display, women are key agents in the acquisition and maintenance of their families' social success, and bear much of the responsibility for creating a family's public image. Whereas many academic treatments of Middle Eastern women link them, explicitly or implicitly, primarily to the private world of the home, I explore the public aspects of their gender position, and posit that new public and semi-public arenas serve as novel venues for competitive consumption, for establishing and reconfirming a family's position. In addition, by arguing that patriarchy sometimes divides rather than unifies, I diverge from ethnographic literature that emphasizes the great extent of mutual support among women. Chapter 3 focuses on the commodification of an imagined ideal of Old Damascus, in the form of theme restaurants. It also examines efforts to preserve Old Damascus, and non-Damascenes' reactions to them, amounting to rhetorical contests between "insiders" and "outsiders." I show that Old City activism, like other realms of Damasceneness, serves as a basis for rivalry and contestation. Chapter 4 examines consumption as a mode of social distinction during the fasting month of Ramadan, a time when public expressions of Damascene identity—and reactions against them—reach their peak. Televised serial dramas become the focal point of social life during the holy month. In the case of the widely viewed *Damascene Days*, state producers may have intended to present Damascus as a symbol of the entire nation, but the series instead occasioned subversive and contentions reactions. Chapter 5 looks at books and documentary films about Old Damascus, exploring the ambiguous and often controversial position both these products and their producers occupy within the intellectual elite. In chapters 3, 4, and 5, I focus the reader's attention on the ways in which public cultural forms serve as weapons in contemporary struggles over competing authenticities.

This ethnography foregrounds what people say, a methodology adopting Anthony Giddens's concept of practical consciousness (Giddens 1979; Ginsburg 1989: 12–14). Following Giddens, I believe in my Syrian informants' ability to express valuable social and political critiques. I recognize no absolute distinction between discourse and practice; in Damascus—where the word is highly valued and the major forms of expressive culture are literary—social and cultural life takes place largely in and through language. Thus I have presented significant, sometimes lengthy passages in my informants' own words.

The central aim of this work is to provide an ethnographic account of the relationship between popular and public cultural forms and modes of elite consumption and social distinction in Damascus during the "ethnographic present" of the early 1990s. This study contributes to a growing corpus of anthropological literature on the uses of public cultural forms in processes of identity formation and contestation in urban contexts. It is my hope that my analysis of authenticity and its uses in identity contests will inform future work on the emergence, or reconstruction, of sub-national identities elsewhere in the world. I examine not merely patterns of consumption but discourses surrounding consumption, which I argue operate as modes of distinction.

There is no "enemy" in this ethnography of elites. This is not a story of economically or socially disenfranchised groups battling a hegemonic state or dominant class. Rather, it is an examination of powerful elites who vie for cultural prestige and social position by identifying with or rejecting a variously constructed Old Damascus. I have tried to deal as evenhandedly as possible with all sides of an emotionally charged and politically sensitive issue. The result is somewhat *Rashomon*-like, juxtaposing the views of various social actors differently related to the Old City in its myriad forms. I hope to have given voice to the many sincerely held positions that make up the Old Damascus debate.

1

"His Family Had a House in Malki, So We Thought He Was All Right"
Socio-Spatial Distinction

> Damascus' beauty is hidden; it doesn't give you everything from the first moment; its beauty comes to you little by little.
> **—Damascene television director Ghassan Jabri**

> Damascus is like a beautiful girl who desires to be sought.
> **—Damascene author Nadia Khost**

> Damascus is a whore, but a high-class one—she doesn't give herself except to those who'll pay a lot.
> **—ʿAlawi journalist**

"Damascus" and "Old Damascus" mean various things to people differently placed within the social configuration of the city. Their meanings have also changed over time, as the Old City has lost and regained prestige value. Nostalgia for a supposedly more homogeneous urban identity in Old Damascus is linked to transformations in Syrian society over the past three decades. Old Damascene neighborhoods, once abandoned to poor migrants, are now the subject of a heritage industry with the old urban elite at its helm. The winding narrow streets and inward-looking houses that a few decades ago represented vestiges of backwardness have now become the center of contemporary concern.

Evocations and reminiscences of Old Damascus often involve references to Old City houses and neighborhoods, and the very different way of life they were once home to. Until the late nineteenth century, most domestic architecture in Damascus was built in the traditional Arab style, with a single entrance and a central courtyard onto which the rooms of the house opened. Grand houses consisted of several courtyards, but rarely more than two stories. Even poorer houses had wells, and sometimes fountains in their courtyard. Trees, bushes, or some form of greenery colored and shaded this central open space. In the early part of the twentieth century, urban notables began to leave their Arab-style, Old City houses for the newly built modern flats of the "garden districts" toward the slopes of Mount Qasiun. Elite families of the period welcomed and actively encouraged urban modernization. Old City activist Siham Tergeman describes this migration:

> It started with a few families, who built factories—the first private [indus-trial] production in Syria. They became very rich, and wanted to live in villas [apartments in detached houses]. So they went to the orchard areas and built villas, one after another, and this is how the neighborhood of Abu Rummaneh came into being. All the rich Damascene families moved there. The families still living in the Old City started to imitate them, so al-Rawda and al-Jisr al-Abyad were built. In their era the French built a few neighborhoods, like that of the Franciscan [parish], built in the French style, with iron balconies. These houses were what the Damascenes began to want, and they became fashionable for the upper classes (*al-akabir*), the "high society." They wanted to move to apartments, because Arab-style houses were tiring, needed a lot of work, with their trees shedding leaves, and stairs the women had to climb up and down.

It is difficult to develop a precise profile of Old Damascus's current inhabitants. While some Damascene families—particularly those in Christian areas—have remained in their Old City houses, most have left. Rural migrants from a variety of regional backgrounds—including Palestinians—have replaced them, living several families to a large merchant house. Most are lower-middle-class artisans and skilled laborers. Many would leave the difficult, crowded condition of the Arab-style house if given the chance, and move to the comfort and convenience of modern apartments, as the elites had decades earlier. Prominent Damascenes have not chosen to join these poorer families by moving back into the Old City. Yet they have come to revalue the Old City's unique architectural heritage, and now promote it as a great national resource. A city steeped in millennia of civilization is the legacy Damascenes embrace as an identity worthy of prominent position in a global arena of cultures.

Damascus in History (and Before)

Damascus is believed to be the oldest continuously inhabited city in the world. Just south of the Old City, in the Ghouta orchards, lies an early Neolithic site dating back to 7790–6690 B.C. The first textual mention of the city dates to the eleventh century B.C., when it served as capital to a small Aramaean kingdom (AlSayyad 1991: 29). Known as Damashqa to the ancient Egyptians, it was part of the Assyrian Empire in the eighth century B.C. After Alexander the Great— known in Arabic lore as the "Two Horned" (Iskandar dhu al-Qarnayn)—conquered the city in 333 B.C., it became part of the Seleucid Empire ruled from Antioch. The Seleucids hellenized Damascus, imparting the Greek language and influencing artistic and architectural styles. Pompey's armies conquered the city in 64 B.C. Under the Romans and Byzantines, Damascus flourished as an important commercial center. Outlines of Greco-Roman Damascus are still visible in the grand arches and columns scattered throughout the Old City. The city reached the peak of its prominence as the capital of the Umayyad dynasty, A.D. 661–750, led by Mu'awiya ibn Abi Sufyan. As seat of the Umayyad caliphate, Damascus ruled over an empire stretching across North Africa to Spain. When the seat of Islamic empire shifted to Baghdad in A.D. 750, Damascus lost its eminence, becoming a provincial town within the Abbasid Empire. The city was subsequently governed by a series of rulers: Fatimids (A.D. 934–1071 or 1075), Seljuks (1071–1174), Ayyubids (1174–1260), Mameluks (1260–1516), and Ottomans (1516–1918). The Hashimite Prince Faisal's brief reign lasted from 1918 until 1920, the beginning of the French occupation. After independence was granted in 1946, Damascus witnessed a long series of military coups d'état which ended only with the al-Asad takeover in 1970.[1]

For centuries Damascus has been an important stop along a major *hajj* (pilgrimage) route to Mecca. An oasis once surrounded by lavish orchards, the city has long been renowned for its beauty throughout the Arab and Muslim worlds. As Islamic lore has it, the prophet Muhammad went as far as the city's outskirts, looked out onto Damascus, and refused to enter, believing it unseemly to visit paradise before death. Damascus was also known for the quality and quantity of its water; the seven tributaries of the Barada River allowed every house to have its own well. Damascenes describe the beauty of pre-Ba'thist Old Damascus in terms appropriate to the *Arabian Nights*—interiors of courtyards, fountains, mosaics, trees, and songbirds, extolled in loving detail. These romantic images of a fabled pre-modern urban beauty inform contemporary Damascenes' conceptions and expressions of identity. Some nineteenth-century Western travelers, looking at more public spaces of streets and markets, paint a different portrait, one of dirt, noise, and squalor (Twain 1996; Porter 1870).

Damascus remains associated with an urbane, cultivated lifestyle, as the classical Arabic term *mudamshaq*, "sophisticated," from Dimashq (Damascus), suggests. The city is also referred to as al-Sham, "the North," a term that once connoted both Damascus itself and the entire Ottoman province of Syria, the bilad al-Sham (the Lands of Damascus). Sham has become a less formal and somewhat emotive term, one often preferred by Damascenes themselves, particularly those involved in the nostalgia movement which will be discussed in following chapters. In colloquial Arabic, Damascenes are referred to as *shuwam* (sing. *shami*).

A number of fanciful-sounding derivations are given for the name "Damascus," Dimashq, the term preferred for formal and academic usage. *Damashaq* is said to mean "fast-moving camel" in Arabic. Another theory holds that the city was named after Damasheq, a great-great-grandson of Noah, who some believe built the city. The Romans, it is said, called it *dumuskus,* or "double musk." "Damascus" is also believed to be derived from the Aramaic *edeim,* "land," and *mask,* "red" (Saadieh 1991: 24).

Elements of these historical memories are increasingly woven into contemporary imagination. Such re-imaginings escape interpreting Damascus strictly through the prism of the "Islamic City," a model that informed an earlier body of literature attempting to define an essential or unique urban form supposedly engendered by the predominance of Islam (Hourani and Stern 1970). A concept that guided years of urban historical and geographic writing, the Islamic City is less useful to an ethnography of a contemporary Middle Eastern city and its people.[2] My work avoids relating Damascus to an ideal Muslim city. I emphasize instead the city's unique forms and concerns on the one hand, and the problems and issues it shares with much of the urbanized world on the other.[3] The shape of the city is increasingly determined by emerging social distinctions that are a facet of modern urban life everywhere, but perhaps particularly acute here.

Residential Patterns

Like many cities in the developing world and beyond, Damascus has experienced a steady and significant population increase throughout the twentieth century. Between the 1890s and 1945, the city's population nearly doubled, reaching almost 300,000 (Thompson 2001: 94). During the post–World War II, post-independence period it multiplied fourfold, rising to 1,347,000 in the early 1980s. Census figures from the mid-1990s place the number at 3.5 million, although unofficial estimates run as high as 5 million. In order to house the large numbers of newcomers, dormitory suburbs were rapidly and cheaply built or expanded, and older two-story buildings were replaced with high-rise apartment blocks.

Several analyses of social differentiation in the urban Middle East relate residential patterns to transformations in status and identity. In her seminal study of Cairo, Janet Abu-Lughod identified a dual process of cultural homogenization and socioeconomic differentiation resulting in the decline of "traditional urbanism," as the economic activities, forms of social relations, and systems of values that were typical one hundred years earlier became increasingly challenged (1971: 219). Cairo, she argued, was unifying culturally; the medieval city was modernizing, and the elite "Gold Coast" was "baladizing" (becoming more local) as wealthy Egyptian nationals replaced foreign elites (ibid.: 219–220). The disparate cultural and technological worlds into which Cairo had been divided were merging, alongside an "increased economic differentiation within the unifying framework of industrial urbanism." The life paths of Cairenes of different ethnic, religious, kinship, and occupational groups intersected more than ever before (ibid.: 237). Classes, Abu-Lughod predicted, would continue to replace communities based on religion, ethnicity, and regional origin, at least in terms of residential patterns, even though class-based identities could not provide the "organic social solidarity" offered by the latter groups (ibid.: 237).

Sami Zubaida extends this thesis to Middle Eastern cities generally. The old quarters, he argues, were stratified both vertically and horizontally (1989). Urban growth, changes in the sources of wealth, status, and power, and the adoption of lifestyles based on European models led the middle classes to move out of the old cities and into class-homogeneous residential quarters. The old quarters, where they still survive, have become lower-class areas, heavily populated with waves of rural migrants and maintaining a mix of residence and small-scale commerce and craft (ibid.: 114–115).

More than a quarter century has passed since the publication of Abu-Lughod's work on Cairo, and it is now important to ask to what extent classes have indeed replaced other forms of collectivity in the urban Middle East. In Damascus, unlike the Middle Eastern city prototype described by Zubaida, economic stratification was evident even in the Old City in the early part of the twentieth century, when certain quarters, such as Suq Saruja and al-Qanawat, were associated with the upper classes (Khoury 1984: 512, 534n.). Subsequently, the sectarian, ethnic, and regional homogenization Abu-Lughod predicted for Cairo has taken place only within the wealthiest segment. For those groups with social rank below the very top, such affiliations continue to play a significant role in residential patterns.

Cities and Difference

Widespread urbanization throughout the twentieth century has rendered contemporary cities sites of intense social differentiation. Issues arising from the close quartering of diverse peoples feature prominently in studies of urban forms. Sociologists of the Chicago School of the 1920s and 1930s saw cities and ruralities as distinctly different phenomena. Urbanization entailed cultural breakdown, as authentic rural traditions disintegrate within new urban contexts (Park, Burgess, and McKenzie 1925). An "urban-folk continuum" measured degrees of citification: from a rural ideal of homogeneity based on face-to-face relations to an urban dystopia of disintegrated heterogeneity (Redfield 1941). Sociocultural dissolution was deemed the inevitable and predictable result of increased settlement size and density. Cities were considered a social problem. The Chicago School saw urban life as social pathology; its fluidity, mobility, and complexity creating instability, unrest, and the dissolution of social relationships and group solidarities.

Until very recently, assimilation was the expected outcome of rural to urban migration, and the retention of rural ways was believed to doom migrants to social and economic marginality (Erman 1998: 541). Social dissolution and cultural breakdown are no longer viewed as inevitable results of urbanization. More recently analysts have pointed to continuities between village and city life. Janet Abu-Lughod's work described the "ruralization" of Cairo, as large migrant populations changed the character of many working-class neighborhoods (1961).

The integration of rural migrants into urban life has continued to occupy urban geographers, sociologists, and anthropologists, particularly those who work outside Western industrial societies. Numerous studies deal with the problems encountered both by the migrants themselves and their host cities. In the Middle Eastern context, much of this work focuses on immigrant enclaves: Cairo's City of the Dead (Watson 1992), the *bidonvilles* of North Africa (Petonnet 1972; Bourdieu 1979), the North African *banlieues* of France (Kepel 1987), and the *gecekondu* of Turkey (Karpat 1976; Erman 1998). Most other studies of urban life center on a single poverty-stricken neighborhood, or set of such neighborhoods of Cairo (Wikan 1980, 1996; Early 1993; Singerman 1995; Singerman and Hoodfar 1996; Ghannam 1997; Hoodfar 1997). My work explores the tensions that processes of migration have created within wealthy areas of Damascus, as the close quartering of competing elites has intensified agonistic modes of distinction.

Old Cities, New Cities

In the Arab world, old walled cities surrounded by modern neighborhoods are a visual legacy of colonialism and post-colonial modernization projects. Studies of such "dual cities" point to continuities between colonial urban planning and contemporary social and class structures. The classic case studies have dealt with North African cities, where French planners built new residential areas outside indigenous medinas. Perceived differences in culture were deemed to require residential segregation. According to Louis Herbert Lyautey, governor of Morocco from 1912 to 1925, and chief architect of the dual-city approach:

> Large streets, boulevards, tall facades for stores and homes, installation of water and electricity are necessary, [all of] which upset the indigenous city completely, making the customary way of life impossible. You know how jealous the Muslim is of the integrity of his private life; you are familiar with the narrow streets, the facades without opening behind which hides the whole of life, the terraces upon which the family spreads out and must therefore remain sheltered from indiscreet looks. But the European house, with its superimposed stories, the modern skyscraper which reaches ever higher, is the death of the terrace; it is an attack upon the traditional mode of life. All the habits and all the tastes [of these two ways of life] oppose one another. Little by little, *the European city chases the native out;* but without thereby achieving the conditions indispensable to our modern way of life, so sprawled out and agitated. *In the end it is always necessary* [for the European] *to leave the indigenous town* and, in haste, create new quarters. *But*

by then it is too late: the damage has been done. The indigenous city is polluted, sabotaged; *all of its charm* has gone, and the elite of its populations has left. (1926 speech, quoted in J. Abu-Lughod 1980: 143, italics added by Abu-Lughod)

In much of colonial North Africa, urban planning followed Lyautey's thinking: new neighborhoods with modern facilities were constructed to house European colonial populations, and locals were confined to old-city quarters. Although never colonized, late Ottoman Istanbul experienced a similar process, as upper-income Turks joined European residents in Western-style neighborhoods north of the Golden Horn, leaving the older residential areas of the city's southern end to poorer classes and new migrants (Çelik 1986: 38–39, 160).

Elegant modern settlements encircled North Africa's old cities, signifying physical and metaphorical surrender to the colonial power (Çelik 1997: 37). In many cases, old cities were neglected, even "mummified," in the guise of respect for local heritage (Hamadeh 1992: 251; J. Abu-Lughod 1980: 151). Timothy Mitchell argues that the desire to preserve the old city as an exotic relic reflects a logic peculiar to the modern West. Nineteenth-century Europeans *enframed* urban space, organizing it along the principles of an exhibition, as a site to be viewed. Old-city quarters became visual museums, and the new city's wide boulevards and monumental facades provided grand vistas (1988: 34–62). In colonial ideology, the dual city formed a visual juxtaposition and physical representation of two cultures, two ways of thinking: one primitive, disordered, inward looking, dirty, and disease-ridden, if picturesque; the other modern, organized, open, clean, and efficient.

As in Damascus, post-independence national elites adopted colonial logic, leaving traditional quarters for the European-style housing left by former colonists. Poor rural migrants moved into the abandoned medina, dividing its houses into smaller, densely populated units (J. Abu-Lughod 1980: 227). These new residents often lacked sufficient resources to repair their crumbling houses, and controlled rents discouraged landlords from undertaking costly maintenance. The divide between old and new city in the post-colonial setting signifies class and regional distinction, an "urban apartheid" of rich and poor, urban and rural. Contemporary urban identities are often imbued with colonial constructs of social difference (Çelik 1997: 182).

As their cultural frame of reference globalizes, Middle Easterners have come to value their old-city quarters as elements of national culture (Öncü 1997: 56). For contemporary Algerians, the medina embodies the anti-colonial struggle and remains a symbol of resistance and decolonization (Çelik 1997: 187). Many cities have undertaken conservation and reconstruction projects designed for the tourist gaze (Çelik 1986; Bianco 2000; LeVine 2001; Mitchell 2001). Traditional elements are folklorized and embraced as part of modernity. They signify a rich heritage, but one relegated to the past through juxtaposition with the new city. What makes Damascus unique is the Syrian state's ambivalence toward the Old City and its elite. Syria's small tourist industry, which showcases a bounty of ancient ruins, provides little counterweight to the regime's security concerns. Like the casbah of colonial Algiers, Old Damascus and its potential to shelter resistance movements is perceived by some to pose a threat to the current rulers. The Old City and the counter-claims to authority and legitimacy it represents prevent the regime from wholeheartedly embracing it as a jewel of national culture. Old Damascus presents both a physical and an ideological threat.

Damascus and Distinction

Markedly hierarchical and religiously, ethnically, and regionally diverse, Damascene society confronts the social scientist with a bewildering array of social groupings and affiliations. Anthropological and sociological studies of Middle Eastern cities have analyzed such formations with only partial success. The classic "mosaic" approach, first expounded by Carleton Coon in the 1950s, depicts Middle Eastern societies as constellations of socially, culturally, and spatially distinct groups, based on religion, ethnicity, tribal, or regional origin (1951). The mosaic metaphor accurately conveys the region's diversity and complexity, yet it is ultimately static and ahistorical. Status and social relations in the urban Middle East are not determined by any fixed characteristics (D. Eickelman 1998: 116). Religious or ethnic affiliation, kinship ties, and residential or occupational groups form crosscutting and often conflicting social networks, rather than isolated or distinct units.

Fredrik Barth's groundbreaking emphasis on the processes of boundary formation and maintenance is helpful in the case of Damascus, where the cultural content of group differentiation may be minimal (1969). Actual differences are less important than how and why such differences are produced and maintained. What is significant is the perception of difference, and its social and political uses. Perceived differences are not cultural essences handed down through generations, but rather social constructs which may refer to the past but are very much a product of the present. Social groups invent traditions, formalizing and ritualizing references to the past (Hobsbawm and Ranger 1983). Traits which become the basis of group identification may have little or nothing to do with older traditions or affiliations, although pseudo-historical explanations may be invoked to camouflage their inventedness (Sollors 1989: xvi).

The relationship of group identity to class structure is central to the Syrian context, where sectarian and regional affiliations are often alloyed with those of hierarchy. The distinction between horizontal and vertical solidarities is a common theme in social science literature. This contrast is basically one of community and class—of societies based on primary identifications of kinship, tribe, and patronage, and those with elaborate divisions of labor and secondary and often impersonal forms of association. A distinction between two ideal types presupposes an evolutionary movement from the former to the latter. The Syrian case illustrates the problems entailed in this approach. It qualifies the concept of class, not because of the persistence of older modes of identity and association, but because of their continual political and ideological reconstruction in relation to new circumstances. Class distinctions are increasingly relevant, yet they crosscut and intersect rather than replace those of region, religion, and ethnic group.

While the socialist ideology of Syria's ruling Baʿth Party has consistently denied the significance of class, sectarian, regional, and ethnic divisions, such differences are nonetheless increasingly significant. In Damascus, these distinctions are being reworked and re-emphasized through new social practices and public cultural forms. The Old City features in these processes both as a physical space to be preserved and an ideal invoked in heritage commodities and urban power struggles. Historic Old Damascus, its physical presence and the public sentiments its former residents and their children express for it, represents spatial and discursive resistance to the monuments of state hegemony found in the new city. Here Damascus contrasts sharply with Baghdad, whose largely destroyed old city provides no architectural subversion of Saddam Hussein's "politics as art," monuments to the president and his deeds (al-Khalil 1992: 33–40). In Damascus, the "visual schizophrenia typical of the Baʿthist city" (ibid.: 50) reaches its apex.

Old Damascus

Damascus extends up the southern slope of Mount Qasiun. At night the upper reaches of the city resemble a mound of colored lights. Old Damascus lies to the southeast of the mountain. Parts of the Old City have been torn down to make way for concrete high-rises and modern boulevards, but much remains standing, including Muslim, Christian, and Jewish residential quarters inside the Old City walls, markets, and light craft industry. The elaborate entrance of Suq al-Hamidiyyeh in the western wall faces one way out onto the masses of traffic off the four-lane Revolution Street (Shariʿ al-Thawra), the other way into the supposed idyll of the Old City. Here on summer days a traditionally dressed juice seller pours tamarind juice from a brass urn strapped to his back, under a mammoth portrait of the country's president. Lining the beginning of the main street of the *suq* (marketplace) are brightly lit tourist shops, facades strung with embroidered *aghabani* tablecloths, gold and silver jewelry, musical instruments, inlaid wood handicrafts, brass trays and urns, and nylon sequined belly dancer outfits. Bored merchants spot a foreigner in seconds, leap up, and follow, describing their wares and offering the "best of prices." Next come fabric stores, sweetshops selling stringy pistachio-encrusted mastic ice cream, jewelry shops, hawkers peddling socks and handkerchiefs, stores selling ornate sequined and beaded dresses. One small cul-de-sac offers nothing but wedding gowns. Uniformed soldiers spending off-duty hours, peasant women—their bright patterned dresses peeping out from under black shawls—shopping for household goods, chador-draped Iranian pilgrims on their way to Shiʿi shrines, and dazed tourists trying to escape the merchants' hard sell all push against each other in a stream of movement toward the heart of the Old City. Further down, the suq's metal roof gives way to Roman arches, stalls lined with religious books and trinkets, more tourist shops, and finally the main entrance of the Umayyad Mosque—former temple of Jupiter for the Romans and church for the Byzantines, still one of the grandest monuments in Syria.

A right turn from the mosque into the first side street leads to the gold suq, with its streams of glittering chains. Al-Bzuriyyeh, the spice suq, lies just beyond, with sacks upon sacks of ground and whole spices, nuts, and medicinal herbs and teas. Continuing on around the mosque, one passes the wood suq, old-fashioned cane chairs lining the path, and several new tourist shops selling "Roman" beads and the Persian tiles and pottery that Iranian visitors peddle to finance their pilgrimages. Just ahead, across from the mosque's back door, is the Old City's best-known café, al-Nawfara, where a *hakawati* (storyteller) still performs every Thursday evening to a crowd of local men. Recently, university students have begun to join the audience, young women as well as men, and the occasional foreigner. On one visit, the *hakawati* stopped his stylized recitation midstream to reassure me that the Christian enemy to which he referred did not include me, but those of long ago. Café al-Nawfara, like so much of Old Damascus, is becoming folklorized, turned into a living museum of olden days for Syrians seeking a momentary glimpse of a quaint past. Once an integral part of the elite's everyday life, then a "no go" zone of embarrassing backwardness, the Old City, with its storytellers and handicrafts, has become an "experience" of local color.

Beyond al-Nawfara lie the Muslim residential quarters of al-ʿAmara, which once housed the local Muslim religious leadership, and al-Qaymariyyeh, once home to a wealthy merchant class, the wax simulacra of which can be seen at the Azm Palace, now a state-owned folklore museum.[4] To the south lies the commercial Midhat Basha Street, the biblical Street Called Straight, a continuation of Suq al-Bzuriyyeh. Along its way workshops produce *muzayik*, intricately patterned inlaid wood furniture, and craftsmen fashion copper and brass vessels. Walking east, one reaches the Christian quarters of Bab Tuma and Bab Sharqi, with their new restaurants and ancient churches facing the eastern wall. The Jewish Quarter (Harat al-Yahud) and the Muslim neighborhood of al-Shaghur lie along the southern wall.

Over the centuries the Old City overran its ancient walls. The quarter located just south of the wall, al-Maydan, dates from the sixteenth century. To middle-class and upper-middle-class Damascenes, al-Maydan represents Old Damascene authenticity.[5] Renowned for tiny eateries producing local delicacies, an old-fashioned accent, and "traditional" architecture and social relations, al-Maydan is considered the quintessential popular Damascene quarter. Yet al-Maydan has long been Old Damascus's most geographically and religiously heterogeneous quarter, a first stop for rural-to-urban migrants, especially those from the Hawran region of southern Syria.

To the west of the old wall is the sixteenth-century quarter of al-Qanawat, formerly a district of notables, its bygone wealth still reflected in elaborate woodwork on balconies and windows. Suq Saruja, a quarter torn in half to make way for Revolution Street, lies to the north. Once home to Ottoman functionaries, this fourteenth-century quarter, nicknamed "Little Istanbul," still boasts some of the most spectacular old Damascene houses. Old notables are for the most part gone from these quarters. Poorer migrants from outside Damascus have replaced them, dividing their once grand houses into crowded single-family units. The old elite of Damascus now reside in the wealthier European-style neighborhoods beyond the Old City walls, in the spacious, airy apartments of the New City.

New Damascus

From Bab Tuma, the Old City's northeastern gate, the middle-class Christian neighborhood of Qassaʿ stretches out, its main street lit by the neon signs of clothing shops. An average four-room flat in this area sells for around 12,000,000 SP, a sum which should be considered in relation to the annual salary of a university-educated civil servant: 60,000 SP.[6] Like much of central New Damascus, this area was developed during the French Mandate period, along the guidelines laid out by architect Michel Ecochard. Further to the east is the suburb of Barzeh, originally built to house the mostly ʿAlawi military families arriving from the countryside, and now home to a small intelligentsia of university teachers and journalists. Here property values are lower: 4,000,000 SP will buy a flat, and special mortgage plans assist civil servants.

Westward from Qassaʿ, we move through the modern, middle- and lower-middle-class areas of Maysat, ʿAdawi, and Baramkeh, bypassing the middle- and lower-middle-class districts of northeastern Damascus—Rukn al-Din, Sheikh Muhyadin, al-Akrad, and al-Sharka-siyyeh. Properties in these regions range from 6,000,000 to 8,000,000 SP to buy, and 60,000 to 120,000 SP per year to rent. Baghdad Street leads to 29 May Street and Bawabat Salhiyyeh Square, the first landmark of elite Damascus, a commercial district home to the National Bank of Syria's headquarters, the five-star Cham Palace Hotel, and Gharaoui, Damascus's most exclusive chocolatier. This is Damascus's Broadway or West End, with the Qabbani Theater, the Cham Palace Theater, and further down the street the Kindi Cinema (one of the city's few cinemas not devoted to martial arts movies). In September, the streets off the square buzz with artists and journalists from all over the Middle East and beyond, when international film and theater festivals alternate from year to year. North of Bawabat Salhiyyeh is Shahbandar Circle and al-Mazraʿa, a middle-class neighborhood whose respectable inhabitants have watched turn into a red-light district of liquor stores and all-night "real estate agents" servicing Arab tourists from the Gulf.

Running alongside the Cham Palace, where writers and artists drink tea and finger worry beads in a glass-encased café, is Maysalun Street, lined with numerous European language and scholarly bookstores and ice cream parlors full of mirrors and marble.[7] Flats in this area sell for 10,000,000 to 13,000,000 SP, and rent for 500,000 to 600,000 per year. A right turn at the Franciscan (al-Fransiscaine) church and girls' school—one of the most prestigious in the city—brings us to the Old Damascene-inhabited neighborhood of Shaʿlan, just south of Zanubia, or "al-Sibki," Park, about a mile away from the Old City. Here, at the intersection of Shaʿlan Street and Hafiz Ibrahim Street, lies one of the city's best produce markets. Stores spill out into fruit and vegetable displays, donkeys bray, and shoppers haggle, while from an air-conditioned shop selling pirated tapes of the latest Western popular music the latest tune from Sweden, so far removed from local mores, blares: "All that she wants is another baby, she's gone tomorrow boy, all that she wants is another baby."

West of Shaʿlan lies the palm-tree-lined Abu Rummaneh Boulevard, known officially as al-Jalaʾ (Evacuation) Street, named for the withdrawal of French Mandate forces. This is Damascus's embassy row, home also to the Arab Cultural Center and the French Research Institute (IFEAD). On summer evenings, prickly pear sellers line Abu Rummaneh with their greenery-covered stalls, while patrons consume this most Damascene of delicacies late into the night.[8] Expensive, old-money apartment buildings occupied by Old Damascenes line the smaller streets on both sides of the boulevard, where average four-room flats sell for 15,000,000 to 25,000,000 SP, and rent for 800,000 to 1,000,000 SP per year. Scattered between apartment buildings are elegant restaurants, stores selling "imported" or smuggled foods, and upscale furniture and clothing boutiques. Shiny marble neoclassical facades announce foreign goods at exorbitant prices. In 1995, these were joined by a score of brightly colored Benetton franchises selling Syrian-produced clothing.

To the east of the boulevard is al-Rawda, where I lived for the first year and half of fieldwork. This neighborhood of florists and art galleries—the Chaura and the Atassi—is also home to the exclusive Health Club. Northwest along the slope of Mount Qasiun lies the al-Jisr al-Abyad neighborhood. Expensive houseware shops sell gilded china and ornate European curios. Here stands the stately old Italian hospital, with its graceful carved-wood window frames. Al-Jisr al-Abyad is part of the larger area referred to as al-Salhiyyeh—originally a medieval village, later home to Ottoman and then French functionaries, and one of the first destinations for wealthy migrants from the Old City. Afif Street leads westward toward the district of al-Muhajirin, a former suburb built at the turn of the twentieth century to house Muslim refugees from Crete and now a Damascene stronghold. Average four-room apartments in this region sell for 10,000,000 SP, and rent for 500,000 to 600,000 per year. The further west one moves, the more expensive the real estate becomes. 'Adnan al-Malki Square marks the beginning of the highest rent zone in Syria, with flats running from 20,000,000 to 40,000,000 SP. The most elite districts—those generally associated with new money—lie to the west of jasmine-scented Malki Avenue. Here in West Malki and New West Malki, a flat runs 40,000,000 to 50,000,000 SP, and rents for 2,000,000 SP per year. Like many upscale residential areas in the Middle East, West and New West Malki are religiously and regionally mixed. Landmarks are status symbols: one who lives near Malki's Shami Hospital lives royally. Malki is home to the American-run Damascus Community School, whose pupils are mostly wealthy Syrians, those few who can afford its $7,000 annual tuition fees. The DCS is also home to the American Language Center, the most expensive—and therefore most prestigious—English-language teaching center in the city.[9]

At the bottom of Malki Avenue sits Umayyad Circle, named for the dynasty at the apex of Syrian—and particularly Damascene—history, and ground zero of the city's elite. The shooting streams of water in this massive roundabout's fountain change direction every few days. Umayyad Circle discourages pedestrians, with its skimpy pavements and confusing traffic movements. But then this is not the sort of circle people walk on, and those who travel there are not the sort who walk. Around the circle stand the imposing modern Asad National Library, the General Association of Radio and Television, and a new performing arts center. On its Western flank stands the hub of elite social life, the Sheraton Hotel. This is where the city's upper echelons construct and reconstruct themselves, where rites of passage are celebrated and familial and professional alliances are forged. This is where life-making, or -breaking, gossip flows. The Sheraton's two major competitors, the Meridien and the Qasr al-Nubala (Nobles' Palace), lie just off the circle on the way toward Abu Rummaneh.

Although vast sections of Damascus's famous gardens have been replaced with low-cost housing, greenery is never too far away. Tishrin Park, host to an annual flower festival, stretches alongside the Sheraton to the northwest of Umayyad Circle. The road running along the park leads eventually to the mountain gorge just outside the city called Rabweh, in whose cliff-side restaurants urbanites continue a beloved age-old tradition, the *sayran* (pl. *sayarin*), a Friday "outing" in summer. A tributary of the Barada River provides the requisite water, since for a *sayran* to be successful there must be shade, water, and beauty (*fay wa may wa shakl hasan*). Modern forms of transport now take people further outside Damascus for *sayarin*, into the cool, green hills of Zabadani and Bludan. In the early spring, the vast orchard region of al-Ghuta just south of the city begins to bloom, providing the ideal setting for the year's first *sayarin*.

Along the western flank of the Sheraton, the broad Mezzeh Autostrade runs through the former "Valley of Violets." It passes by the main Damascus University campus and dormitory area, now renamed "Basil City" in memory of President Hafiz al-Asad's "martyred" son, to reach the suburb of Mezzeh. Like Salhiyyeh, Mezzeh was once a suburban village, said to have been founded by Yemeni migrants during the Umayyad caliphate, A.D. 661–750. A working-class Old Mezzeh still survives, but over the past two decades New Mezzeh has engulfed it with large buildings housing the wealthy. Many of these well-to-do residents are new to Damascus, having returned to Syria from lucrative careers in the Arabian Gulf. Others more rooted in the city have escaped smaller flats in the crowded city center. The suburb becomes more affluent as one moves further along the highway, as concrete high-rises give way to the palatial apartments of Villat Sharqiyyeh, where property values equal those in Malki. To the south is the slightly less monied Villat Gharbiyyeh, with flats selling for 13,000,000 to 15,000,000 SP and renting at 1,000,000 per year. New Mezzeh has itself become a leisure site with numerous elegant shops, restaurants, and hotels. North of Mezzeh is Dummar, a dormitory suburb of middle-class professionals and university lecturers.

This is a sketch of *elite* New Damascus, and includes only those regions that weigh anything at all on scales of wealth, power, and prestige. For the elite, the rest of Damascus exists only as a foil for wealth and privilege. It is not *their* Damascus. These areas of the city are telling markers of social class. In the television series *The Other Side* (*al-Wajh al-Akhar*), a teenage girl ashamed of living in the Old City takes a bus to al-Muhajirin each day after school to convince her classmates she is living there instead. Iman Abdul Rahim of the Ministry of Tourism tells a similar tale of social-spatial "sizing up":

> I went to a meeting of a club that gathers together Damascenes.[10] The director is an elite Damascene (*bint ʿaʾileh shamiyyeh*), from a very well known family, she's a Quwwatli. You can consider it the number one or two family in the country. She struck up a conversation with me, asking questions, and from these questions she was able to form an 80 percent accurate picture of my social position. The first question was "Where do you live?" Before "What did you study?" or "Who is your husband?" If you say, "I'm living in Malki," or "I'm living in Abu Rummaneh," your position immediately changes, even if you are wearing very casual simple clothing. People immediately know your class.

Place of residence indicates social group in the way occupation often does in the industrial West. Damascus is large enough for people to invoke broad social categories, but also small enough for inhabitants to form a shared knowledge of places and their reputations. Status is linked to place and, to a lesser extent, people. In the marriage market, that most central institution of Syrian social life, Damascus residents put a premium on wealthy neighborhoods. The most incisive question to a potential bride or groom is no longer "Who is your father?" or "What do you do?" but "Where do you live?" Connoting both great wealth and old wealth, Malki has a particularly deep social resonance. Much sought after is the potential bride or bridegroom who lives in this neighborhood of the old elite. As my Damascene neighbor said of her violently abusive former husband, "his family had a house in Malki, so we thought he was all right." Another Damascene informant tells a similar tale:

> My husband and I went to see a doctor in al-Maydan. My husband didn't bring his identity papers. The doctor was very short with him, said he was careless, and told him to go and get them. "I'm not going all the way home and back," my husband said, "because it's already late, and you'll be closed by the time I return." "Why," asked the doctor, "where do you live?" My husband replied "Malki," and this changed his attitude completely, and he's a doctor! Immediately he respected him, and started calling him *beik* (sir).

In contemporary Damascus, residential neighborhoods are telling markers of social status. The right address alone elicits the respect due a *beik*. My work reveals an urban geography of social distinction in which areas signify not merely the degree of wealth but also the type of wealth, since sectarian and regional identities are interwoven with those of class. As will be seen in the next chapter, the social differences so clearly inscribed in residential boundaries are also constructed and reconstructed through the leisure practices and expressive cultural forms occurring within these spaces. In these consumptive contests, women are key players.

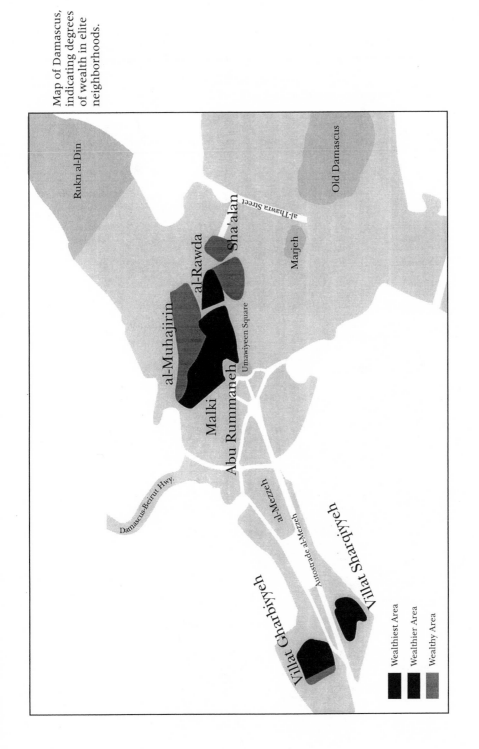

Map of Damascus, indicating degrees of wealth in elite neighborhoods.

Rukn al-Din

Old Damascus

al-Rawda

Sha'alan

al-Thawra Street

Marjeh

al-Muhajirin

Umawiyeen Square

Malki

Abu Rummaneh

Damascus-Beirut Hwy.

al-Mezzeh

Autostrade al-Mezzeh

Villat Gharbiyyeh

Villat Sharqiyyeh

Wealthiest Area

Wealthier Area

Wealthy Area

Residential Old
Damascus

Residential Old Damascus

Suq al-Hamidiyyeh

Suq al-Bzuriyyeh

Abu Rummaneh Boulevard

'Adnan al-Malki Avenue

2

"That Color Looks Great on You"
Consumption, Display, and Gender

In my imagination young women were
divided into two classes; those who were to be
purchased, and those who were to purchase.
—**Maria Edgeworth,** *Castle Rackrent*

We make conversation: we husbands talk
about production; the ladies, about
consumption.
—**Italo Calvino,** *Time and the Hunter*

The Commodification of Social Life

In Damascus, social identities are increasingly negotiated and contested through competitive consumption. Women emerge as central
players in contests over position and prestige; what they wear, where
they dine, and who they marry may signify, reinforce, and even create class affiliation. The commodification of social life engenders a
context in which Damasceneness is continually invoked, and sometimes undermined.

The ability to purchase expensive consumer goods, and to be seen
in fashionable venues, has long been an important mark of elite status for women in Damascus.[1] Under the socialist economic policies of
the 1960s, 1970s, and 1980s, minimal domestic industry combined
with import bans to render commodities scarce. Access to consumer
goods, such as fashionable clothing, distinguished those with connections to powerful individuals (for whom sanctions against smuggling
did not apply) and the wealthy who traveled abroad. The Ba'th Party

attempt to rid Syrian society of social hierarchy not only failed, but actually produced new class divisions. During the 1990s, a boom in local production and loosening of import regulations led to an increasing availability of both locally produced and foreign consumables on Syrian store shelves. The commodification of many aspects of social life accelerated, as more commodities and public leisure sites widened opportunities for social distinction through consumption.

The kind of consumption in which people in Damascus engage both reflects and constructs social differences. My exploration of this phenomenon draws on Pierre Bourdieu's analysis of distinction, which links preferences in cuisine, art, music, and home furnishings to income, educational level, and social background (1984). Bourdieu's once groundbreaking and now commonplace argument demonstrated that taste is a matter not of individual proclivity but of social position. "Good taste," the socially acquired preference for high over low cultural forms, serves as cultural capital, an asset not directly material but enhancing and reinforcing class position.

The relationship between consumption, display, and social identity is explored in a significant body of recent literature. Much of this material shows how the range of commodities now available allows the differentiation and ranking, by presentation and consumption, of persons who have no "natural" relations, such as kin or locality, but instead must state their social position before an audience who otherwise might know little of them. Elite Damascus presents a seeming paradox. Style, leisure activities, and displays of wealth have become increasingly significant with economic liberalization. As one informant puts it, elites in Damascus are "inventing occasions to show off their wealth." Yet these have not eclipsed the importance of family name. Damascus is still very much like a small town for the middle and upper classes; all appear to know one another. But like the inhabitants of Herbert Gans's "ethnic village" urban enclave, Damascenes do not actually know one another. They know of and about one another (1962: 15, 75). Damascenes often have at their fingertips detailed information, or speculation—family background, income, profession, education—about persons they have never met. Information networks are vast; social networks are much smaller. Because people may not know one another personally, may only know about one another, seeing and perceiving others become significant. Here consumption comes into play. Elite names remain elite, and new names become elite through public displays of wealth. Older forms of social identification are not disappearing but are being reworked, through consumption in a new arena, a public culture of hotels, restaurants, and cafés. To paraphrase a line from Lampe-dusa's *The Leopard,* things are changing so that things can remain the same (1960: 40).

In a "community" where people may not know one another but do see one another, appearances take on great importance. Syrian men are image conscious—those who can afford it wear expensive clothing, cologne, and gold jewelry and drive flashy cars; but it is women who most often represent familial wealth and status through physical beauty and adornment. Feminist critics in the West argue that with the continual bombardment of narrowly defined images of female beauty in the contemporary media, physical appearance has become the most important measure of a woman's worth. Such comments are made in the context of advanced industrial societies, where the pressure on women to reach unattainable heights of physical perfection is perceived by some as part of a backlash against feminist successes (Wolf 1991).[2] In Syria, a similar situation is devel-oping, as increasing access to Western media combines with ever tightening restrictions on women's social presence outside the home, although Western-style feminism has never occurred.

The Syrian media's commodification of women's bodies is swift-ly catching up with that of Western counterparts. With the privatiza-tion of the Syrian economy over the past decade, a rapidly growing domestic advertising industry has developed. When the Arab Adver-tising Institute (*al-Mu'assasa al-'Arabiyya lil-I'lan*) was set up in 1990, there were only three Syrian television advertising agencies; by the middle of 1991 this number had increased to sixty-five. In addition, four international agencies set up offices in Damascus in the mid-1990s.[3] Televised images of heavily made-up, tightly clothed women now join those long depicted on the pages of Arabic women's maga-zines. Between advertisements, foreign and locally produced se-rial dramas convey a similarly homogeneous, exaggerated, hyper-real feminine ideal—the glossy mouths, lacquered hair, and power shoulder pads of 1980s American soap operas adopted by Syrian women of all ages and social groups.[4] Holding center stage in con-sumption and display contests, women provide an ideal focus for a discussion of the commodification of image and identity.

Chastity as Capital

Compounding the importance of image for Syrian women is the premium placed on the appearance of chastity. An unpopular sub-ject among gender specialists who prefer to emphasize Middle East-ern women's empowerment, the issue of control over female sexuality is profoundly affecting Syrian society in novel ways. Elite Syrians themselves are reluctant to discuss this situation, even in forums focusing on gender. A lecture on feminism at the American Cultural Center provides a case in point: a young Syrian female Ph.D., adorned with the emphasized femininity of a Hollywood starlet, discussed Simone de Beauvoir and Hélène Cixous. Neither she nor the post-lecture commentators mentioned the local obsession with female sexual purity. Instead, a young actor spoke passionately about the need to preserve the family. A long debate, reminiscent of American notions of "political correctness," centered on whether or not male authors are able to write from a woman's point of view, and whether or not a writer could depict experiences he or she had not had. A Damascus University professor spoke of sexism in language. No one mentioned the vast majority of women who are forbidden— by parents, brothers, husbands, or the watchfulness of neighbors— to attend a lecture like this one, held in the evening, since returning home after dark prompts suspicion.

The appearance of sexual purity becomes a form of capital for a young woman. Its absence can be disastrous for her future prospects. It can also become ammunition for opposing families to hurl at their enemies. In order to preserve their chastity capital, young women should not be seen interacting with men, particularly one-to-one, before they are engaged. Their moving about the city alone, especially after sundown, is frowned upon. The economic implications of these sanctions are profound. To paraphrase Bourdieu, women's subjective situation—restricted movement outside the home—is both a precondition and a product of their material dependency (1979).

Although premarital social and even sexual contact between men and women is not unknown, discretion is key.[5] Elite districts of Damascus—which provide relative anonymity—are peppered with small, dark, heavily curtained coffee shops where courting couples can sit together unnoticed. Headscarf-clad young women hold their boyfriends' hands as they speak intensely over inexpensive cups of coffee and tea. Dates take place either surreptitiously or under the guise of fictional marriage engagement.[6]

Young women for whom interaction with men is restricted adopt strategies of attraction through display. Semi-public spaces provide venues for showing oneself to others. The Health Club in Abu Rummaneh, for instance, is an entirely unisex workout place in a neighborhood largely populated by upper-middle-class, conservative Damascenes. The women who can afford to go there drive or are driven. They tend not to walk on the streets, even in conservative clothing. Yet inside the club they wear heavy makeup and skimpy leotards—often with spaces cut to reveal large sections of bare stomach, back, or thigh—and leave flowing their invariably long hair. In contrast, non-Syrian women appear in leggings or sweat pants and long baggy T-shirts, their faces bare of makeup and hair tied back. The club's single, brightly lit, mirror-paneled room seems designed with display in mind, as aerobic classes take place in a cleared area in front of the weights and exercise machines. Those pumping iron—mostly men—can watch the bobbing behinds, delineated clearly in thong-backed leotards, of the women taking step aerobics or body-toning classes, as technopop blares in the background. All the leotards sold in the club's small boutique have low-cut scoop necklines and thong-backed bottoms. The Health Club is one of the arenas between public and private where young women, and to a lesser extent young men, take advantage of the in-between-ness to show off as much body as possible. This contrasts sharply with the hidden intimacy of the curtained coffee shop, as Health Club patrons hide themselves from sight on the way to and from a space specifically designed to reveal.

Most semi-public spaces, including professional ones, provide opportunities for attraction. Flirtatiousness is the norm. A Damascene professional told me that a diplomat from the American Cultural Center had suggested starting classes in office conduct for Syrian women. She told the diplomat that no one would attend them, as women who work do so to attract husbands, not build careers. Most jobs open to women, however prestigious, do not pay enough to enable them to become economically self-sufficient. Unmarried women, even wealthy ones, rarely set up independent households. Jobs are seen as temporary measures on the way to marriage or as supplementary income afterward. For young single women, they are primarily a venue for display, the ultimate aim of which is to secure a successful future in the private, rather than public, sphere. For married women, they supply extra income, social contact, and a chance to exhibit their husbands' affection and economic status through self-adornment.

Beauty and Wealth on the Marriageability Scale

In elite Damascus, competitive display is often geared toward attaining desirable marriage partners. Marriages, like the wedding ceremonies commencing them, signify and engender social position. A daughter who obtains a prestigious mate raises, or at least reinforces, her family's lofty rank. Brides are chosen for a variety of assets, among which beauty and wealth are most significant.

Damascenes value feminine beauty, and associate it with the city. A beautiful woman is said to have drunk the water of Damascus (*sharbaneh mayat al-sham*). As old notable author Rana Kabbani notes, Damascene beauties are "famous for their bedroom eyes and al-abaster skin" (1998: 134). Yet wealth sometimes eclipses beauty, as great fortunes can now obliterate distinctions between new and old money. A young Damascene professional woman from an old elite family described these standards to me:

> If there's a lot of money involved, beauty makes no difference. It only mat-ters when they are of average wealth, or borderline. For example, you have *bayt* (family) X, who are not Damascenes. Their daughters are ugly (*bisha'at*), by the beauty standards of the country. They're not attractive, they all have hairy complexions. But they have lots of money, so they married *awlad 'ayal* (Damascene elites).

When I asked if *awlad 'ayal* also consider money the most important characteristic, my informant replied:

> Of course! They are even more interested in money. Sons of old noble fam-ilies are more interested in new money, in the new money classes. It's the opposite of what you might think. The interest in money among upper classes is equal, new money or old. It's more important than anything else.

Such a characterization from an articulate informant with a wealth of local knowledge contradicted my own assumption, and many Syrians' contention, that the old urban elite marry only among themselves. I asked my informant how intermarriage occurs, given that, as she had told me earlier, the Old Damascenes "consider them-selves superior":

> How does this work? A boy (*shabb*) of the rich classes—new money—mar-ries an old money girl (*bint*). If he has a lot of money, her family won't consider it a problem, even if this money has come through different means. If an old money boy marries a new money girl, the matter is differ-ent. If she's not pretty, she must be very, very rich.

Damascene author Rana Kabbani concurs:

> For all their feminine wiles, Damascene women are hardheaded when it comes to the beneficiaries or victim of their beautification: men. Given the choice between Romeo and rich Count Paris, they will choose the latter. Their perfectly sugared arms need gems to show them off. (ibid.: 135)[7]

While beauty is a key asset for women, wealth is what renders a groom desirable. As my Damascene informant observed: "Boys' looks don't matter. A boy, old or new money, may be short and bald, but if he has a lot of money, he can marry the prettiest girl in the country. So looks are only important for girls."

Syrian women of elite classes are aware of and not always complacent about this double standard. At a dinner party of middle-aged couples, one of the husbands called his wife—ten years younger than himself—an old hag. Suddenly all the women disappeared into the back rooms of the flat, then re-emerged with all the portable mirrors they could find and handed them to their husbands.

Beauty remains important, yet wealth is beginning to replace other attributes of desirability. Complex distinctions are made between beauty, money, and status, as a middle-aged Damascene housewife explained:

> For example, X [an elite old Damascene] wanted to marry a girl from a very, very rich family—you can call them one of the millionaire families. But she wasn't at all pretty. But here her family begins to calculate: ok, he's a good-looking boy, and their daughter is ugly, and he's not poor, he has money, so it's an appropriate match. Had she been pretty, they would have engaged her to someone a bit better than him, someone richer. So the girls of this family all married good-looking boys who had less money than they. They do a trade-off—those who have money want beauty. Now, given the country's standards, if an old money boy can choose between a very, very pretty girl and one who is very rich, he will choose the richer. It didn't used to be this way. Fifteen years ago, when my husband's [old elite] brothers got engaged, they were looking for pretty girls. Pretty young girls, in order to have pretty children. But those who are becoming engaged now are always looking for very rich girls. . . . Standards have changed. Before, the best they could have was a pretty girl, a young daughter-in-law. Now they chose a very rich girl. There's been a change in peoples' thinking with respect to wealth.

Location of the family house is a key class indictor. The housewife continues:

> Recently my husband's youngest brother went to meet a girl who lived in Suwaiqa.[8] She was amazingly beautiful, the standard of a beauty queen, and a nice girl—he himself said all this about her—a fourth-year English literature student, who speaks English and has been to America. And she was 21 or 22, an appropriate age. But his family refused. My husband was shocked, such a pretty, nice, educated girl of an appropriate age. But they want someone who lives near West Malki, the closer the better.

A mate's desirability is not defined by the groom alone; choosing a partner is a family matter in which mothers and sisters are central.

The marriage market in elite Damascus exists within a male-dominated economic system, but is not itself male controlled; powerful matrons direct the movement of people and statuses. Contemporary Damascus here resembles nothing so much as the drawing rooms of Jane Austen and Maria Edgeworth. Beauty and fortune are explicitly weighed and measured—usually by women themselves—to determine a woman's worth. Indeed, one Damascene informant, like Lady Bertram of Austen's *Mansfield Park,* repeatedly expressed surprise and indignation at an acquaintance who, although neither attractive nor rich, had married well. Not unlike nineteenth-century Britain, contemporary Syria is undergoing rapid social and economic transformations, with older kinship-based forms of distinction giving way to materially based ones, or at least a material idiom replacing that of kinship. Elites are redefining themselves, yet some things remain the same: the centrality of marriage and kin and the basis of family honor. The contrived chastity of contemporary Syria parallels the contrived gentility of Austen's England.

Clothing Makes the Woman

For all women in Damascus, the ability to purchase a look that highlights beauty, and suggests wealth, is crucial. For single women, appearance is central to obtaining a desirable spouse. But the pressure to present a stylish image does not disappear after marriage, since a wife's grooming and attire then signify her husband's and family's status. Competitive display is evident at elite in-spots: at the Sheraton Hotel pool, wealthy women change bathing suits several times during an afternoon of sunbathing. A married woman, expensively coiffed and dressed, is one who has made an enviable match. Wedding rings are a clear status marker. The Damascene professional observes:

> I was at a party recently, sitting at a round table with ten other people. When I saw their hands on the table, I could tell immediately what class they belong to, from the diamond rings on their fingers. When a woman is very rich, she always wears diamond rings; one with five large diamonds and one a solitaire, a big, clear diamond. And that's it, even if she is from a different governorate, she's clearly from the very rich. These two rings alone would cost a million SP. You'll find it is a very important thing among the richest girls in the country, how much their solitaires cost. It means the bridegroom can afford everything else. Even if I don't know anything else about you, without asking you anything, I can tell your class from your ring.

Here style marks intra-elite distinctions:

Also, someone may have a ring as heavy as a diamond ring, but which has no diamonds in it, and it's immediately clear that she is new money, not from old money. Gold [alone] indicates that she does not have nobility (*'araqa*) in her family. Diamonds are higher. Why? Because diamonds are a luxury, while gold is a means of saving.[9] Diamonds are 100 percent luxury. They show that your husband can spend a million lira on just a ring.

Acquisition practices among the elite are ranked, with those who can afford to shop in France or Lebanon at the top, those who buy at the better Damascene stores in the middle, and below them those who must resort to the cheaper synthetic local imitations of European catwalk fashions available in less expensive boutiques. Natural fabrics are rare and worn only by the uppermost stratum, or sometimes the Western educated. Certain fabrics mark old elites from their newer counterparts, as my young professional informant notes:

Upper-class, old-money Damascene girls wear *guipere*[10] dresses. Then it's known how much was spent on the fabric for the dress, even if its style is ugly. *Dentelle* (lace) as well. And of course, mink. It must be a long black coat, with recognizable sections in it.

Women move beyond superficial adornment of clothing to resculpt their bodies. Rana Kabbani argues:

For plastic surgery, Damascus must rank second to Rio in terms of popularity. A new monied generation is heavily into liposuction, facelifts, breast enhancement, eyebrow, eyelid, and lip tatooing, and other cosmetic improvements. The richest surgeon in town is the nose-job king whose motto is "the husband is the last to nose." (1998: 135)

"The Problem of What to Wear"

Competitive self-adornment, the essence of social display in most major Middle Eastern cities, has received scant scholarly attention.[11] Lindisfarne-Tapper and Ingham's recent study of dress in the Middle East focuses almost exclusively on "traditional" clothing and issues of modesty (1997b). Meneley touches on the issue in the context of Yemen, where differences in fabrics determine whether or not a dress of the currently fashionable style is "genuine" (*asli*) (1996: 110–111). My own work is not intended as the extended treatment that clothing in the Middle East warrants; instead I examine sartorial statements as strategies for social mobility.

Young women dress to impress not only men, but even more importantly, other women, given the central role mothers and sisters play in finding a young man a bride. All-female social events are opportunities to introduce a marriageable daughter, niece, or sister. An extraordinary amount of time and money is spent thinking about, talking about, and purchasing new clothes and hairstyles.

Dress style among both young and middle-aged women tends to run to two extremes. On the one hand, there is a strong tendency toward highly marked sensuality or sexuality: tight, figure-hugging, and sometimes cleavage-revealing clothing in vivid colors—red and black are a favorite combination—heavy makeup, teased and moussed long hair, high heels, multiple gold or gilt accessories. One evening, as we sipped coffee in the Sheraton's al-Nawafeer Café, one of my two women companions glanced around at the parade of glitter and bemoaned the recent changes in taste. "The aristocracy used to have class," she remarked; "now everything must be bigger, busier, heavier, and shinier."[12] On the other hand, there is an increasing number of *muhajjabeh,* who, with their white headscarves and simple blue or gray overcoats, eschew all local conventions of attractiveness.[13] Women find it difficult to maintain a stylistic middle ground between the invisibility of the *hijab* (Islamic dress) and the flamboyance of the coquette. As one Damascene woman put it (in English), "we have cockteasers and *muhajjabeh,* and nothing in between."

The following anecdote illustrates this sartorial dilemma. A young, unmarried Syrian woman, working among foreign men at the UN Observer Forces Headquarters, told me she tries to dress conservatively at work to avoid attracting sexual attention. She is Christian, so the scarf for her is not an option. But when she goes out in the evening, more flamboyantly dressed, her women friends always compliment her and ask why she does not dress that way all the time. In this context, the choice to eschew makeup and wear an overcoat and scarf can be seen as a socially acceptable form of retreat from the endless pressure to objectify oneself. The wearing of the *hijab* signifies a dignity and moral authority placing the wearer above display contests. There is very little middle ground. To affect an understated style is to invite criticism from all sides.

Wolf quotes a long series of comments made about women's clothing in the Western workplace, arguing that any style is open to criticism (1991: 38–47). This problem is acute in Damascus, where appearance is so often and so openly discussed. Only a few women manage an in-between-ness, often those who have professional and social contacts with the French. For the old elite of Damascus, proficiency in French language and culture represented refinement and cultivation. Just as the study of French literature is giving way to business and technical English at Damascus University, the Francophone and Francophile circles are shrinking in a swell of strongly marked materialism.

Display Cases

For married women, the tradition of the afternoon reception, *is-tiqbal,* provides an opportunity for displays of skill, taste, and wealth. On the same day each month, a woman invites her circle of friends to her home for an *istiqbal.* The afternoon is preceded by a flurry of activity, as the matron, her daughters, daughters-in-law, and household servants clean the house thoroughly and bring out the best china and silver. Women of the extended family and their guests dress in their finest and most fashionable clothes. Most often light refreshments are served, sometimes a full meal. Whatever is offered is as elaborate, expensive, and labor intensive as possible. Freshly squeezed juice, homemade preserves, sweets laden with *samneh* (sheep's milk butter), and nuts are standard. An *istiqbal* is intended to reveal a woman's beauty, taste, and housekeeping skills, and her husband's wealth and position. Guests arrive wearing their own status markers. Husbands take part both in shopping for the event, and discussing it afterward, thereby gaining a glimpse of their colleagues' fortunes: "A woman serves the most expensive foods and drinks that she can, according to her husband's ability and position. Hospitality (*al-diyafeh*) is important because it demonstrates how much he is worth." As a Damascene proverb holds, "a wife is a man's face" (*martu wajihtu*). "The *istiqbal* is his advertising agency," as one Damascene informant put it.

More frequently, competitive display takes place beyond such domestic spaces. Major gathering spots, such as the big hotels, also provide venues for seeing and being seen. Many upper-middle-class families—those who cannot afford villas in Marbella—vacation at the Meridien or the Cham Côte d'Azur hotels on the Syrian coast, at Latakia, during the August peak season. In the evenings, people stroll from one hotel to the other, so as not to miss any action. At dusk, throngs of holiday-makers pass one another on the tree-lined avenue connecting the two. These hotels provide little in the way of activities or entertainment; their lobbies, restaurants, bars, and cafés are packed with vacationers who at first glance appear to be doing nothing at all. They are actually very busy, doing an important part of the work of contemporary elites: looking and being looked at, talking and being talked about. Everyone dresses carefully in new clothing. Young women take advantage of the resort atmosphere to display every curve in fluorescent Lycra mini-dresses.

This mating game continues year round at the Sheraton pizzeria, where up-to-date fashions reveal cleavage and thigh. Young men and women gaze at each other from the safety of groups; they rarely converse one-to-one publicly. Young women are allowed, indeed encouraged, to attract men, but are forbidden to socialize with them. The aim is to attract a husband with her body, since young people of opposite sexes are rarely permitted enough time together for anything else to matter. Discouraged from openly attracting male attention through wit, warmth, intelligence, or charm, women become silent images. Display, contained within certain spaces, is more acceptable than interaction.

The decision to wear a headscarf in public—which a growing number of women are making—can be seen as retreat from a competition that is becoming increasingly unaffordable, as economic liberalization swells inflation and floods the market with luxury goods out of reach for most. Yet given that many relatively well-to-do young women have adopted the scarf, economic explanations alone do not account for the phenomenon. Nor does it always reflect a newfound religiosity. Rather, the scarf is often a way of opting out of the display game and its objectification. Several Damascene women I met opted for the *hijab* after traumatic encounters with men.[14] It is here that standard sociological explanations of veiling as political protest intersect with personal histories.[15] As public culture's objectification and commodification of women's bodies mirrors their abuse in private, women increasingly shrink from both spheres.

In a context where image rather than achievement determines status, the presentation stakes are high. Every aspect of a woman's appearance is subject to scrutiny and evaluation by other women. Losing or gaining a pound, drying one's hair differently, wearing a skirt instead of trousers or a slightly thicker line of eyeliner, all elicit comment; sometimes, but not always, in compliment form. A song by the Iraqi heartthrob Kadhim al-Sahir that was wildly popular during my second year of fieldwork set to music a comment I heard throughout my stay in Syria:

That color looks great on you	*Hadha al-laun ʿaleik yujannin*
It matches the color of your eyes	*Yushbeh laun ʿayunak*

At Damascus's exclusive Nadi al-Sharq (Oriental Club), two young women greet each other with high-pitched excitement and kisses on both cheeks. "They are not on good terms," whispers my companion into my ear. In marked contradiction to the social harmony among Middle Eastern women often depicted by feminist anthropologists,[16] behind the appearance of intimacy often lurks bitterness and hostility. Syrian women have confided in me the difficulty they have making female friends amid continual rivalry.[17] The constant competitiveness is wearing; nothing about the other goes unnoticed. Women compare themselves continually and mercilessly in an agonistic mode of sociability tinged with hostility.[18]

In elite Damascus, women alternate flattery with criticism, cruelty with kindness, and as one put it, "build you up in order to knock you down again." Cutting remarks are sandwiched between grand gestures of affection and generosity, so one seldom knows where one stands. One favorite form of female sparring is the backhanded compliment: "You've gained weight, but it looks good on you"; "You look better in skirts than in trousers"; "You don't look short because you're fat." Outright insults are also not uncommon. Once I was with a friend on holiday in Latakia when she met an acquaintance she had not seen since the previous year. "Are you pregnant?" asked the woman. "No, just heavier," my friend replied. Instead of cowering in embarrassment, the woman continued, "But this is really quite a change, isn't it? You really have gained weight!"

Knocking others down alternates with propping oneself up. Self-congratulation is standard. It is not uncommon to hear Syrians recounting their many suitors, describing the beauty of their singing voice, showing off things they have made, repeating compliments they have received. It is statistically impossible for me to have met so many people who, they claim, graduated first in their class in all of Damascus, all of Latakia, all of Syria. One of my Arabic tutors once asked me if I, myself, had been at the top of my class. Taken aback, I asked what she meant. "We have heard that Oxford and Cambridge accept only the best students." I tried to explain how students are accepted into research programs, as far as I understand the process. A culturally appropriate answer, however, would have been: "Yes, they do accept only the best, and I am one of them." A talented and successful architect I know turns this tendency on its head by boasting of having been at the bottom of his class, possibly to point out the meaninglessness of success in the Syrian educational system, with its emphasis on rote memorization, its disorganization and corruption.

Interestingly, the closest parallel to the levels of rivalry I witnessed in Damascus is to be found in the ethnography of Greece (Campbell 1964; Herzfeld 1985, 1987). It is no longer fashionable to speak of the Mediterranean as a cultural unit. Yet in many an encounter with Syrian women, I was reminded not of the giggling harem parties suggested in most literature on Middle Eastern women, but rather of the contests among Campbell's Sarakatsani shepherds (Campbell 1964). Michael Herzfeld's description of agonism among rural Greek men is equally fitting for Syrian women: "Glendiot men engage in a constant struggle to gain a precarious and transitory advantage over each other" (1985: 11). Male ethnographers of Greece see agonism as a masculine characteristic. According to Herzfeld, women conceal while men perform (ibid.: 139). One can imagine that Greek women, like the Yemenis Meneley describes, do not behave so demurely among themselves.[19]

Buried within many ethnographies of Middle Eastern women—and usually left unanalyzed—are hints at something less sisterly afoot. In her study of working-class women in Cairo's City of the Dead, Helen Watson notes:

> The women swap news and gossip as they do whenever and wherever they meet, but, unlike doorstep encounters and communal laundry sessions at the water pump, conversation among women in the curtained-off room is much more informal, unbridled, candid. The basic facts about an impending marriage may filter through the community by many different female-controlled channels, but piquant details and "off the record" remarks are reserved for a select audience of close friends at all-female get-togethers. The women may dismiss the quality of a bride-to-be's trousseau, then apply the same sharp tongue to her face and figure. (1992: 13)

Such "off the record" remarks by Cairene women reflect an essential quality of Arab women's interaction. Status consciousness, competition, and one-upmanship are among the most salient features of female social life. Unsurprisingly, many of these contests are played out over physical appearance. This is true even in Oman, a society considered unique in the Middle East for its social reserve and lack of open conflict (C. Eickelman 1984: 112; Wikan 1982: 10, 14). Quoting from her field notes, Christine Eickelman describes an encounter rife with divisiveness:

> I was sitting with a group of young girls and married women in a side passageway when Ibtasima arrived, carrying her youngest child. She is a

young woman of slave descent. On seeing me, she joined the group. One young woman asked [me], "Miryam, who has the prettiest child? This woman [she pointed to Ibtasima, who is clearly of African origin] or this woman [she pointed to a young shaykhly woman with a very white-skinned child of about the same age]?" "What a question!" I answered. "All babies are beautiful." My answer pleased Ibtasima so much that she turned to me with a grin of triumph and invited me for coffee at her house. I accepted and walked away with Ibtasima in dead silence. (1984: 135)

The intensity of relationships among women is often misread as social harmony, but closeness does not always involve mutual support. As Georg Simmel notes, "the extreme violence of antagonistic excitement is linked to the closeness of belonging together" (1955: 50). Anthropologist Suad Joseph includes in an edited collection on the Arab family an anonymous contribution from a Syrian painter whose fraught relationship with her sister was captured in a biographical film:

The interview with my eldest sister, Isabelle, came to me as a shock. She expressed an intense involvement with me that I had not previously noticed. I knew, of course, that she had been hovering over me, but what I did not know was that this concern came from an irrepressible jealousy and not from the normal concern an older sister would have for her younger sister. That she had always interfered, that she had always been there to comment, report, fuel all arguments I had with my mother as I was growing up—this hostile behavior had been prompted by jealousy. (Scheherazade 1999: 93)

Writing from exile, the Aleppine painter now recasts her sister's behavior in American pop psychological terms, as "abuse."

My sister abused me both physically and mentally. And to tell myself that that abuse came from her jealousy of me did not make it any less painful— a jealousy that did not relent and ruined years of my life. When I complain about it to my mother, she says, "No, no, you are the only one she ever loved." But what is love in that case? It is forever mingled with manipulation. (ibid.: 105)

Intensely emotive power struggle, rather than warmly supportive bonding, often characterizes relations among women in the strongly patriarchal societies of the Middle East. Ethnographers often present striking interactions of discord with little comment, and fail to reflect upon their implications for a presumed harmony among women. This silence may reflect a deep ambivalence on the part of the anthropologists sensitive to the portrayal of groups who, like Arabs and Muslims, have been so vilified in the Western media and popular culture. Indeed, much of this writing comes in the wake of Said's *Orientalism,* a study of negative imagery and stereotyping in literature and scholarship on the Middle East. Said's excursion into Foucauldian questions of knowledge and power in colonial and post-colonial academia has often been so literally read that a political correctness has arisen, making it controversial to portray Arabs or Muslims in anything but the most positive light. Competition and contestation must therefore be downplayed.

Furthermore, some writing suggests nostalgia for a sense of community missing from most women anthropologists' Western middle-class experience. A yearning, perhaps, for a true sisterhood. This image of a harem utopia has a long history in Western women's writings. Lady Mary Wortley Montagu, an eighteenth-century British diplomat's wife and diarist, evoked just such a scene of sisterly camaraderie. A biographer describes Lady Mary's reaction to a Turkish bath visit: "It was like an artist's fantasy . . . to find unadorned, unimproved femininity free from lewdness or narcissism or rivalry: this was a most happy denial of what her own culture had led her to expect" (Grundy 1999: 138). A century later, Victorian women assumed that physical proximity reflected egalitarianism: "the sociability of the *haremlik* had another and, to the Victorians, more 'positive' side: the mixing together of women of different classes, different age-groups, and, usually, different races" (Melman 1992: 154).

This trope of female solidarity and inclusiveness recurs in contemporary ethnography. In the acknowledgments to one of the most successful recent studies of Middle Eastern women, Lila Abu-Lughod quotes from her field notes: "It is a quiet life I will miss. There is no loneliness, always someone to sit with. I feel so much a part of something here. I don't remember ever feeling that before" (1986: xiii).

Some recent material moves beyond assumptions of sisterhood. Susan Waltz's (1990) study of political efficacy among Tunisian women points to ways in which women themselves reinforce patriarchal structures. Here the most effective and successful women politicians recounted distance or hostility from their mothers and encouragement from male role models such as fathers and brothers. Highly efficacious women "uniformly experienced the active intervention of their father, or a father-figure, to reroute the path of their socialization" (ibid.: 31). Likewise, Amalia Sa'ar emphasizes a distinction between the ideology of the family as supportive, empathetic, and affectionate, and the experience of the family, which for women is often lonely, isolating, and sometimes threatening (2001: 723). Her work on Palestinian families presents striking instances of "mothers and sisters who not only fail to support their daughters or sisters in times of distress, but who become outright hostile the lonelier and more isolated the latter become" (ibid.: 735). As in Damascus, individual women may themselves have vested interests in maintaining the existing social order. Women's support networks often fail to cultivate professional success, and sometimes have a detrimental effect. Close relationships do not always provide emotional succor.

Anne Meneley's work on Yemen (1996) and Unni Wikan's early work on Cairene women remain the only extended ethnographies dealing with female competition in the Middle East.[20] "Nobody here wishes anybody any good," says one woman of her community (Wikan 1980: 5), and Wikan's informants articulate what mine express through display: "I'm better than you! I eat drink and dress better than you!" (ibid.: 27). She describes a context in which differences in material possessions are perceived as differences of human value (ibid.). Friendships are volatile and short lived (ibid.: 63). Wikan attributes these women's pervasive materialism, mutual distrust, frequent slander, and self-praise to the difficult and degrading conditions of poverty; yet all are prevalent among the elite of Damascus. I argue that such agonism also serves as response to the pressures facing elites, who, in ever changing circumstances, fear falling down the social scale.

Fieldwork at a Beauty Contest

Foreign women living in Damascus find themselves thrust into the competitive fray, as they are drawn—perhaps unwittingly—into local women's status contests. Local women often feel that foreign females get more male attention than they deserve, merely because of what they represent (sexual freedom, exoticness, novelty, and, of course, a potential way out of Syria). While many young foreign women bemoan the hostility they experience from Syrian women in service jobs, this is structural rather than personal.

Although relatively young and single, I fell far short, literally, of the local ideal. Damascenes hold that "height is two thirds of beauty" (*al-tul tiltayn al-jamal*); I stand four feet ten inches tall. Nevertheless, unwanted sexual attention occurred frequently, despite my care to dress modestly and interact carefully. Indeed, one woman questioned why I was wearing a rather dowdy tan suit with a mid-calf-length skirt on a hot summer afternoon. "These are my interview clothes," I answered. I sometimes sensed puzzlement and hostility from male informants for my reluctance to flirt.

Relatively young unmarried women from elsewhere find relationships with Syrian women difficult to form and often nearly impossible to maintain.[21] As noted, Syrian women themselves find relationships with each other volatile. Yet no other anthropologist writing about Middle Eastern women has described such an experience. Perhaps this omission stems from an assumed anthropological goal of acceptance in the society studied. Ethnographies often follow a standard narrative: fieldwork was difficult at first, the natives were understandably suspicious, but with sensitivity and perseverance, barriers dissolved, and the anthropologist became an accepted, admired, even beloved honorary member of a community, building mutually rewarding relationships spanning years of repeat fieldwork visits. Clifford Geertz refers to this ethnographic device as "the myth of the chameleon fieldworker . . . a walking miracle of empathy, tact, patience, and cosmopolitanism" whose personal qualities provide entry into the most closed of communities (1976: 222).

Positive sentiments are emphasized in much ethnographic writing by women on women. In some ethnographies, "informants" are always referred to as "friends" (Early 1993; Meneley 1996).[22] One anthropologist goes so far as to suggest that women, due to their supposedly superior social skills, are better at fieldwork than men (Wiener 1999). A sense of gratitude to individuals who have opened their homes and hearts, often gaining little in return, is entirely understandable. Links and commonalties are stressed. Anything that appears to suggest failure to bond might be construed a failure of the ethnographic endeavor.[23] Yet if the goal of ethnographic writing is to elucidate facets of the societies about which we write, to explore the different experiences and expressions of our common humanity rather than illustrate the social skills and popularity of the ethnographer, then aversion and conflict should be central. Antipathy is as relevant as empathy. A closed door can be as telling as an open one, a snub as significant as a kiss.

There remains an underlying empiricist assumption that the ethnographer's task is to seek information contained within a bounded cultural isolate. The quality of that information is deemed to improve as she is accepted into a network of mutually supportive women, who open up, revealing their realities, dreams, hopes, and fears. The extent to which the anthropologist is accepted as an honorary daughter or sister is assumed to determine success in getting the facts. Anthropologists of Arab birth or extraction emphasize this, and one goes so far as to suggest that an outsider would be unlikely to attain the same level of veracity:

> A sociological myth is a paradigm rendered obsolete by a different model that has greater empirical validity. I suggest that when an ethnographer's access to information is severely curtailed, then paradigms must of neces-

sity be constructed on the basis of hearsay, appearance, and unverifiable inferences. In the case of the study of domestic relations in Arab society, such paradigms are the consequence of the limited access of male ethnographers to relevant data. I believe that under these conditions, only female researchers can possibly have easy access to the data needed. More specifically, I would argue that female indigenous researchers will have a particular advantage in this respect, although I am prepared to admit the possibility that a foreign female anthropologist might, under the most favorable fieldwork conditions, also gain such access in the long run. But this would be at the expense of spending much time in the effort. (Altorki 1988: 64)

This despite the recent problematizing of the very notion that different "cultures" exist (L. Abu-Lughod 1991). If we are no longer to take for granted the existence of another "culture," then how can we talk about gaining access to it? If "other cultures" are mere analytical constructs (ibid.), then why does one need a father's introduction into them (L. Abu-Lughod 1986: 12)? Decades after Fredrik Barth shifted our attention toward the processes of boundary construction, and away from the often arbitrary cultural content within them, ethnographers of the Middle East are still concerned with access to an inner core of "data." The issue is not one of access to information, but to networks, to processes of inclusion and exclusion, that themselves are as revealing as the cultural information they may yield.

Some women anthropologists stress the extent to which they assumed, and were accepted in, the role of daughter (L. Abu-Lughod 1986; Altorki and El-Solh 1988). As Reem Saad points out, while playing this role successfully may demonstrate the skill and sensitivity of the ethnographer, it does little for women who live in the Arab world, since the anthropologist, with academic authority behind her, serves to legitimize practices of patriarchal dominance (1994: 54). While an ethnographer cannot and should not flaunt local mores, their wholesale acceptance and enthusiastic adoption ought to be regarded with some suspicion. Access into the intimacy of social relations carries responsibility. As Herzfeld argues, "if we take seriously our hosts' wish to be treated as moral equals, as indeed we should, such avoidance of criticism is not only condescending but inconsistent as well" (1997: 167).[24]

It is interesting to contrast the harmonious fieldwork interactions described in Altorki and El-Solh's *Arab Women in the Field* with those in its predecessor, Golde's *Women in the Field* (1986). The latter is an honest account of rupture and dissonance in field sites as diverse as Latin America, Eastern Europe, and the Pacific. Golde describes the difficulty of forming relationships with the often jealous and hostile unmarried women of a Mexican village (1986: 87). Weidman was the object of women's jealousy in Burma (1986: 256). Unlike the uncritical "dutiful daughters" of Middle Eastern anthropology, she admits to being less than enthusiastic about her fieldwork role: "I was not especially proud of what was involved in playing the Burmese game well. I did not like the rules themselves, and I liked even less what they required of me" (1986: 261).

My own field notes bemoan the "data" I may have lost as a result of the suspicion and resentment I evoked in other women. In one incident, a friend suggested taking me to a meeting of the Arab Club, then canceled. "My [male] cousin is busy, and I can't find another man to go with us. And I know the two women who told me of the meeting will be jealous if we go there on our own." More crucially, the female leader of Friends of Damascus denied with a sneer my request to attend the organization's next activity. A male member of the group made this request on my behalf in my presence. As Willy Jansen shows in the case of Algeria, adult women who lack male partners are socially ambiguous, falling between proper gender categories (1987: 10). They are, in keeping with Mary Douglas's classic formulation, dangerously "out of place" (1966).

Western women researchers often feel that all Syrians, but particularly women, try to knock them off some imagined high horse. My earliest fieldwork memories involve accompanying another American researcher on her last round of interviews and witnessing the frequent scorn directed at her perfectly proficient colloquial Arabic. I also sensed that Syrians sometimes suspected each other of giving offense and tried to shield us from potential hostility.

When I did manage to sustain relationships with women, they often vied with one another for my affections, and chided me for perceived slights or preferences. They would remark "I was worried that your Arabic was suffering because you're spending so much time with X" (who spoke English), or, more blatantly, "Sometimes I think you like X and Y better than me." I began to conceal my relationships with women from other women, but felt guilty for my disingenuousness. Later into my fieldwork, I realized that I had adopted local women's strategies for social survival. What I discovered was that the intense competitiveness I sometimes encountered did not signify a failure to bond or gain access. Rather, these experiences of seeming rejection heralded my acceptance into circles of cultural intimacy where both hostility and affection characterize close relationships. Acceptance as friend, or even fictive sister, means having to operate amid strong contradictory emotions.

I played audience to my informants' frequent self-aggrandizing, and refrained from returning in kind, lest I provoke even more resentment. I smiled, congratulated, stroked egos, and bit my tongue. I tried to take slights and insults in my stride, reminding myself of their ethnographic relevance, for I, like the women I studied, was often put in uncomfortable positions of competitive display. One particularly memorable instance occurred on New Year's Eve of my second year of fieldwork. My closest friend invited me to spend the evening with her family. She was organizing a party for about sixty people, hiring a hall, a caterer, a band, and a dancer. I agreed early on to attend. Just before I left for the United States for Christmas, and again during the week after my return, she urged me repeatedly to try and find a date for the occasion, on the grounds that all the guests would be in couples. I continually refused, finally pointing out that her unmarried sister and brothers would be there without dates. That settled, she asked who would be doing my hair.

Knowing it was my birthday on the first of January, she ordered a cake as well. It was laid out in the middle of a semi-circle of tables early in the evening, a pink and white double heart with my name written on it. Shortly after midnight the band started to play "Happy Birthday" and I was called over to blow out the lone candle and cut the cake. But it did not end there; I was obliged to dance a "birthday dance" with the caterer/master of ceremonies, on the platform where the band was still playing "Happy Birthday." It went on for an endless five minutes. My friend's obvious delight made the embarrassment worthwhile. I sat down, thinking I could now fade into the background and relax for the rest of the evening. Then a dancer wiggled onto the stage in an amazingly revealing costume. True, there was an opaque net covering her middle, but the strapless bra top consisted of two wired peaks of beaded fabric which fit, as with some ball gowns, an inch or so away from the body, so that she was covered almost up to the shoulder blades while standing still and completely exposed as soon as she moved. Her body moved from side to side, but the costume remained centered. No one appeared offended.

Thankfully she finished quickly, and we all got up to dance to the current pop music hits, including, of course, "Hadha al-Laun" ("That Color"). I was just beginning to relax and enjoy the evening when the master of ceremonies called for beauty contest nominations. My first impulse was to run to the ladies' room, but young women were heading toward the stage with no coaxing, and I was afraid I would miss something interesting. I thought I would get away with hiding behind my friend's brother, where I could not be seen from the stage. I nearly succeeded; there were five girls lined up in front of the band, and the contest was about to begin, when my friend and her two brothers, followed by the rest of her family, began to urge me to join in. I thanked them and declined. They persisted, and people from neighboring tables joined in the coaxing. Finally my friend walked over and pulled me up. I continued to resist, but now realized that nothing short of a tantrum would relieve me from participating. I told my friend I would take part only if she did. Reading this as acquiescence, she said that she could not join in because she was fat and pushed me onto the stage. So there I was, on the eve of my thirtieth birthday, in a conservatively flared black cocktail dress and pearl earrings, tacked onto a line of vibrant mini-skirted, spike-heeled, moussed, and painted nineteen-year-olds. Then we had to prance around the stage individually while the band played behind us. I tried to console myself with the thought that I was joining a long anthropological tradition of participating in unpleasant and humiliating rituals. It seemed endless. First there was the "public opinion" vote, in which audience members were asked to clap for their favorite contestant. I noticed that my friend's brothers cheered for each of us equally, calling out all of our numbers. The audience, either out of sensitivity or embarrassment, failed to choose a clear winner. Then it was time for the judges to decide. I was eliminated first, as numbers one, two, three, four, and five were asked to come forward (I was number six). Finally they chose a winner, and the new blond "beauty queen" (*malikat al-jamal*) pranced around the stage in her crown and sash, as the defeated contestants left the stage in tears. As a group of us rode home in a hired minibus, my friend noted that the annual beauty contest had long been a sensitive issue. The next day she rang to apologize for any offense the incident caused, and confided that the outcome of the contest had been decided in advance, to rectify hurt caused by the previous year's result.

Attractiveness, the means to procure it, and the access to spaces in which to display it are surpassing other measures of worth among the elites of Damascus. I am not suggesting here that Middle Eastern women are uniquely competitive. Indeed, the resonance with Wolf's work on contemporary America and Britain, let alone the eighteenth-century Britain of Austen and Edgeworth, precludes any impulse to particularize. Nor am I suggesting that Syrian women are more competitive among themselves than men are. For both women and men, contestation is a key mode of identity expression and social interaction in contemporary Damascus. What I take issue with is the projection onto Middle Eastern women of a female solidarity and level of mutual support and friendship which they do not enjoy, as my findings demonstrate. Antagonistic relations among women are part of a system of oppression (Simmel 1955: 94–96). Women are often their own harshest critics, and hold each other to a stringent set of moral values and aesthetic standards. As Simmel notes, "Women's position on the defensive does not allow the wall of custom to be lowered even at a single point (ibid.: 96). If patriarchal structures and the increasing commodification of social relations and physical appearances everywhere pit woman against woman, this is even truer of places with strong male dominance, like the Middle East. As Wolf puts it, "solidarity is hardest to find when women learn to see each other as beauties first" (1991: 56).

As both judges and contestants, women direct the contests that shape the social world of Damascus. They create and are created by new consumptive patterns and leisure practices and the social hierarchies these engender and maintain. The emergence of new classes, and the intermingling of old and new money, has heightened competition within the elite marriage market, which in turn pressures women into conspicuous displays of both bodies and adornments. As in all contests, some are more successful than others.

An examination of marriage practices, consumptive patterns, and display modes among women in Damascus reveals an uneasy accommodation between old and new elites. Informants from various class, sectarian, and regional groups often invoke an endogamous principle to describe Damascene, particularly elite Damascene, marriage practices: "Damascenes never marry non-Damascenes." Yet I observed numerous instances of elite Damascenes—often women—marrying wealthy non-Damascenes—often regime-connected ʿAlawis. If young women serve as preservers of family honor and emblems of family prestige, it is unsurprising that their marriage to men from socially, if not economically and politically, inferior groups produces strong "we" images. Marriage, entailing as it does the alignment of families and the melding of cultural and economic capital, is a primary locus of identity and sociability. I argue that it is the aspect of social life in which the accommodation of competing elites is most keenly felt, acutely denied, and discursively resisted. It is also where the tension between old ideals and new realities becomes particularly apparent. Damasceneness is not always maintained in marital alignments, but it is continually invoked in public cultural forms, such as Old City theme restaurants and events promoting Old Damascus, which form the subject of chapter 3.

3 Old Damascus Commodified

> She washed my face, dressed me in a gown
> she had made by hand and tattered sandals
> that fell off my feet on the road. So she car-
> ried them and carried me part of the way.
> Before we arrived, she put me down to fasten
> them on my feet, telling me to keep them on
> no matter what, as it was improper to walk
> barefoot. Not only because I was her son, but
> because we were from the city, and city
> children were different from country children.
> —**Hanna Mina,** *Fragments of Memory*

Ties to an elite Old Damascus, genuine or spurious, have become cultural capital in Bourdieu's sense—very like women's adornment —in a context of rapid social transformation and increasing emphasis on public image and display. The Old City itself, until the 1980s a nether-region associated with the backwardness of the past, is now considered a source of rich authenticity for Damascenes at home and abroad, who boast of the Old City's glory to foreigners and other Syrians alike. For instance, Rana Kabbani, Damascene author and media figure now living in London, promotes Old Damascus's wealth of traditional, "natural" beauty products to the readers of British *Vogue* (1998: 134–135). In a global context with an increasingly high premium on local cultures, Old Damascus is again a status marker. Damascenes and others experience the Old City through a variety of expressive cultural forms and new leisure practices. Selective participation in this reinvented Old Damascus, and the various discourses surrounding it, reflects the many tensions permeating the social field of the city. Damascus, in its various manifestations, is the axis around which insider and outsider lines are drawn and claims to prestige and merit are laid. Heritage operates as a tactic in status wars, as a mode of social distinction.

Until the early 1990s a middle-class or upper-middle-class Damascene might never have ventured into the Old City of Damascus, a place then associated with peasants and tourists, with the backwardness of the past. Today that same urbanite, whose parents or grandparents abandoned the Old City and all it stood for, spends long leisure hours in this former backwater, in one of several recently opened restaurants. Here we have the transformation of old residential quarters into a leisure center for the new middle classes.

The opening of restaurants in Old Damascus also reflects the development of modernity through the growth of new leisure practices. Once an integral part of communal life, leisure activities are now separated from work, privatized, and commodified (Rojek 1995: 191). Restaurants are a case in point. Dining out has become the most popular pastime among the urban elite. Just two decades ago, restaurant-going in Damascus, as in much of the Middle East, was largely restricted to foreigners, travelers, and students. Aside from their coffeehouses and street stalls, few Middle Eastern countries have developed elaborate restaurant traditions (Roden 1988: 3). Morocco and Lebanon, both heavily influenced by the French, are notable exceptions. Syrians used to denigrate the quality and cleanliness of their restaurants, and considered working in them among the lowliest of occupations. Dining was a homebound, family-centered activity. In the mid-1980s, there were relatively few restaurants in Damascus, all of them in the New City. These ranged from humble student sandwich shops to upscale French-style establishments with airy patio seating, such as those in Malki's leafy Restaurant Square. By the early 1990s, restaurants had become central to the experience of past and present, near and far, seeing and being seen, being and becoming. They form part of a new local public culture through which sub-national identities are expressed and negotiated.

In the late 1980s, restaurants began to open in the Old City's largely residential Christian quarter. Set in old merchant houses, these establishments have abandoned the Western or "continental" restaurant model that inspired the last generation of Damascus restaurants. Instead, they aim to provide a restaurant experience that is deliberately "Eastern," and beyond this, distinctively Damascene.

One of the oldest and best known of these is Le Piano Bar, described in the introduction. A less self-conscious and more elaborate reconstruction of the past is the Omayyad Palace Restaurant, located in what is said to be the vaulted basement of the long-destroyed Umayyad Palace in the Qaymariyyeh quarter (behind the wood suq, south of the Umayyad Mosque). "Damascus Generosity and Hospitality invite you to the Omayyad Palace," reads the restaurant's glossy brochure, in English and Arabic. The diner is ushered down a carpet-lined staircase into a cavernous room lavishly decorated with numerous carpets, a bubbling fountain, plants hanging from skylights, patterned marble floor, mother-of-pearl-inlaid and brocade-upholstered chairs, low brass tables, locally blown glass, copper urns, and glass cases filled with pottery, scarves, and old photographs. Waiters in baggy black trousers, black-and-silver-striped shirts made from local cloth, fezzes, and imitation Docksider shoes serve drinks. The evening begins with a folklore troupe dancing to taped music. The dancing continues for half an hour; then patrons are invited to an extensive, almost exclusively "oriental" buffet. Tea, coffee, and hubble bubbles (water pipes) arrive after the meal, as a "traditional" band, dressed in *jalabiyyehs* (traditional kaftans) and fezzes, plays old songs. Whirling dervishes and Sufi music round off the evening.

In Old City theme restaurants such as the Omayyad Palace, objects once tied to a set of kinship-based practices and relations are aestheticized, set up as "décor," and sold as an experience of an imagined past. The modernity of such an experience is obvious; nothing could be less truly Old Damascene than a restaurant meal, and Mawlawiyya Sufis would never perform in a setting so profane. But through leisure practices such as restaurant-going, Damascus dwellers become linked to a new community of fellow diners, all sampling the "authentic" tastes, sights, and sounds of commodified heritage. The Damascene's own past is exoticized as a tourist experience.

A restaurant heavily frequented for *ghada*ʾ—the afternoon meal, traditionally Syria's heaviest—is the Old Damascus. Located in the upper story of a building in the Old City Muslim quarter of al-ʿAmara, this establishment serves the standard Syrian restaurant fare of *mezzeh* or *muqabbilat* (an elaborate array of hot and cold starters) and grilled meat, as well as the stews and grains which are the mainstay of Damascene home cooking. Decorated in the marbles, painted and carved wood, and inlay that would seem quintessentially Damascene, the Old Damascus's authenticity has nevertheless been called into question. Architectural historian Nazih Kawakibi—whom I encountered on my last visit to this restaurant—considers the building a stylistic travesty:

> This building is awful because it is [a copy of] the Tarbiyat Misqal of Cairo, of Egypt. The person who designed this elevation copied it from the one in Egypt. He opened a book, and he copied this, and he built it. Is this an appropriate building in Damascus? No! The *muqaranas* [system of projecting niches in Islamic architecture] is a fountain, and the entrance of the *turbeh* [mausoleum] is from the wrong direction. You can go back to the references and compare. It's very ridiculous.

At the end of 1994, these three restaurants—along with the oldest and now overshadowed Abu al-'Izz—were the only ones in Old Damascus. By early 1996, six more had opened, all in Christian areas. Most elaborate is Zaytuni, which showcases beautiful mosaic, vine-draped courtyards. The 1001 Nights charms with its cozy indoor seating room draped and upholstered in carpets and tapestries. The Old Town "Music Restaurant," as its calling card reads, copies Le Piano Bar, with pianist and video screens. La Guitare is a slightly less formal and more Mediterranean version of its neighbor Zaytuni. Vino Rosso (al-Nabidh al-Ahmar), a first-floor eatery in Bab Tuma, sports a vineyard theme and serves pizza and other Western foods along with mezzeh. The Casablanca, a few doors down from Le Piano Bar, serves a seafood cuisine not at all typical of Damascus.

Restaurants and other contemporary leisure activities reflect the increasing commodification of everyday life. Dining out, as Joanne Finkelstein notes, "demonstrates a strengthening of the consumer ethic and the importance of commodities in the mediation of interpersonal relations" (1989: 6). Restaurants commodify human emotions, in this case nostalgia and loss. They supply fantasy through "architecture of desire" (ibid.: 3). Dining in the Old City offers a glimpse, however fleeting and misrepresented, of a life lost. It also reconnects the old urban elite with the architectural forms central to both their memories of the past and their criticisms of the present.

Commodified representations of Old Damascus are not limited to the Old City itself. Old Damascus theme restaurants and cafés have sprung up in elite districts of the New City over the past decade. These include the very casual and inexpensive Shamiyyat, a basement restaurant just off Abu Rummaneh. Old Damascus is evoked here by means of painted faux wood paneling, brass coffee pots, baskets, and other old-fashioned kitchen implements that adorn its ceiling and walls. Serving hearty Damascene stews and mezzeh twenty-four hours a day, Shamiyyat is a favorite of visiting Lebanese officers and students from the nearby French Institute. A few yards away is the more elegant Dimashqiyyah, with its white and gold facade and waiters in traditional costume.

Bows to the past have also been made in the New City's older establishments. The posh Nadi al-Sharq (Oriental Club) has added an Eastern-style café to the front of its otherwise Western-style restaurant. The Meridien Hotel created Café Tric Trac, a mosaic-filled garden café popular for water-pipe smoking and backgammon and card playing on summer evenings. Tables are filled with *al-mas'ulin,* "the officials," the powerful and well connected in government, military, and business.

The Damascus Sheraton, the city's most elegant hotel and favorite haunt of local elites, has most fully exploited the Old Damascus theme with several recent additions. Al-Narabayn is an upscale version of al-Nawfara, the popular café behind the Umayyad Mosque in the Old City. In the summer, al-Narabayn moves outdoors, becoming al-Nawafeer, a name reminiscent of al-Nawfara. In these establishments, families and groups of teenagers pay exorbitant prices for coffee, tea, and simple foods long associated with the poor. Patrons pass long hours, buffed, coiffed, and glittering in gold, talking and playing backgammon, seeing and being seen. It is an experience of heritage that I argue combines constructs of authenticity with the creation and reaffirmation of the status hierarchies and social relations central to Damascene life.

Hotel restaurants serving local food in local ambience enjoy increasing popularity. The Sheraton replaced its elegant French restaurant, which fared poorly, with the more successful "Oriental" Ishbilia (Seville). Here too, the atmosphere is consciously "Eastern," right down to the waiters' long waxed moustaches. In 1989 the Sheraton invented a local tradition with its weekly Layalina, an outdoor, summertime "Oriental" food and entertainment extravaganza, which replaced the smaller and more expensive events at which French or continental food was served. This new event takes place in the hotel's swimming pool area, which, because of its long, grand staircase designed for bridal processions, is the most sought after location for summer weddings.[1] Layalina is held on Monday nights because hairdressers in Damascus are closed on this day, thus limiting the possibility of the Sheraton losing wedding bookings. During its first year, Layalina's buffet served Western continental food. Then the Sheraton management, eager to lower costs and attract more customers, tried local cuisine, which is less expensive to prepare. This strategy proved a hit. In addition to the "open buffet," an employee in old-fashioned costume sells falafel—a street food not habitually eaten in restaurants, particularly of the Sheraton's caliber—from a carriage like those used in the old quarter. Another makes *al-labnat*, a sweet that used to be sold outside schools. All of these innovations were sound business decisions, according to Sheraton manager Sami Farah. "People are fed up with classical European food," he explains, "they want mezzeh, grills, and arak."

The Meridien Hotel answered the Sheraton with its own summer evening reinvented tradition: Sayran, named for the picnic custom of Old Damascus. Sayran is also held weekly, on the hotel's grounds, and decorated with Old City touches. Old-fashioned music and traditional foods complete "a party just like my grandmother used to throw," as one Damascene patron put it.

"Old Damascus" restaurants and cafés, both in the Old City itself and in the elite New City neighborhoods beyond its walls, are distinctly local phenomena. Foreign expatriates and tourists visit these eateries, but the most frequent patrons are Syrian. Syria's tourist industry alone would be far too small to sustain the large number of successful Old City theme establishments which have sprung up in Damascus throughout the 1990s. Yet the popularity of Old Damascus restaurants among Damascenes and other Syrians should not be seen as a rejection of the non-Damascene, the foreign and the Western. Rather, constructions of local culture are taking their place, self-consciously, among global cultures, with Café Tric Trac literally next to the Meridien's Mexican restaurant, and al-Narabayn next to the Sheraton's pizzeria.

Such cosmopolitanism, involving a command of both local and foreign idioms, has long been a mark of social distinction for Syrian elites. What is new is its expression in public culture, in the development of leisure sites, in the commodification of the local and the global. For Damascenes, these restaurants recall, and partially recreate, the prestige of the city's, and their own, past. But such new arenas also exemplify the contradictions of the present. They are open to all who can afford them, providing entrée into upper-crust consumption venues for newer competitors. Ironically, the Damascene elite has not only had to work with, and sometimes for, their former social inferiors, but they now serve them in the very heart of old elite culture—the Old Damascene merchant house turned restaurant.

The Myth of Return?

Restaurant and cafés remain the Damascenes' only mode of physical return; the Damascene elite has not resettled Old Damascus. Even the most ardent Old Damascus activists and aficionados live in elite districts of New Damascus—Siham Tergeman and Nadia Khost in Mezzeh—and few express any desire to move back to the Old City.[2] The Damascene house, they argue, is unsuitable for modern living and expensive to maintain. According to prominent old notable Najat Qassab Hasan:

> Now we say that the old house is in the realm of nostalgia. We want it to remain, but tell any Damascene "here is an old house, go and live in it" and he will not go. The comforts available in the modern house are impossible in the Old City. The rhythm of life changed. A woman no longer lives with her husband's family. It's impossible because a new generation has emerged that wants its freedom. Now love of Old Damascus has become a kind of love poetry (*ghazal*) to the past, a longing. . . . Life is like a river, no one can return water to its source. Life goes on, time crushes everything like a bulldozer. But we can remind each other; we can remember.

Damascenes often point to a lack of modern conveniences as the major drawback to Old City living. According to well-known Old Damascene author and political figure Nasr al-Din al-Bahra, "The modern woman of Damascus doesn't like the Old City lifestyle. Houses are very big, and need a lot of work. In extended families all the women used to do the cleaning; now servants are needed, and this is very expensive."

Damascenes may not want to live in Old Damascus, but they remain emotionally connected to it. "I don't live there," said Damascene cinema director Nabil Maleh, "but I belong there somehow." This preference for the imagined idea, rather than the reality of a past way of life, is a common feature of nostalgic expression. As David Lowenthal notes:

> Few admirers of the past would choose to return to it—nostalgia expresses longings for times that are safely, rather than sadly, beyond recall. . . . People tend to believe that life in the past was "happier"—that families were closer, that pollution was absent, that peace and order prevailed. But desirable as these attributes may seem, and conducive to happiness as they may have been, few would now embrace them at the cost of modern comforts. (1989: 28)

Speaking of his fellow Damascenes, philosopher Sadik al-Azm echoes Lowenthal:

> Nostalgia is one thing; but reality is something else. There is something false about nostalgia. If you took those people who are nostalgic, if you were to take them back, and put them in a real-life situation of how it was, they themselves would rather have their nostalgia than *it*.

Yet Nadia Khost claims that it is indeed possible to combine the best of the old and the new: "Of course there must be renovations—modern heating and plumbing. While Arab construction lasts, it can also be developed. It *is* possible to renovate the Arab house to suit modern needs." The modernization of Arab-style architecture had already been successful, Khost argues, in the quarter of al-Maydan, where buildings destroyed in the battles against French occupation were restored in the Arab style, but "improved to a certain extent."

Some argue that they left the Old City forcibly, and would return if they could. Old Damascus activist Siham Tergeman argues that she cannot return to live in the Old City because of plans to destroy it.

> The house I was born in and grew up in is next to the Shami Mosque. I urged them not to tear it down, but to turn it into a museum, and tell people that someone was born here, lived here, loved here, who wrote about, immortalized Damascus in this modest house. "Never," they said; a merchant has bought it and will pull it down to build a high rise. It still survives, but they've got it. I haven't found a way to defend my own house.

Nadia Khost feels similarly:

> Moving to Mezzeh was almost unacceptable to me. The house I was born and raised in, in Suq Saruja, was on land which ended up under Revolution Street. I honestly hate this street, I can't bear it, even now, and it's been there a long time. The most beautiful houses in Damascus—their decorations, trees, fountains, and sitting rooms—all ended up under Revolution Street, severely limiting the number of historic buildings along the hajj route.[3] So it was necessary for us, the inhabitants of Suq Saruja, to look for new housing, in a new city of which we were critical. I would prefer to live in the Old City, but it is limited and threatened. I believe that when the entire Old City—both inside and outside the wall—is [legally] preserved, we will return.

While most Damascenes do not want to live in the Old City themselves, they do want it inhabited. This attitude prompts criticism: "Sure, it's easy for them to tell poor people to live in pre-modern conditions, in dilapidated houses" remarked a Circassian painter, "when they themselves live in Mezzeh."[4] An ʿAlawi journalist put it this way: "It's not possible for the past to live in the present. It's impossible. Even if the past was pleasant and good; it was good for *its* time. It won't work now. People have cars now, they're useless in the Old City. Salah al-Din al-Ayyubi [Saladin] didn't have a Mercedes."

Exhibiting Old Damascus

Photographs are among the most important means of reconstructing a lost place of the past. A motif of bygone splendor, contrasted with contemporary degradation, permeates documentary exhibitions of Old Damascus. Annual photographic exhibits commemorating local historian Khalid Moaz are held at the Arab Cultural Center in Abu Rummaneh. The memorial of 1992 displayed photographs of Suq Saruja by well-known Damascene artists. The 1994 exhibit was devoted to "Lanes and Alleyways." Perhaps most significant was 1993's "Gardens and Orchards of Damascus," featuring photographs taken by Moaz in the 1930s and 1940s, and those by his son, architectural historian Abd al-Razzaq, of the same sites in the 1980s and 1990s. For example, an image of a *shaykh*'s tomb surrounded by trees would be juxtaposed with a photograph of the same tomb surrounded by concrete construction, vividly demonstrating Damascus's aesthetic deterioration.

A more imaginary Old Damascus is a favorite theme for other visual artists. Damascene Asma al-Fayumi, wife of director Ghassan Jabri, paints an impressionistic Old City of vivid shades of blue, with the stylized figures of large-eyed young women and white peace doves characteristic of much contemporary Arab painting. Another is Mahmud Jalal al-ʿAsha, whose work I first admired in the home of Damascene novelist Nadia al-Ghazzi. Originally from Suq Saruja, and now residing in the middle-class neighborhood of Tijara, al-ʿAsha creates bas-relief sculptures in layers of wood depicting Old Damascene scenes. The Old City serves as a source of authenticity for Damascene artists who construct the local in global frames. Transnational visual art forms, such as painting and sculpture, are adopted to convey a strong sense of place. Their exhibition, often feted with elaborate opening events, offers yet another opportunity for Old Damascene community reimaginings.

Friends of Damascus

Many photographic and artistic exhibitions concerning the Old City are sponsored by an organization called The Society of Friends

of Damascus (Jam'iat Asdiqa' Dimashq). Here a sense of Old Damascene community is reconstructed, and the distinctions between old
and new elites highlighted. In-group connections are forged and
maintained, and marriage matches of elite pedigree made. Established in 1977 by "people who were very keen to have the city as it
should be," as the group's president, Burhan Qassab Hasan, put it,
the Friends of Damascus founded the Museum of the City of Damascus and sponsors lectures, exhibits, and concerts. Each year on the
Night of Power it holds a Sufi—Mawlawiyya order—*dhikr* in an Old
City house.[5] Friends of Damascus has a 50/50 gender ratio, and most
members are over fifty years old, although Qassab Hasan's young
colleague, Iyad 'Anbari, is working to lower its age profile. Qassab
Hasan estimates that 30 percent of the organization's 1,000 members are non-Damascene. "We don't place restrictions [against non-
Damascenes] but we prefer to have Damascenes because they like
Damascus more." Yet in practice membership is restricted; a candi-
date must be nominated by two current members. Qassab Hasan argues that such regulations are in place because "we need people who
work, not who have fun." He applauds the organization's preservation work:

> We stopped the tearing down of houses. . . . We are doing our best. All the
> government officials co-operate with us. Many would like to see Damascus
> as it was before. Whether they like it or not, when we say we want to do
> this or that, they have to agree.

Some members argue that the group's efforts are restricted by
the governorate (Muhafazat Dimashq). Others point to a shift in the
organization's priorities and a growing accommodation between old
elite ideals and new market demands, as high-rise apartment blocks
housing many families generate greater profits than Arab-style houses. As one activist member observed:

> Friends of Damascus organized conservation work in the beginning. They
> began with a very good project for the general preservation of the Old City.
> For example, they called for the banning of lorries—be they civilian or mil-
> itary—from the Old City. But Friends of Damascus's practice has moved
> from this preservation project to a cultural and touristic one. They no
> longer make demands. It is well known that the preservation of the Old
> City is a hard, bitter, painful struggle against the estate agents/merchants
> (*al-'aqariyyin*) and the engineers of the Governorate of Damascus who do
> their bidding. Friends of Damascus is not prepared, is unwilling—given its
> social, cultural, class, and moral structure—to do battle with them.

This accommodation is reflected in the organization's activities; the lavish dinner parties with which Friends of Damascus is often associated used to be held in Old City houses, but now tend to take place at the Sheraton, Meridien, or Cham Palace Hotels. Much as with the Daughters of the American Revolution in the United States, many feel that the organization's primary goal is not the preservation or restoration of the Old City but the maintenance and promotion of the old social elite. Meanwhile, ardent Old Damascus activists often express irritation and frustration at the organization's lack of success in getting laws passed to protect large areas of the Old City. Themselves Friends of Damascus members, they point to a preference for socializing over activism. "It should be called 'The Society of Friends' rather than 'The Society of Friends of Damascus,'" said one. According to another:

> They do nothing, just waste time delivering lectures. Delivering lectures means nothing; we need to move! You know, all the members are aged and retired, so they are enjoying passing time. In Ramadan they will break fast at the Cham Palace [Hotel] with a piano. This is ridiculous! They should act in a very different way, they should educate people about Damascus, conserving, preserving. They should publish articles, they should change their ideas, and the way they do the work, in order to be much better.

Yet another pointed to such "passing time" as the organization's raison d'être: "What do they want, these Friends of Damascus members? They want what you could call prestige. They want to form and maintain relations among themselves, and with ministers and other prominent people." A former member takes this criticism further: "I don't know why you are interested in Friends of Damascus," she asked me. "It's becoming more of a matchmaking company than a society. Most of the women there are old maids looking for husbands."

Many Syrians of non-Damascene origin living in Damascus see Friends of Damascus as a sinister organization whose bigoted and xenophobic members aim to rid the city of all "outsiders." According to an 'Alawi poet originally from the coastal region:

> Their idea, which is not directly expressed, is that Damascus was invaded by many migrants who deformed its old or inherited identity. They consider those who have come to Damascus to have corrupted the majesty of the Old City. They would like us to leave.

The Committee for the Preservation
of the Old City of Damascus

The al-Asad regime maintains an ambiguous and often contradictory stance on Old Damascus, sometimes embracing it as a gem-
stone in the crown of national culture and resource to be exploited,
at other times rejecting it as a relic of the feudal past and potential
sanctuary for opposition. These conflicting viewpoints converge in
the work of the Committee for the Preservation of the Old City of
Damascus (Lajnat Himayat Madinat Dimashq al-Qadima), a division
of the Governorate of Damascus (Muhafazat Dimashq), which itself
falls under the Ministry of Local Administration (Wizarat al-Idara al-
Mahaliyya). Established in 1986 by a decree from the prime minister, this government agency directs the study, preservation, and conservation of the Old City. Its staff of engineers oversees additions and
repairs to private houses as well as the protection and reconstruction
of monuments. The committee is headquartered in the lavish Maktab 'Anbar, once an exclusive school educating young men of the
Damascene elite. Twice a month the committee meets with representatives from governmental foundations, ministries, and Friends
of Damascus. According to director Muhammad Bashar al-Jabban,
Friends of Damascus representatives carry the most weight in these
meetings: "We listen to their opinions, and usually take their suggestions, if they are in keeping with the law." The committee does its
best to balance the stylistic integrity of Old Damascus with the demands of modernization:

> We keep to the old styles, in both form and content. But we allow some
> upgrading (*tajdid*), new types of appliances, to help people remain in their
> Old City houses, to live in them, and be able to benefit from them. We pre-
> serve our heritage, our characteristic architecture, and try to modernize it.

Here again, Old City activists express frustration with the committee's failure to protect large areas of Old Damascus. They note that
while it has been somewhat successful in protecting buildings within
the Old City walls, much Old City architecture, like the quarter of al-
Qanawat and the largely destroyed Suq Saruja, lies beyond the committee's jurisdiction. According to one activist:

> They don't know what they're doing. The committee should be full of
> well-educated people, and they should have many advisors: architects,
> writers, poets, etc. It is now in the Maktab 'Anbar, under the supervision of
> the municipality, so it's been changed into a prefecture of the municipality,

and it's full of structural engineers, and those other engineers and archi-
tects who are not doing well with the municipality itself. It's become an
exile, all those they are angry with are sent to Maktab 'Anbar. . . . They
paint the [Old City] walls with white plaster or lime, but this means nothing, it only protects the exterior. We should go inside, we should know the
infrastructure. . . . We should protect Damascus from the Committee for
the Preservation of the Old City of Damascus!

A Damascene architect concurs, and expresses a more sinister view
of this government agency:

It became clear to me, and anyone will tell you, that they are selling pieces
of the Old City. When I discovered that these ornaments, painted wood
panels for example, were being sold, I went to the engineers at Maktab
'Anbar and said to them, "This is outrageous, we must find a way to stop
this." "It's very difficult," they told me. "On the contrary," I said, "it's not
difficult at all." But what I slowly discovered was that they themselves
were brokers, middlemen, selling pieces of the Old City. For instance, there
was a Frenchman who bought a piece of painted wood, and put it in his
bedroom. I saw it with my own eyes, in his flat in Paris. Do you know X, a
Syrian engineer? This engineer, a member of the Committee to Preserve
the Old City of Damascus, went to Paris to bring it to him. He was helping
him buy this piece of painted wood, and was working on its restoration in
his flat! . . . This sort of thing goes on all the time. You can't imagine how
ugly this business is.

Friends and Enemies

For many Damascenes, celebrating the Old City is a form of resistance against the new social order—specifically, a political elite
whom they blame for the supposed deterioration of Damascus.
When I asked a Damascene television director why people have become so interested in Old Damascus in recent years, he replied:

Not all the people, only the true Damascenes. Why, because they feel they
are in a minority. Damascus is a town invaded by its own countryside. It's
under attack from the provinces. People are here because the social life in
the countryside is awful. They run to Damascus to have a better way of
life. More, as they think, civilized than in their own lands.

Such group self-aggrandizement is a common feature of urban social
conflict. Norbert Elias and John Scotson argue that when faced with
newer competitors, established groups often attribute to their own
members "superior human characteristics" (1994: xvi). Their informant "insider" group settled in a northern English village only two
generations before the arrival of those they deem "outsiders." One

can thus imagine how much more fervent are feelings of superiority among Damascenes who count their roots in the city in centuries rather than decades. Damascenes often assume that other Syrians envy them their association with an old aristocratic culture. As a prominent Old City activist argued, "The people of Damascus are 'super,' an elite (*nukhbeh*) civilization. All those from the countryside (*ahl al-rif*) are jealous of them." A Damascene film director concurs:

> Starting in the 1960s there was an invasion from the countryside. It's not true that everyone from the countryside is part of the regime, but the Damascenes think they are. Those from the countryside had a strong tendency to think of themselves as equal to the Damascenes, but they discovered in a short time that they were not. So they tried to become Damascene by changing their dialect and by pretending to have been born here. But in the eyes of the original Damascenes they remain outsiders.

The television director described what some Damascenes see as a conspiracy on the part of the Baʿth Party (which, he notes, was "founded by Christians") to pull down Muslim sections of the Old City, pointing out that the quarters which have been spared are predominantly Christian and Jewish. The activist expressed a similar view:

> Ecochard[6] was Christian, and he took inner Damascus, Damascus within the walls—Christian Damascus before the conquest of Islam—and said, "*this* is the authentic Damascus" and protected it. After the Islamic conquest other quarters developed—al-Maydan, al-Qanawat, Suq Saruja—these are all Muslim neighborhoods. Now they are tearing down the Muslim neighborhoods, and leaving the Christian city. That's the truth! You're asking why they're destroying them; it's because they're following Ecochard's plan, either from ignorance, or on purpose. . . . I'm not sectarian (*taʾifi*), but when they tear down the Muslim quarters I begin to ask why.

Some Damascenes see the government's destruction of Sunni quarters of the Old City as an attempt to break Damascene Sunni unity and any political threat it might impose: "The regime is frightened, so they want to tear it down to the very last Arab house." But this fear is based on a misperception, Damascenes argue. According to the activist:

> This city is not conservative, like people imagine it is. It's not religiously conservative. There's no Muslim Brotherhood. . . . But there is still fear of religious fanaticism (*taʿassub*). They're trying to paint the Old City, those simple people who pray, fast, and go to the mosque, as fanatics. They aren't Muslim brothers; they're religious: they go to pray and then return

to their shops. That's different. But they've begun to tear down their houses because they are intertwined (*mutashabikeh*); no one can get in between them. They want to tear them down in order to build streets they can see through. This is how I understand it; they're afraid for themselves. But this is a mistake. Damascus is a city whose people are lovely (*hilwin*). They just want to live. They love life, commerce, and peace.

Debates over city planning reflect conflicting visions of Syrian modernity. Some Damascenes see themselves almost erased in the Baʿthist reconfiguration of the city:

> Damascenes say that the redevelopment of Damascus was undertaken to destroy the old image, so that nothing would remain except their [the ʿAlawis'] advent. There is a lot of cynicism involved in destroying Damascus to build a new Damascus that will be recognized as the regime's contribution to civilization, a more modern Syria, a better one.

With the destruction of old quarters, Damascenes feel a sense of social continuity has been broken, even though they have long since moved out of the Old City and into the wealthier districts of the modern city. "The Damascene people found themselves lost," as one put it. In the following observation from a Damascene author, "my quarter" refers to a childhood home:

> In my quarter, the state started buying up houses and putting people on the streets. The simple people, those of middle income (*al-mutawassitin*), the poor, they are throwing their belongings, their furniture out onto the street, buying their houses for 7,000 SP, and selling them for 70,000,000 SP. They began to separate people, sending them outside Damascus—some to Barzeh, some to Qatana. This old neighborhood—and I'm telling you because I want you to understand and write about it—had a single character, its people living together. Me, my father, my grandfather, and great-grandfather all lived in one house. My father knew our neighbors, my grandfather knew their grandfathers, the whole quarter knew one another, like one big family. So when they destroyed the quarter and its residents left, this spirit was lost.

Contemporary tensions are often attributed antique origins. Some Damascenes trace the animosity between themselves and the ʿAlawis back to the Umayyad dynasty:

> The countryside rules Damascus, and they made the decision to destroy Umayyad Damascus. The rulers are ʿAlawi. There has been animosity between the ʿAlawis and the Umayyads from the days of ʿAli Ibn Abi Talib and Muʿawiya. Muʿawiya was a great statesman in Islamic history, who left religion aside, and built a state, a bureaucracy, and an army and forged re-

lations with Europe. 'Ali ibn Abi Talib was a religious man. So a war took place between a religious man and a statesman, and Mu'awiyya won, he whom they call the sly fox, a son of Damascus. And this leadership lasted for 1,400 years, until today. Now it is being contested. Now it is being destroyed. This is a very big, deep, and difficult matter. It's not easy at all for you.

Many Old Damascus supporters are not among the city's wealthiest citizens, and do not represent marriages of new money and old status. Many are intellectually oriented upper-middle-class professionals—lawyers, doctors, and journalists—with comfortable, but in no way extravagant, lifestyles. Their families usually have long-established roots in the city; their names are well known and often associated with Damascene exclusivity. Yet they are not always *awlad 'ayal,* members of the old notable families. Many have business interests, but feel no sense of identification with businessmen—some of whom are themselves from old notable families—whom they blame for working along with the government to destroy the Old City:

> There was a pact between the Damascene capitalists and the leading 'Alawi officers, so Damascus became the center of their [the 'Alawis'] businesses and their control, and it was easier for them to become part of an established culture, rather than to create a parallel culture. So Damascus is their domain now.

Interestingly, some of the most prominent Old Damascus activists are former leftists who once believed in the nationalist and pan-Arabist projects and have since become disillusioned. Najat Qassab Hasan, for example, was a prominent member of the Syrian Communist Party in the 1940s. In the words of a young translator:

> I've noticed over the past five years that I have become proud of being Damascene. I see this also with my father, who was one of the founders of the Ba'th Party. The Ba'thists used to think Syrians were all simply Syrian. Now many of them regret this. Now they feel that they are distinct from all the villagers, but especially from the 'Alawis. They think: the 'Alawis may have the money, they may have the power, but we have the tradition.

This change of political affiliation is often pointed to by critics of the Old Damascus trend as evidence of typical Damascene weakness of character. Non-Damascenes hold that the Damascenes have always had a mercantile mentality, backing whoever was in power as long as they were left to conduct business peacefully. 'Alawis in particular like to point out that they themselves make up most of the opposition, and the political prison population. While they take on the dirty and dangerous business of politics, ʿAlawis argue, the Damascenes focus on making money. But according to a Damascene screenwriter, this stereotype fails to capture the whole picture:

> We often hear the older generation of Damascenes described as merchants who cared about nothing but business, and had no appreciation of education, art, and culture. We hear this so much that we ourselves believe it. But it's not true.

Although they no longer hold the reigns of political power, the Damascenes remain associated with control over resources. For non-Damascenes, the "merchant princes of Damascus," as an ʿAlawi professor put it, still control commercial enterprise. According to an ʿAlawi writer, members of his sect are not automatically preferred for government and other positions:

> The most important jobs go to Damascenes and Christians. They say that this regime is ʿAlawi, but I don't think so. Or, you can say that there is a coalition of ʿAlawis who are benefiting, but not the rest. There are ʿAlawi villages that still don't have electricity. If you ask a Damascene, he will answer in a way that reflects his prejudices. He will say that they [the ʿAlawis] have come and dominated everything, stolen everything, etc. But those who came in from other areas live in the suburbs, in illegal, substandard housing, while those in the center are Damascene and Christian.

An ʿAlawi dentist questions the assumption that high-ranking members of the military are wealthy and powerful, and argues that money has replaced sectarianism in securing influence:

> I seriously do not see ʿAlawis as a ruling party or bloc. If you look at rich ʿAlawi families, they're very few compared to the Sunnis who really have money and influence. If you're an officer in the army, what does that mean? Even if you're an officer close to the president, your salary is low. You have no power to make decisions—the president does that. Real power is over people. I went to some ʿAlawi officers for help when my brother was in prison, and they asked for money! These days it's not really about religion. Many of those closest to the president are not ʿAlawi. And I don't see my relatives involved.

The university, too, used to be a Damascene preserve; the ʿAlawi professor remembered a Damascene colleague complaining that all the outsiders had ruined the university. "Do you mean me?" the professor asked. "No, not you, but all the others," the colleague replied. The ʿAlawi writer told a similar story:

I asked one [a Damascene], "why are you so interested in restoring an Old City, rather than building a city of the future?" I felt that there was something ideological in his answer. He said that before the many projects that changed the architectural character of Damascus, people lived calmer and more balanced lives. They think that what happened to people in Damascus is that they became dehumanized, lost openness, communication, and trust. Yet Damascenes are very closed: they don't visit non-Damascenes; they don't invite non-Damascenes to their houses. You can't make friendships with the women, and with the men you can only make friendships that are not friendships at the same time. There is something sectarian that motivates those who show interest in Old Damascus. They isolate themselves as a special group from Damascene bourgeois families, and they consider people who come to Damascus as invaders who corrupted or changed the majesty of the Old City.

Damascenes see themselves as generous and open. According to Damascene author and Old City activist Siham Tergeman, "Damascenes are noted for their hospitality." Non-Damascenes see them as miserly and closed.[7] Non-Damascenes also consider Damascene Sunnis socially, politically, and religiously conservative. Sexual segregation and the wearing of the *hijab* are offered as evidence of Damascene backwardness, strangeness, and close-mindedness. "The strangest thing happened on my way to visit you," said an 'Alawi friend originally from a village near Tartus. "A woman I met on the stairs asked me to turn my head away." "That's my neighbor," I explained; "her parents live two floors below, and she tends to consider the stairs private space and doesn't wear her scarf when going up and down." "Maybe so," he replied, "but I've never had anything like that happen to me before. Don't you think it's strange?" An Iraqi woman married to a Palestinian turns the Damascene preoccupation with sexual purity on its head: "The Damascenes have dirty minds. If I greet my [male] neighbor, they assume something is going on between us." "I can understand why people of other governorates are hostile toward the Damascenes," argued a Latakian, who continued:

The Damascenes in general are not very generous; they're frugal. People from other governorates are angry because the Damascenes always had money; but this is because they've always been good merchants. This is the quality of the Damascenes that they hate, that they are inhospitable, and too careful with their money. We [non-Damascenes] are a real mixture, our horizons are much more open. We sometimes argue with real Damascenes because they are so limited. They stick to certain foods, certain customs. I'm always asking myself why.

Damascenes who decades ago left their traditional homes for the European-style flats outside its walls are returning to Old Damascus in quintessentially modern ways. They are reclaiming the Old City, physically, by promoting preservation and conservation of its quarters and by establishing and frequenting leisure sites such as Le Piano Bar. They are also recreating an idealized Old Damascus and the social connections it once—supposedly—embodied through institutions such as Friends of Damascus. Old City-themed art exhibits and other events of reimagining provide narratives of social identity that run counter to the nominally inclusive constructions of the state. I argue that nostalgic constructs, and the reactions to them by excluded groups, serve as modes of social distinction, as various social actors vie over prestige and recognition in a context of shifting values. Old Damascus, as both physical space and imagined ideal, forms a significant fault line between the different groups sharing the city. Selective consumption and rejection of Old Damascus is the stuff of boundary construction and reconstruction. These practices of social differentiation peak during the holy month of Ramadan, to which we shall now turn.

Le Piano Bar, exterior

Le Piano Bar, interior

Omayyad Palace Restaurant

Café al-Nawafeer, exterior, Sheraton Hotel

Café al-Nawafeer, interior, Sheraton Hotel

Café al-Nawfara, Old Damascus

4

Ramadan Lived and Consumed

Ramadan is a month of repentance, the month
the Holy Qur'an descended, the month of
the Night of Power . . . a month of good Arab
Islamic days . . . a month of friendly relations,
mutual respect, and piety . . . when rich and
poor are equal . . . a month bringing together
qualities and virtues, more than any other
month of the year.

—**Munir Kayyal,** *Ramadan in the Damascus
of Olden Days*

For devout Muslims, Ramadan is a time of self-purification. Fasting
(*sawm*) from dawn to dusk is one of the five pillars of Islam. This ap-
plies not only to food and drink, but also to tobacco, non-essential
medications, and sexual relations. Those unable to fast must com-
pensate with a donation of food to the poor (*kaffara*) for each day
they omit. Believers must also avoid sinful thoughts, arguments, and
malicious gossip. Ramadan is also a season of heightened almsgiving
(*zakat, sadaqa*)—another pillar of the faith. For pious Muslims, the
holy month is imbued with profound metaphysical meaning. Yet in
Syria and many other Muslim societies Ramadan holds other meanings, which, despite their obvious social significance, have received
scant anthropological attention. Anthropological discussions of Ramadan center almost exclusively on religious precepts, as if the month
held only deep religious significance for all its participants (Antoun
1968; Fallers 1974; Yamani 1987; Buitelaar 1993). It has become
customary for academics to treat Ramadan fasting and feasting as
expressions of popular religiosity and Islamic egalitarianism. Syrians

agree that fasting is designed to promote empathy for the poor, and feasts are often donated to the needy. Yet such customs may reinforce, rather than undermine, social hierarchy. In Damascus, practices of identity assertion and boundary construction peak during the holy month, when expressions of Damasceneness, and reactions against them, are most publicly and loudly expressed. Representations of Old Damascus feature in a variety of Ramadan consumptive practices and cultural forms whose various meanings are debated in the media and in conversation.

Ramadan and Damasceneness

According to Damascenes, the city has a particular association with Ramadan. According to Munir Kayyal:

> The City of Damascus was unparalleled in traditions distinctive from those of their kind in [other] Arabic and Islamic civilizations. These traditions were not wholly in conflict with what the True Religion (*al-din al-hanif*) teaches; they were regarded as part of the heritage of the blessed month of Ramadan, and Ramadan without them loses much of its beauty and splendor. (1992: 88)

Ramadan remains linked to what are seen as typically Damascene practices, extolled by Damascenes and sneered at by others. A Damascene English teacher argues that the very religious, whom she equates with the poor, fast out of belief, but elite Damascenes fast as a mode of distinction:

> All the people of other governorates (*muhafazat*) [of Syria] consider Damascenes to be the least religious among them. Damascenes link the matter of the appearance of religiosity to nobility (*akabriyyeh*), to the fact that they are aristocratic (*'ariq*), authentically Old Damascene. Since the people who have come in from other governorates don't fast, the Damascenes began to fast, and to fast habitually.[1] They do anything that might exhibit this activity. This is what led to the idea of the café, and the idea of eating *iftar* (the fast-breaking meal) outside the house, in a restaurant. It all becomes popular. For example, now during the last ten days of Ramadan, it becomes difficult to find a table in any restaurants at *iftar* time. This [practice] allows people to go out for a social occasion and appear religious at the same time.

Fasting is common among Damascenes who are in other ways non-observant. It is a way of fitting in for non-Damascenes married to Damascenes, or the upwardly mobile seeking status markers. One informant tells of her non-religious Palestinian father beginning to fast only after he married into her mother's old notable family. Non-

Damascenes consider fasting among non-practicing Muslims hypocritical. An ʿAlawi friend living in the largely Damascene neighborhood of Muhajirin took to eating breakfast on his balcony each morning, in defiance of what he saw as Damascene pretentiousness. Another informant, who grew up in the regionally diverse neighborhood of Baramkeh, then moved to Muhajirin after marriage, confirms this association of Damasceneness and ostentatious fasting. In *Damascene Talk* (*Hadith Dimashqi*), Najat Qassab Hasan admits that some Damascenes, in keeping with their well-known phrase "everything has its place" (*kull shiʾ li-halu*), separate occasional religiosity from everyday practice, fasting with great piety, then drinking alcohol again as soon as the month ends (1988: 194–195). Public displays of Ramadan "customs and traditions" are linked to Damasceneness in the minds of Damascenes and non-Damascenes alike.

Reinvented traditions offer Damascenes opportunities to display local identity and to consume conspicuously. As among Muslims elsewhere, food consumption reaches its height during Ramadan. For several weeks before the month begins, food stores display items to be consumed at the *iftar* table, such as *qamr al-din* (apricot leather), tamarind, and *ʿaraq sus* (licorice root), which are used to make fast-breaking beverages. An "organized" (*murattibeh*) Damascene housewife stocks up on these and other non-perishable provisions (*muneh*) as early as possible. "They *still* stockpile, even now," remarked a journalist from Hama, who sees this activity as evidence of Damascene backwardness and miserliness. Yet prices rise considerably as the month approaches. Iman Abdul Rahim, director of International Relations at the Ministry of Tourism, tells this story of pre-Ramadan grocery shopping:

> The funny thing is that it's obvious that the month of Ramadan is the month of fasting. People are supposed to eat less. But people eat more, consumption multiplies, and everything becomes more expensive. Two days ago I was talking to my greengrocer. Lemons were 50 SP [$1], cucumbers were 40, as were zucchini, and the eggplant I bought for *maqlubeh*[2] was 60. All this is a lot. I told him, "Ramadan hasn't even begun yet," and he replied "Happy holidays" (*kull saneh wa inti salimeh*).

Food eaten during Ramadan is the best and most elaborate of the year. The government has tried to stem the tide of rising consumption by regulating the amount of luxury foods—such as meat and nuts—that can be shown in television advertisements, so as not to taunt the poor with images of items completely out of their reach. Yet the relaxation of importation laws in the early 1990s has flooded the market with expensive items, further marking off those who can afford them from those who cannot. These differences in consumption power are most salient during Ramadan. Those with freezers will store peak-season summer vegetables for Ramadan when it falls in winter.[3] They will also produce labor-intensive dishes, such as *kibbeh*—cracked wheat and lamb patties stuffed with minced lamb, spices, and nuts—ahead of time and freeze them. More meat and other luxuries—such as dried and fresh fruit, nuts, and sheep's milk butter (*samneh ʿarabiyyeh*)—are eaten than at any other time of year, and there is meant to be a new dish every day. Only during Ramadan do Damascenes eat sweets daily; bakeries are full of traditional pastries, syrup-laden and filled with cream, nuts, or dates, which are produced at no other time. Trays of sweets are ordered weeks in advance.

Among the Damascene elite, a typical *iftar,* or *ftur* as it is sometimes called, begins with *fatteh,* a rich soup of broth, chickpeas, yogurt, bread, garlic, sesame butter (*tahineh*), and *samneh,* often topped with pine nuts or meat, sometimes with tiny lamb-stuffed fried eggplant. *Fatteh* involves mixing hot broth with cold yogurt, and must be consumed immediately. Hours before sunset women work in the kitchen, preparing everything that can be done ahead of time—all but the *fatteh*. Children wait at the window, ears turned to the local mosque, or in front of the television, waiting to hear Sadaq Allahu al-Azim recited, marking the end of the fasting day. "*Saqqi,*" they will shout, "pour" (the broth out over the bread), as *fatteh* must be served as soon it is assembled. The table will already be laid with an array of juices, *ful* (fava beans), fresh bread, and salads such as *fattush* (greens and tomatoes with squares of fried bread). After this comes lamb or chicken and vegetable stews, often in yogurt sauces (which are believed to be hydrating), baked macaroni with local white cheese, *samneh*-laden rice, kibbeh, fruit, and tea. Last are sweets specific to Ramadan, such as the cream cakes *warbat bi-qishteh* or the triangle-shaped cream and pistachio-nut-filled *namura*.

The peak of the social calendar, Ramadan is a period of intense sociability. The first ten days of the month are relatively quiet, to allow adaptation to the demands of fasting. Then the invitations (*ʿazaʾim,* sing. *ʿazimeh*) begin. Mothers often hold the first *ʿazimeh,* inviting married children and their families, usually for a Thursday evening *iftar,* allowing for a long night of revelry before Friday's day of rest. After this is the eldest daughter's or son's turn. Some are quite elaborate affairs serving fifty or sixty guests. Recently the *ʿazaʾim* network has begun to extend beyond the family, as wives invite their husbands' colleagues and working women invite their own. As with the corporate Christmas party in Britain and America, company directors have begun to hold *'aza'im* for their employees. According to one informant, "Ramadan has become an opportunity, an occasion to have a big *'azimeh*."

Ramadan socializing has begun to spread beyond the home, into the young but burgeoning world of Syrian public culture. The last Thursday night before the beginning of the holy month is Takrizat Ramadan, an evening of indulgence before fasting begins, akin to Mardi Gras in Catholic tradition. Najat Qassab Hasan describes this occasion:

> Among the strangest of preparations for fasting is one the Damascenes call Takrizat Ramadan, when they proceed to celebrate by eating what they like, and most likely with an outing (*sayran*) or an evening party. For those among them who drink alcohol (*al-khamra*) indulgently on ordinary days, but who are absolutely prohibited from drinking during the fasting month, "Takriza" becomes a night of drunkenness and drink (*lailat sukr wa sharab*). Afterward they rise and bathe to purify themselves, and resolve to refrain from drinking. (1988: 194)

The traditional *sayran* involved a picnic in one of the outlying regions of Damascus, in the orchards of the al-Ghuta or by the river in Rabweh. Now Takrizat Ramadan has become an occasion not just for drinking and eating and enjoying oneself, but for doing so at public consumption sites. Families today are more likely to spend the afternoon at a restaurant table than on a picnic blanket. Such social display does not stop when fasting starts; Takrizat Ramadan is just the beginning of a monthlong competitive consumption spree for Damascene elites.

Ramadan is far more publicly marked in Damascus than it is elsewhere in Syria, as a visit to the northern cities of Aleppo and Latakia during the month confirmed. Restaurants in Damascus, humble and posh, foreign style and local, tend to close during the day, and to serve set menus for *iftar*, with Radio Damascus piped in on the sound system to announce the exact moment of fast breaking. In contrast, many more of those in Aleppo and Latakia stay open all day, serve their standard offerings in addition to or in lieu of a set *iftar*, and let the diner decide when to break fast.

Upscale Damascene restaurants produce glossy booklets listing the month's *iftar* offerings. The Meridien Hotel's Café al-Manshiyyeh's 1994 brochure cover features an aerial photograph of Old Damascus, with the Umayyad Mosque at its center and a Qur'anic verse as its caption. Inside are season's greetings from Saudi Arabian Airlines. Qur'anic verses alone adorn the Nadi al-Sharq's booklet front cover, with an interior shot of the Umayyad Mosque inside among the menus. These brochures make no mention of the price of their meals, but they each charge 1,000 SP per head, about a week's pay for a university-educated government employee. Some restaurants, like the suburban Sahara al-Siyahi, also distribute stand-up calendars charting the changing schedule of sunset.

Elegant restaurants and hotels serve either five- or six-course meals, or set out elaborate "open buffets," long tables piled with delicacies. Usually a "traditional Damascene" atmosphere is evoked. On the thirteenth of Ramadan 1994, the Meridien Hotel served:

> Juice—Assorted Starters
> Vegetable Soup
> *Fatteh* with Stuffed Eggplant
> Stuffed Zucchini in Yogurt Sauce
> Cracked Wheat with Lamb and Marrow
> Buffet of Middle Eastern Sweets and Seasonal Fruits

The Nadi al-Sharq's menu for the sixteenth offered:

> Beverages—Starters
> Cream of Asparagus Soup
> Sheep's Feet *Fatteh*
> Chicken and Rice in a Cream Sauce
> Lamb Cutlets
> *Basmeh* with Cheese (cheese "stamps," cheese-stuffed pastry)

After breaking fast, many Damascenes frequent upmarket cafés. This practice dates back only to the early 1990s, when the elite hotels opened their cafés. Before this time, women almost never ventured into cafés, which were mostly limited to working-class men. Now post-*iftar* café hopping is all the rage. By midnight, the Sheraton's al-Narabayn (or al-Nawafeer when Ramadan falls in summer), the Meridien's Tric Trac, and the Nadi al-Sharq's patio café are packed with smartly dressed socialites, women as well as men. "Just like in the old café, in the old quarter," said Abdul Rahim of the Ministry of Tourism:

> This is something the Sheraton never used to have, ever. But then they got the idea for al-Narabayn. It shows that people are certainly going back to being more Eastern. They've begun to go, the wealthy families, to the most

elegant places, the Sheraton's Narabayn, the Oriental Club. You won't find an empty table.

Some Damascene establishments have begun to serve *suhur,* the meal taken before sunrise, in addition to *iftar.* The Oriental Club, one of the city's most expensive restaurants, is perhaps the most popular *suhur* location. Despite its name, the club's décor is vaguely art deco, broken only by a Bedouin tent-like coffee area near the entrance. Reservations for *suhur* must be booked well in advance for those who lack connections. Patrons arrive at about 11:00 P.M., groups of older couples wearing suits, parties of younger men and women dressed more casually but equally expensively. They sit at high tables draped in green linen, playing cards or backgammon, smoking water pipes or cigarettes. A waiter in traditional costume serves tamarind juice from a large brass urn strapped to his back. A musician begins to play an oud.[4] The vice president's son arrives with a circle of diamond-and-gold-bejeweled young couples. "People are here just to be seen," explains my Damascene companion; "they could play cards at home." The buffet, similar to those offered for *iftar,* is served from 1:00 A.M.

The association of Ramadan and public consumption is again reinforced at the very end of the month. On the night before the beginning of Eid al-Fitr, the holiday marking the end of Ramadan, stores stay open late into the night—and some all night—for shoppers to purchase new holiday clothing. Syrian television broadcasts live interviews with shoppers, asking where they are from and what they are buying, and wishing them a happy holiday.

Not everyone is happy with what some see as the growing commercialization and serialization of Ramadan. Some argue television watching (described below) and conspicuous consumption are displacing the spirituality and expression of social connectedness which they feel once characterized the season. Their notions of ascetic Ramadan piety are just as beholden to modern constructions of nostalgia as are the Damascenes' commodified representations of the Old City. Ramadan practices provide an opportunity for social and political critique. For a librarian from Latakia,

> Ramadan is supposed to be a month for God. Why do you fast? You fast because you are supposed to see what it is like for the poor who may be able to eat only once a day, and then only something very simple. The whole tradition is now upside down. When we fast, we shouldn't then turn around and eat great varieties of food, fill the table, and eat, eat, eat like grasshoppers. We ought to be more moderate, because this month has

a meaning. Instead we are eating as much as possible before and after fasting. And then, instead of praying or reading the Qur'an, or having meaningful discussions, we just sit in front of this apparatus and watch one series after another, one series after another. . . . If I had any power, I would do something about all these programs. First of all, nobody can sit in front of the television from the moment it starts until the moment it ends, and watch all this nonsense which comes one after another, one after another, like a race. And in between all the news and comments and I don't know what. This month wasn't meant to be like that, not at all. But look what we've turned it into, and not just here in Syria, but all over the Arab world. . . . In Islam, music and dance are not really accepted, but now just as you are sitting down to break your fast, just as you say the *bismillah*, these people are offering you songs and dances!

The librarian suggests that the media and public culture during Ramadan contribute to support for Muslim fundamentalism:

This is why we have fundamentalists. When they criticize such programs, you can't say they are wrong. Of course, fundamentalists are wrong about many other things. But our people are simple people; you must remember that we have a very high percentage of people who are very simple, and you can easily turn their minds when you deal with religious topics.

Public displays of religiosity have become more prevalent. Damascenes have begun to frequent mosques in large numbers during Ramadan, a practice some see as an expression of status rather than piety. According to the librarian:

People are eating, and then running to the mosque. I don't know the *tarawih*,[5] maybe they have to do thirty or forty bends, up and down, up and down. They go to do gymnastics in the mosque! Of course they go to pray, but I call it gymnastics, because really if you have just eaten after a long day of fasting, it is very difficult to do this up and down movement. You can pray the *tarawih* any time you like, at home, but now even women are going to the mosque, and this is a new tradition. Women used to pray at home, but now they are all going, women and men, in their prayer gowns, to the mosque. You can see them in the streets.

According to a Damascene English teacher, mosques have become part of a public culture of display:

The *tarawih* prayer has become a big social event, especially over the last five years. When I was young, I never heard of women going to mosques to pray the *tarawih*. Now, especially during the last ten days [of Ramadan] the mosques are full of women. It's become an event (*munasabeh*); women go to see each other at the mosque.

Mosques, like so many other semi-public spaces, have become court-ship grounds. The English teacher points out:

> Mothers have begun, for the first time, to take their daughters to the mosque, all of them. It's become a social occasion. It's become an occasion to see people, and to find a mate, a type of reception. Eligible bachelors, merchants, and sons of notables (*abna' al-'ayal*) traditionally have very strong ties to their families, and generally are matched by their mothers. So all the girls have begun to display themselves in front of these mothers.

Some point to the values of solidarity with and sympathy for the poor that they feel Ramadan is meant to evoke, and object to the proliferation of images of conspicuous consumption bombarding those who can barely make ends meet. Syrian Ministry of Tourism's Abdul Rahim pointed to Sharihan, the Egyptian actress and dancer whose Ramadan television variety show, very popular among Damascene audiences, epitomizes the change in values:

> During the credits, which go on for about five minutes, she wears about one hundred different dresses. Each second or two she comes out with a different dress, each worth more than 5000 Egyptian pounds. They must be full of decorations, elaborately made. Many Damascene girls wish to emulate Sharihan, but few have the means.

Ramadan, Abdul Rahim argues, has become associated with elite status and wealth:

> Here in Damascus, Ramadan has become an elite tradition (*ramadan sar taqlid al-akabir*). It's not that the poor don't fast, but it's the understanding people have. The elite (*awlad al-akabir*) use Ramadan as a way of distinguishing themselves (*ka zahira betmayyezun*).

Ramadan Television

Ramadan has become a season of nostalgia for Syrian Muslims, very much like Christmas in some American circles. Families gather, expatriates return, and the days of old are evoked around the *iftar*—"fast breaking"—table and on the television screen. On Ramadan evenings Damascenes exchange their suits and dresses for long, old-fashioned caftans and robes (*jalabiyyehs* and *'abayas*) and visit relatives and friends to watch together the season's nostalgic and folk-loric television offerings. Most Damascus homes receive only two television channels: Channel One, which airs programs in Arabic, and Channel Two, which at other times of the year broadcasts foreign-language material.[6] During the fasting month, Arabic programming takes over much of Channel Two's airtime.

Syrian television has entered a boom period. Formerly country cousins to Cairo in television and film production, Syrian directors, producers, screenwriters, and actors are beginning to develop reputations beyond their country's borders. As actor-director Hatim ʿAli remarked, "We have new ideas and new subjects," while "the Egyptians are repeating themselves" (Lancaster 1998). Syrian programs are shown on television networks in numerous Arab countries and on the newly launched Syrian, Middle Eastern, and Europe-based satellite channels, such as Middle East Broadcasting Network (MBC). Arab viewers find Syrian programs refreshing in their often satirical treatment of Arab society and polity. By avoiding the specific, directors manage to slip past the censors some very cutting social and cultural commentary.

The 1994 Ramadan broadcast schedule included a nightly half-hour variety program entitled *Intoxication with the Past* (*Min Nashwat al-Madi*). Opening credits featured a close-up of a man's arms playing an oud in the ornate reception room of the Nizam House, Sir Richard Burton's former Old City residence and a masterpiece of Damascene architecture. In this same room, with its characteristic green-and gold-painted carved wood panels, a host interviews actors and musicians about traditional performing arts. Guests often break into a cappella song or dance. One program begins in the radio station archives, with the host sifting through transcripts of old songs. Segments filmed in the Nizam House are interspersed with performance clips from different regions of the country, modern groups singing popular music from the 1940s and 1950s and self-consciously "folkloric" performances, usually of men in local costume—black or white *shirwal* (baggy trousers) suspended by multicolored sashes—doing line dances such as the *dabkeh* around bubbling fountains in open courtyards.

Similar in content but with a stronger emphasis on material labeled "heritage" (*turath*) is the Folklore Series (Musalsal al-Folklur) *Our Popular Memory* (*Dhakiratuna al-Shaʿbiyya*). Here local experts, usually men identified as "doctor" or "professor," speak about customs and traditions (*ʿadat wa taqalid*) from behind desks or before monuments. Unlike *Intoxication with the Past*, which mixes song and dance from many different regions in a single episode, *Our Popular Memory* chooses a particular location for each program and features not only performance, but local culture of all sorts: monumental architecture, public baths, markets, houses, household furnishings, cooking implements, and costumes. A third program, *Ramadan Days* (*Ayyam Ramadaniyya*) presents holiday traditions from around the country as timeless, although some of these are no longer widely practiced. In addition, various chat programs feature Syrian celebrities sharing memories. On *Red Anemones* (*Shaqaʾiq al-Nuʿman*), Syria's leading comic, Durayd Lahham, spoke wistfully of bygone social relations: "In the old quarter, you would turn up the volume of your radio, not to annoy your neighbors, but so they could enjoy it with you." In *Ramadan Cuisine* (*Tabaq Ramadan*), a chef from one of Damascus's elite hotels takes viewers through the preparation of both traditional holiday specialties, such as the date-sweet *maʿmul*, and such recently adopted fare as lasagne, sponge cake, and chocolate éclairs. The latter is aired just before sunset and is followed with religious programming: the call to prayer from various Damascus mosques, and "Television Mufti" Muhammad al-Buti's *Qurʾanic Studies.*[7]

These programs reflect the ways in which the government takes advantage of the opportunities Ramadan presents for national culture construction. They form part of the ruling Baʿth Party's efforts to incorporate diversity under a rubric of Syrian, and beyond this Arab, nationalism. Routine visits to the suq to buy spices are videotaped and framed as part of "our national heritage." How closely Syrians watch these programs is difficult to ascertain. Many households, especially those fasting, will turn the television on around sunset, to hear the exact moment to break fast, and to keep hungry guests and lively children occupied while food is heated. But most tend to treat as background noise the programs aired just before and after sunset, in distinct contrast to those which captivate viewers later in the evening. The later period, which might be called "Ramadan prime time," begins approximately one hour after the beginning of *iftar,* and is reserved for the year's most eagerly anticipated local television production, the Ramadan dramatic series (*musalsal*).[8]

Syria produces many low-budget serial dramas each year, often on contemporary urban issues, but showpiece productions, usually on historical themes, are most commonly aired during Ramadan. Often a second locally produced series is shown later in the evening, in a similarly desirable slot. Watching these series has become as much a part of Ramadan for Damascenes as breaking fast with apricot juice.

These programs play a pivotal role in ongoing debates over representations of local and national culture. Dramatic depictions of Old Damascus do not engender feelings of connectedness among the different social groups making up Syrian society, as Benedict Anderson suggests the novel does (1983). Rather, they exacerbate regional and sectarian tensions, provoking resentment and hostility rather than kinship and fraternity.

Given the locally specific social and political context of these conflicts, much of the formalist, semiotic, and sociological media criticism produced by Western writers is of little use in exploring how Syrians actually engage with their own television productions. Only recently have anthropologists and media studies specialists turned their attention to the role that locally produced television programs play in social, ideological, and political contests within specific non-Western contexts (Lull 1991; L. Abu-Lughod 1993, 1995; Mankekar 1993, 1999; Das 1995; Lutgendorf 1995; Rofel 1995; Armbrust 1996). These works explore the ways in which indigenous dramas and local responses to them serve as modes of social distinction. They illustrate the now commonplace observation that global cultural forms, such as television, are locally appropriated and transformed to serve culturally specific ends. In Damascus, sub-national identities are being constructed and reconstructed through identification with or rejection of nostalgic representations of the city's past, such as those presented in Ramadan serial dramas.

Damascene Days

During the first half of Ramadan in 1993, a series entitled *Damascene Days* (*Ayyam Shamiyya*) occupied the earlier prime-time slot. Produced by Syrian Arab Television, the series is said to have been inspired by Egypt's successful *Hilmiyya Nights* (*Layali Hilmiyya*).[9] While several television series have been set in Old Damascus, *Damascene Days* is said to be the first to depict social life in the city in the late Ottoman period (1910). It is also said to have been the first such program without a strong political plot. *Damascene Days* attempted to portray daily life in an unnamed Old City quarter, concentrating on family relations, problems between neighbors, and local administration. Customs and traditions associated with rites of passage were carefully depicted. An epitome of local folklore, *Damascene Days* was shown in Cairo—arguably the capital of Arab culture—as part of a program of cultural exchange between Egypt and Syria (*Funun* 18 July 1994) and won an award at the 1995 Arab Television Festival. The series was broadcast in numerous other Arab countries.

Clearly the media event of the year in Syria, *Damascene Days* inspired a shift in my research. My original project focused on the relationship between food and social distinction among the different groups living in Damascus. Set to explore the connection between a growing sense of Damasceneness and a resurgence of interest in "traditional" foods, I watched the first several episodes with an eye on the treatment of food. Witnessing the controversy sparked by the series, I realized that to focus exclusively on food, or indeed any one subject, was to treat as tangential many events and practices that dominate social and cultural life in the city. It was during the airing of *Damascene Days* that I decided to expand the focus of my research to include all manifestations of Old Damascus revivalism.

It is difficult to overestimate the extent to which the fifteen episodes of *Damascene Days* were watched and discussed. As one reviewer put it, streets and shops emptied each night during the hour-long broadcast, and as they left their houses afterward, people imitated the old-fashioned, drawn-out accent of the *Damascene Days* characters (Jabbur 1993: 26). Television sets were tuned to the series even in the presence of large numbers of guests. *Damascene Days* sparked numerous newspaper and magazine articles, interviews, and editorials. During Eid al-Fitr, Syrian Television aired "An Evening with the *Damascene Days* Cast," an hour-long discussion program filmed in an Old Damascene house, during which all those involved in the production, and various other media figures, were asked the same question: what is the secret of the public's love for *Damascene Days*? The series was the subject of endless discussion at parties, in buses and shared taxis, in hairdressers and shops, in restaurants and cafés.

The Story

The central plot involves an impoverished widow and her hummus-seller son who had been forced ten years earlier to mortgage half their house to the quarter's café owner. Son Mahmoud is unable to pay the mortgage, so the café owner now wants to rent the rooms to his waiter. Fearful of a "stranger" moving in, and hoping to raise his status and attract a suitable wife, Mahmoud decides to ask the quarter's wealthiest merchant, Abu ʿAbdu, for a loan. Abu ʿAbdu agrees, but asks for some type of collateral. Mahmoud offers his shop. Abu ʿAbdu asks for something "more valuable than a hundred houses or shops": a clipping from Mahmoud's mustache.[10] At first Mahmoud refuses vehemently, for surrendering mustache hair is tantamount to risking his masculinity (*rujuliyyeh*). After several agonizing days, Mahmoud agrees to Abu ʿAbdu's terms. Abu ʿAbdu wraps the clippings in a handkerchief and stores them in a locked wooden box to which Umm ʿAbdu, his eldest wife, has the only key.

Naziha, Abu ʿAbdu's younger wife, steals the key and hides the handkerchief in an attempt to discredit Umm ʿAbdu. Relations between the co-wives are predictably sour: Naziha brags of Abu ʿAbdu's attentions to her, while Umm ʿAbdu taunts Naziha about her childlessness.

Mahmoud works diligently and is able to repay the loan quickly, but Abu ʿAbdu cannot produce the mustache hairs. Mahmoud is furious; his reputation remains sullied as long as the hairs are missing. Abu ʿAbdu tries to substitute a lock from Umm ʿAbdu's braid, but his deception is discovered, and this attempt to pass off "women's hair" as Mahmoud's escalates the scandal. Umm Mahmoud tries to convince her son that he is better off with the money—fifteen Ottoman gold pieces—than the mustache hair, but material resources will not restore his standing. Indeed, Mahmoud's debasement is the talk of the quarter. Abu Dahir, the quilt maker, refuses to engage his daughter to Mahmoud, as the legacy of lost honor will disgrace generations of the latter's progeny. Enraged and distraught, Mahmoud tries to storm Abu ʿAbdu's house to look for the missing bristles; a crowd rushes from the café to restrain him. The matter is taken before the quarter's council of notables (*al-qadawat*), and the *zaʿim,* the locally recognized leader of the quarter, declares any slur on Mahmoud's honor to be one on his own, thus restoring Mahmoud's reputation. Mahmoud marries Abu Dahir's daughter and prospers. Eventually the mustache hairs are recovered, and a disgraced Naziha is nearly returned to her natal family. In the end it is Umm ʿAbdu who dissuades Abu ʿAbdu from divorcing Naziha; Umm ʿAbdu has grown fond of her co-wife who, she argues, has suffered enough for her deed.

It's a Wonderful (Fantasized) Life

Around this story a rich tapestry of social life, of bygone ways, is woven. Abu Dahir, the quilter, teaches his apprentices ethics, molding character as well as skill. Women exchange gossip through windows in adjoining walls, men in the barbershop and cafe. The barber cuts hair and practices medicine, treating abscesses with garlic and lemon, amusing his customers with jokes and stories. The midwife "tests" a potential wife and daughter-in-law, kissing her to sniff her body and checking her housekeeping skills. The *qabaday*—strongman—a fugitive from the quarter of Shaghur, brandishes his dagger to defend a humiliated Mahmoud, but also cries for the mother he left behind. Men gather in the café each Thursday night to hear the storyteller (*hakawati*) recount heroic tales, while women sing and dance in one another's homes. The series' concerns are intensely personal and familial, its characters charmingly naive. Quarter residents resemble an extended, mostly happy family, who help one another financially and calm one another's anxieties. Disputes are settled with affection. Notables treat their social inferiors with paternalistic concern.

Women visit each other frequently, but before leaving their houses, cover their long dresses with black skirts and drape black shawls over their upper bodies and faces. In only one scene does a woman speak to a man not her relative, and here Mahmoud turns his head away to address the fully cloaked midwife. Women are meant to be invisible, or at least anonymous in public places. In a scene that confounded contemporary Damascus dwellers, Abu 'Abdu scolds his young son for walking in on a group of men visiting in the merchant's reception room; now when fully wrapped mother and son walk together in the quarter, the men will know whose wife she is. Female chastity, a central component of male honor, is carefully guarded: when Turkish soldiers rape the egg seller's daughter, the latter takes the problem to the *za'im*. His solution safeguards honor, but not at the expense of the girl's future, for he marries her to one of his sons and instructs the egg seller to keep the attack a secret. This son was meant to divorce the girl shortly afterward, the marriage serving only to legitimize both her loss of virginity and any offspring resulting from the rape. Instead the boy falls in love with her and keeps her.

Like the nostalgic reminiscences of Friends of Damascus, *Damascene Days* is an attempted reconstruction of this fantasized world of innocence and wholesomeness. Characters appear guileless. Some *Damascene Days* fans argue that people really were this way. *Damascene Days* screenwriter Akram Sharim describes the imagined Damascene of 1910:

> A man [of that time] didn't have self-interest (*ihtimam*); he had love. He loved his house, he loved his children. . . . As a human being he was simple, his way of thinking simple, his way of life (*tabi 'at hayatu*) simple, uncomplicated, pure (*naqi*).

Themes of simplicity and purity, in contrast to the complexity and corruption of contemporary life, emerge and re-emerge in discussions of *Damascene Days*. The series' rosy nostalgia was widely read as criticism of the present. In an interview on "An Evening with the *Damascene Days* Cast," actor Rashid 'Assaf gives his account of the series' success:

The work could be called Damascene daily life (*yawmiyyat shamiyyeh*). The public interacts with it in a very simple way. . . . The work depicts a moment in our people's history, a pure moment in the face of life's pressures, a moment that represents our reaction against divisiveness, and our refusal to accept these pressures. It reflects our search for a better society, a pure society based on trust and belief. This work really dealt with all this, and the way people responded to it shows that this is what they long for.

Damascene Days constructs a static, timeless era of sweetness and naïveté. Massey notes this tendency to associate strong notions of place with static concepts of tradition, essentialist views of the past, and bounded notions of culture, despite evidence of flux, social, economic, and political transformation, and interrelationships and interdependencies among places (1994). The past serves as a "golden age" susceptible to generalizations and simplifications untenable in treatments of the present. A desire for a "simple," politically stable setting to construct a timeless account of social life, a portrait of pristine "customs and traditions," is what attracted Sharim to 1910:

I knew there was an old custom of using mustache hair as collateral, and I wrote it into a story, but then the problem was finding a time period. The Teens and Twenties were inappropriate; there was too much going on politically, like *safar berlik*[11] and World War I. The thirties was the French Mandate period. The forties wouldn't work; it was inappropriate because it was a time of consciousness generally: political, economic, educational, and health consciousness. This consciousness develops in part II. In part I we had a quarter with a locked gate, and a community (*mujtama*ᶜ) within it. So I went back to 1910.

Most Damascene viewers saw in *Damascene Days* an authenticity in keeping with their own sense of identity. Fans of the series stressed the accuracy of the dialogue, which was rich in local idiom, the décor, which showcased inlaid furniture and other local crafts, and social customs, such as those connected to marriage. For Dr. Nadia Khost, writer and leading Old City activist:

Damascene Days showed the positive features of the quarter, its human relations, and presented its beauty. . . . [The series] evoked the magic of the atmosphere of the Damascene quarter, the characters, their clothes, even their way of speaking.

Prominent lawyer and media figure Najat Qassab Hasan, author of the widely read *Damascene Talk* (*Hadith Dimashqi*) and well-known Old Damascus advocate, found the series "beautiful, the best such program; it stopped time." Colette Khuri, Damascene author, People's Assembly member, and unofficial representative of Christian Damascus, thought the series "elegant and refined."

Some saw flattering continuities; Muhammad Bashar al-Jabban, a Damascene civil engineer and director of the Committee for the Preservation of the Old City of Damascus (Lajnat Himayat Madinat Dimashq al-Qadima), pointed out that the series dealt with honor, a concept which "still informs our customs and traditions." Fawwaz Haddad, author of two novels set in Old Damascus, lauded *Damascene Days* for "its efforts to paint a positive picture of Damascus from beginning to end." Positive portrayals of the local past seem to be what Damascene audiences value most highly.[12] As Damascene actor Rafiq Sbai'i, the *za'im* of *Damascene Days*, put it:

> Every human being is protective of his home environment, and wants it to be shown in the best light. . . . In my opinion, art is a beautification (*tajmil*) of reality, and a presentation of that reality in as pleasant a picture as possible. This is the fundamental task (*mahamma*) of the artist, so that it will not be said of us that we "air our dirty laundry in public" and paint ourselves as scoundrels. (Mansur 1994: 62)

The huge success of *Damascene Days* is, in part, attributable to its actors, many of whom, like Sbai'i, are known for folkloric roles. One reviewer described Sbai'i as "a noble Damascene tree, blooming every season because he drinks from roots deeply planted in authentic ground" (R. al-Kisan 1993: 20). Sbai'i's "Abu Sayyah" was the central character of the first drama series set in Old Damascus, *Hammam al-Hana* of 1968. In 1993 Sbai'i could still be seen as Abu Sayyah on variety shows singing old songs, and in an advertisement for government investment bonds. The *za'im* was the favorite *Damascene Days* character, a success which Sbai'i attributes to his experience as a Damascene: "I'm a son of this Damascene milieu (*bi'a*), grew up in it, and lived this folk life (*hayat sha'biyya*) in all its minute details. This I was able to reflect in an authentic portrait (*sura sadiqa*)" (ibid.: 21).

Here is where the elaborate concerns of cultural criticism and film studies often seem distant from ethnographic detail. Membership in imagined communities determines commentary. Praise for *Damascene Days* invariably centered on the accuracy of language, décor, and social customs. The series was evaluated less for production or entertainment value than for historical realism. Some Damascenes qualified their generally enthusiastic responses with reservations about historical mistakes or misrepresentations. When I asked what they thought of *Damascene Days* generally, Damascenes often answered with an estimate of how much of the series they thought was true to life: Damascene ʿAdil Saʿdi claimed it was "80 percent accurate"; while Muhammad Bashar al-Jabban of the Committee for the Preservation of the Old City of Damascus, rated it as "only 40 percent realistic; I can even say a little less." The program's nostalgic depiction of the past served not as mere pleasurable diversion, but as historical document. According to actor Taysir Asadi, who played *Damascene Days* quilt maker Abu Dahir:

> This series will not die; it will live. . . . It will become a document for generations and generations. If someone wants to see what 1910 was like, the way things were, they can go back to the series to get the facts, because everything in it is true. The writer and I went to houses and spoke to many people, in order to ensure that everything was true. (Interview on "An Evening with the *Damascene Days* Cast")

Televisual Authenticity

For Damascenes and non-Damascenes alike, *Damascene Days* constituted an evaluation of Damascene culture and its relationship to the Syrian state. Therefore it is not surprising that Damascenes subjected this representation of their golden age to an exacting set of standards. After lauding the overall quality of *Damascene Days*, many point out what they thought it got wrong. Colette Khuri criticized a deficiency she feels the series shares with others of its type:

> There is a problem with these series: they never speak about Christian people in Damascus. We are 20 percent of Damascus, and we've played a very important role in the nation. It's our own fault, because until now we have not written screenplays. It will happen, because it is history, and you cannot change history. But *Damascene Days* was for Muslims, and all for Muslims.[13]

For Nasr al-Din al-Bahra, Damascene writer, former People's Assembly member, and author of a nostalgic book on the Old City, the makers of the series

> tried to, and achieved, a great deal of realism. Some of the characters were very realistic, like the barber and the quilt maker. But there was exaggeration (*mubalagha*), as in the story of the mustache, and in the treatment of the merchant and his two wives. The two wives would not have sat together with their husband, as they do in the series. Also, the [merchant's] wife beating is exaggerated. It happened, but not everyone did it. The wife calling her husband "*sidi*" (my lord) was rare. Most women called their husbands "cousin" (*ibn ʿammi*). The series was not authoritative, but it was beautiful folklore.

Burhan Qassab Hasan, brother of Najat and president of the Friends of Damascus, also pointed to exaggeration:

> The way they talk; they shout. It wasn't like this. For example, my father would talk to me with respect; he would use the plural. You would think they were at Oxford with you; they were known to be very gentle, very soft. They didn't have this harsh accent. But when they show this, everyone laughs. It's like when in films you always hear actors speaking in cockney accents; it isn't representative.

Exaggeration and inaccurate depictions of gender relations were the most frequently cited criticisms among Damascenes. Many took issue with the wealthy merchant's heavy-handed and violent treatment of his wives. Nadia Khost argues:

> I think viewers' strong positive reaction was due to the fact that it presented characters we know, familiar places. But I take exception to the subject matter. . . . As a woman I object to the depiction of women. The woman in the Damascene quarter had her rightful position. True, she was covered (*muhajjabeh*), but she was queen and mistress of her house; she wasn't a man's slave. She would *flatter* a man (*tulattifuhu*). Damascene women were noted for flattering men. A Damascene woman would say to her husband "welcome, welcome, how *are* you?" or "would you like something." She had many ways of making him feel important, but she too was important; . . . this is a skill, letting the man think he is very important. Don't we still know this skill? Letting the man think he is making all the decisions, when in fact she's the one deciding. This was not made clear in the series, where women of that time are portrayed as they are in the contemporary imagination (*al-dhihn al-mu'asir*): weak, backward, and simple minded.

Many Damascenes pointed to Sharim's non-Damascene identity as the reason for what they see as misrepresentations. "He's an old friend," said one, "but he's not Damascene; he's Palestinian." Privileging direct personal experience over research, Damascenes argued Sharim has not lived in Old Damascus, did not grow up there. The suggestion is that non-Damascenes do not have the right to represent Damascus, however meticulous they are with facts and however positive their representations. According to Siham Tergeman, author of the widely read memoir *O Wealth of Damascus* (*Ya Mal al-Sham*):[14]

> All these writers [of television series] are non-Damascene. The writer of *Damascene Days* is Palestinian. He was asked, "How do you know about these things, proverbs, weddings, women? Women in the period you're talking about, the forties [*sic*] weren't like that. . . ." He answered, "I

knocked on doors and asked for material." This isn't sound; it's weak. You have to *know* Damascus. I didn't gather information. . . . All of this [*Ya Mal al-Sham*] is from family, my memories. I lived the life of Damascus; it's stored up inside me. Don't pay any attention to television series; they're all commercial. You'll only find historical mistakes.

This epistemological debate, research versus personal or inherited experience, arose again in a heated conversation between Sharim and a group of Damascene media figures. The discussion took place at a dinner party given by Damascene documentary filmmaker Hind Midani to show me her film, *Damascus: A Point of View* (*Dimashq: Masafat al-Nazr*). The gathering consisted of Ghassan Jabri, director of *To You . . . Damascus* (*La-ki . . . Ya Sham*), a series aired in the late 1980s about attempts to save an Old City quarter marked for destruction, Jabri's wife Asma al-Fayoumi, a painter of Old Damascus themes, Sharim, Midani, and myself. Midani lives in a modern flat in the Damascus suburb of Dummar, but strands of vine leaves strung along the walls of her sitting room suggest an Old City courtyard. We began the evening with ice-cold vodka, a custom brought from the former Soviet Union, where Midani, like many Syrian artists, undertook postgraduate studies. We sat down to a meal of local specialties, kibbeh, stuffed grape leaves, *burak* (cheese pastries), and Syrian red wine. Alcohol may have helped fuel the heated discussion that followed.

Several times during the screening of Midani's film, Sharim exclaimed, "this is all wrong" (*kullu ghalat*). When I glanced at him for an elaboration, Jabri stepped in to avert a confrontation. After it ended, Sharim argued that films and books depict an Old Damascus of houses and buildings, not of the people who lived there; "The human being never comes through." *Damascene Days*, he argued, was an attempt to rectify this deficiency. He also claimed that Damascenes often get their own history wrong, pointing to an inaccuracy in the work of well-known folklorist and historian Munir Kayyal. Midani responded that Damascenes speak from generations of experience: "We know Damascus because we know its soul; our fathers and grandfathers lived here. The Azm Palace may have had electricity at a certain point, but I know when my own house got electricity." Then Jabri and Sharim began to argue over dates, times, and places. One debate centered on whether or not the prostitutes of the Shaghur quarter—where Jabri grew up—were veiled, then whether or not there were prostitutes in Shaghur at all. Sharim argued that there were not, and Jabri responded with a story from his childhood. Once he was out in the quarter peddling toiletries and strayed over into the red-light district, where the women eagerly bought up his lipsticks and hairbrushes. He then returned home and boasted of his successes to his father who, when he discovered where the boy had been, beat Jabri with a reed cane (*fala'a*) on the soles of his feet (in much the same way the *Damascus Days* quilt maker punishes his mischievous apprentice). Next the discussion turned to when Damascene women stopped wearing the veil, with Jabri arguing it was much later than Sharim claimed. Midani and Fayoumi argued that Sharim was thinking of Palestinian women, who were much more liberated. The argument ended with Sharim leaving the flat in a huff.

Sharim's decision to set his story in 1910, just beyond the cusp of living memory, may have been in part an effort to avert such criticism. I asked him about claims of historical errors, citing complaints about *Damascene Days* wives addressing their husbands as "*sidi*" (my lord). For many Damascenes this term suggested an inaccurate and unacceptable degree of deference on the part of wives. Sharim argued that his critics' information was all from the 1930s. In a published interview Sharim claimed that the series depicted negative and positive aspects of the period equally, and that wife beating was in fact much more widespread than the series indicated. He pointed to the market stalls that used to specialize in the reed canes (*fala'as*) which formed a standard part of Damascene household furnishings. "We did not depict in 1910 what would make [the contemporary viewer] feel that our own era is the backward one!" (Sharim 1993: 18) He and director Bassam al-Malla anticipated a rough time from the local public. According to al-Malla:

> We feared our audience; we knew they would take us to task for any mistakes. This made our work very hard. We really faced a challenge. . . . We worked from a position of respect for and fear of our audience. . . . We considered them smarter than we are; we're not at all smarter than they are. This is one of the most important reasons for the series' success. (Interview on "An Evening with the *Damascene Days* Cast")

It was such fear that prompted Sharim to consult over forty sources, including social history books, local historians, and traditional artisans (Sharim 1993: 18). Some commentators claim to detect the sources Sharim used. Nasr al-Din al-Bahra, for instance, claims that Sharim bases several characters and stories in the series on Ahmad Hilmi al-'Allaf's seminal book *Damascus at the Rise of the Twentieth Century* (*Dimashq fi Matl'a al-Qarn al-'Ishrin*). Another prominent Old City activist, author of a well-known Old Damascus memoir, directly accused Sharim of plagiarism:

My book was taken, the title changed, and a few changes made. They took songs, customs, and traditions, just lifted them from my book without citing it. The writer stole my book. They don't know academic etiquette; they don't know that if you want to take something from a book, you must give the reference. . . . Don't even mention *Damascene Days* to me; it really upsets me.

Paradise Lost

The old quarter of *Damascene Days* is a world turned in upon itself; the inward-looking closeness of the Damascene house mirrors the self-contained and seemingly self-sufficient quarter whose occupants rarely leave its walls. Yet Damascene quarters in the early part of this century were largely residential, housing only small shops and light craft production. Most male inhabitants worked in the commercial district (Khoury 1984: 509). By focusing on those who would have spent their days within the quarter—such as the barber, the egg seller, the hummus seller, the café owner, the quilt maker, the night watchman—*Damascene Days* suggests an exaggeratedly isolated social unit. No characters from outside the quarter—save the fugitive *qabaday* and patrolling Turkish soldiers—are introduced, even though waves of migrants have always moved into and through the Old City. The series depicts a neighborhood of mutual assistance and economic stability, although late-Ottoman Damascus experienced rapid inflation, artisan strikes, and a weakening of family support networks (Reilly 1995: 102–103). Few references are made to any community larger than the quarter, despite the emergence of Arab nationalist ideology at about this time. Also, while many old quarters of the period in fact housed members of similar occupations, the residents of the *Damascene Days* quarter all practice different professions. Muslim quarters tended to be economically homogeneous, which is not at all true of that in *Damascene Days* with its mix of rich and poor (Khoury 1984: 512). Also, despite disparities of wealth, characters share a common belief system, although at this time a gulf was opening between educated elites and urban masses (Gelvin 1998). The Old Damascus of *Damascene Days* is a simplification, a distillation of historical material into a handful of "traditional" prototypical people and places.

The series' set design reinforces this cozy sense of seclusion. True, the old-style Damascene house, like most Arab architecture, is built around a courtyard, and thus has a feeling of inwardness and enclosure, but it also has an upper level open to the sky, from which the courtyards of neighboring houses can be seen. Life in such a house is in many ways less private and more social than it is in a modern flat. By using only ground-floor sets, the makers of *Damascene Days* overstate the closeness of life. Compounding this impression is the dim studio lighting, not at all suggestive of the bright Mediterranean sunshine which makes its way into the narrowest alleys of the real Old Damascus.

Damascene Days constructs a time when virtues of chivalry (*furusiyyeh*), generosity (*nakhweh*), masculine honor (*muruweh*), and masculinity (*rujuliyyeh*) mattered more than money, as indeed they might if everyone knew their neighbor and no wider world intruded. The criticism of contemporary values need never be made explicit. Nowadays material wealth is rapidly becoming the most important measure of status in Syria, and Damascenes blame this trend on a regime they see as dominated by ʿAlawi peasants. For Damascenes, the new elites are barbarians from the countryside who destroyed the older, Damascene-controlled forms of commerce. Damascenes, particularly the intellectuals, argue that their older, nobler forms of social relations and modes of distinction are being replaced with the worship of money. They yearn for the days when mustache hairs were worth more than gold.

The rosy nostalgia of *Damascene Days* appears to contradict what many Damascenes see as the regime's desire to discredit them, to downplay the richness of their local identity. Many Damascenes believe that because the former ruling class was largely Damascene, the current government views Damascenes as a potential threat. Given this perception, questions arose as to why the regime would allow such a celebration of Damascus and Damasceneness to be aired in the most coveted time slot of the broadcast year. Although many Syrian television series are now produced by private production companies, television stations remain under strict government control. Censorship in Syria is so rigorous that in some cases films the government itself has funded, such as those of the award-winning Muhammad Malas, have been banned from distribution. Thus when a series is aired, Syrians speculate about the messages the government might be trying to relay. What then was this regime, long considered to be anti-Damascene, attempting to convey in an ode to Old Damascus? A Damascene filmmaker saw *Damascene Days* as "a positive depiction of a dictatorship, a community united under a strong leader—the *zaʿim*." A Damascene director argued that it was part of the regime's general effort to contain Damascene identity, to keep it from growing into a subversive counterculture. When I asked another Damascene director how preparations for the long-anticipated *Damascene Days, Part II*, were proceeding, he said the regime would never permit a sequel:

> *Damascene Days* slipped through the door, and they were faced with the overwhelming popularity of the series, so they just rode the wave. They started talking about how wonderful Damascus was, and how much they love Damascus. Do they really love Damascus? Of course not! If they love Damascus so much, then why did they make so many revolutions against the Damascene people?

Likewise, the author of a widely read Old Damascus memoir said she has refused offers from a Damascene television director to dramatize her book, because the regime would never allow another *Damascene Days*.

Indeed, the series' flattering image of Damascus and the Damascenes proved contentious. The most vociferous criticisms came not from Damascenes themselves, but from those groups they considered to be outsiders. Non-Damascenes argued that *Damascene Days* sanitized and romanticized life in the Old City, glossing over or collapsing social and economic differences. For instance, both merchant and hummus seller have mother-of-pearl-inlaid furniture, and all characters are positively drawn, save the brutal but buffoonish Turkish soldiers. Yet many Damascenes who remember life in the Old City of the 1930s and 1940s contend that class differences were indeed less accentuated than they are now. Syrians of non-Damascene origin living in Damascus object more generally to the glowing depiction of life in Old Damascus. A Sunni journalist from the city of Hama asked why I considered *Damascene Days* part of my research, since there were "more important," more realistic dramas in which to find the "authentic Damascene quarter" and "Damascene ways of thinking" (*tabi'at al-tafkir al-dimashqi*). He offered as an example *Smile of Sadness* (*Basmat al-Huzn*), a largely ignored series based on Ulfat al-Idlibi's acclaimed novel, in which the main character, an oppressed and thwarted young woman, hangs herself from a lemon tree in the courtyard of her house.

Critics see *Damascene Days* as part of a wider movement by Damascenes to glorify themselves and their past. Many non-Damascenes would agree with James Clifford's view of authenticity as a tactic, an attempt to assert cultural and social dominance (1988: 11–12). They saw in *Damascene Days* (quite rightly, according to some Damascenes) the suggestion that life in the city was better—nobler, less corrupt—than it is now, under a non-Damascene, non-urban regime. They link the series to complaints from Damascenes about the deterioration of the city brought on by mass migration from the countryside, and particularly from the largely 'Alawi coastal region (the *sahil*) over the past thirty-five years of Ba'th Party rule. According to an 'Alawi-born doctor, a long-term Damascus resident:

> It's part of a trend; they want to show themselves as more authentic, and they look down on the minorities. They've failed in so many ways, in politics, in social structure—the family has disintegrated—so they produce *Damascene Days* to prove how wonderful they were in the past. And then there is the association of all Damascus with Ramadan. But why not with Christmas? Do they ever talk about traditions in Bab Tuma?[15] When you say *Damascene Days,* it really means "Ramadan days." It's all about one sect. They try to prove the authenticity of Damascus, but ignore its diversity.

An 'Alawi journalist remarked:

> I liked the story to an extent, but not the work as a whole. It's a clear expression of our identity crisis. The problem is how to think about the past in the present. People took issue with particular points, like if the *qabaday* was realistically portrayed, but for me this isn't important; it's all lies. I shouldn't write history from my own point of view, or depict people of the past as angels. The important thing for me is to write about the past in a way that serves the present. It's not important to produce a series about how a Damascene got married in the nineteenth century. . . . These series reflect patterns of consumption, not culture. They reflect a crisis of the past, present, and future. Isn't there anything positive in the present to base a series on? You can go to any quarter of Old Damascus now and find the same sorts of characters, and make a wonderful series, but a satirical one. They portray themselves as wonderful, but half of them were traitors; historically, half of Damascus were traitors, during the days of the French, and those of the Turks and Mamluks.

Other Versions

In Ramadan 1994, Old Damascus again occupied Syrian Television's post-*iftar* slot, in the series *Abu Kamil, Part II.* Set in an Old City quarter during the last days of the French Mandate—the early 1940s—this unsuccessful sequel to the popular *Abu Kamil,* broadcast several years earlier, firmly contradicted any notion that the regime had become partial to, or was attempting to appease, its Damascene faction. The series was criticized in many circles; viewers found it drawn out, outlandish, and dull. *Abu Kamil II* failed to live up to expectations heightened by the success of the first *Abu Kamil,* and failed to take full advantage of its relatively generous budget and thirty hours of prime airtime ('Ayadeh 1994: 12). The series' Damascene screenwriter, Dr. Fu'ad Sharbaji, shared his fellow Damascenes' regard for authenticity of experience over depth of research:

> Atmosphere (*bi'a*) is not clothing, it is not dialect; it is the whole of social relationships, between people and place, between people and time, between people and the political system. Unfortunately, many producers and screenwriters treat atmosphere as if it is merely accents or traditional costumes, or going to al-Nawfara [café]. But this is not it. . . . You can't learn atmosphere; it's a foundation (*asas*). Atmosphere is a web of knowledge, ideas, sentiments, and spirit. When I wrote *Abu Kamil*, I discovered that I didn't write it on my own; all my ancestors wrote it with me.

Yet many would argue that Sharbaji's ancestors failed him, for while non-Damascene audiences were disappointed and indifferent, Damascene viewers were outraged. Nadia Khost, for example, was "100 percent against *Abu Kamil*." This series, Damascenes argued, was "all imaginary" and "all lies." Many stopped tuning in long before the last of its thirty episodes was aired, making it difficult to find anyone to help me follow the twists and turns of the series' intricate plot.

Unlike *Damascene Days*, which presented Old City dwellers galvanized to help one another and to defend themselves against the Turks, *Abu Kamil II* depicted Damascenes as traitors who collaborated with the French, informed on one another, and fought among themselves. Much of the series' dialogue consisted of hysterical arguing. Many Damascenes saw *Abu Kamil II* as a deliberate affront. According to one Old Damascus proponent:

> The whole [series] is an offense against the Damascene people (*kulu khata' 'an ahl al-Sham*). It's like an insult to the Damascenes, from the contemporaries (*al-mu'asirin*), from the people of the countryside (*ibna' al-rif*) who insult ('*am yahinu*) the people of Damascus. They rejected it—all the [Damascene] families watched and rejected the series. If you know Damascus and its people well, you'll understand what I'm saying to you. We, the people of Damascus, are still here. You can't write a story about me and say, "this is what you said." This is not what I said; I don't say this.

Once again, Damascenes objected to depictions of women. Scenes of a young woman character committed to an insane asylum were considered offensive and untrue. Many found the female lead's freedom of movement unbelievable. According to a Damascene translator:

At this time you didn't have women living alone, or going outside without their heads covered, or letting men enter their houses like that. You couldn't just bring men into your house like that, even if you were at the center of a revolution; . . . at the end, she said to that man, "we can be lovers, we can marry." Nobody can, it's unheard of in Damascus, even now, so how could it have happened then?

Colette Khuri objected to the depiction of social relations among Damascenes:

> In Damascus people believed in each other, and at the time in which *Abu Kamil* was set we used to assist each other. Even now, if there is a difficult period, I am never in need because my neighbors will help me, we help each other. We never fought with each other; we defend each other. Not like in *Abu Kamil,* where they were always accusing each other.

Burhan Qassab Hasan of Friends of Damascus criticized *Abu Kamil II* on several counts: "The whole thing was unreal. You never saw a woman going into a police station. And this accent was used by only one-fourth of people. Now they think their ancestors spoke like that, but it's not true."

Abu Kamil II screenwriter Fu'ad Sharbaji "failed the history test," according to 'Adil Abu Shanab, author of the nostalgic memoir *Damascus in the Days of Old* (*Dimashq Ayyam Zaman*). Sharbaji placed people and events in the wrong times and places, he argued. Abu Shanab and others claimed the French were portrayed too harshly in the series, since in the early 1940s French involvement in the everyday affairs of Old City dwellers was minimal. Underfunded and overburdened with wartime concerns, Mandate forces did not go about searching houses and beating old men as they do in the series (Abu Shanab 1994: 24). The depiction of Damascene collaboration with the French upset many viewers. A prominent Old City activist, whose family hails from another Syrian city, argued:

> It's completely false, because when you look at the social life of the Old City of Damascus, you'll find they rebelled against the French Mandate authorities. People were very honest in Damascus, they didn't have bad feelings toward each other, and they did not behave badly in the way that those in *Abu Kamil* do. Lying, cheating, robbery, all these things are not true. Relations between families and neighbors in the same quarter were so homogeneous and harmonious, people loved each other and protected each other, and they interacted in a very respectful way. The writer of the screenplay wrote very badly. I think he didn't ask any expert for advice, nor did he contact any elderly people who lived in Damascus in the thirties, because many of the elderly thought "this is awful, this is not true, we didn't have this kind of behavior in the Old City in the thirties."

Some Damascenes admitted that collaboration did take place, but not to the extent or in the way the series suggested:

> The relationship between the French and the people of the country, and relationships among merchants weren't like that. . . . It did happen that people benefited from circumstances, but not in this atmosphere, not in this way. The big families, the leading merchants worked with the French. It's true; they did work with the French, but within a nationalist atmosphere (*dimn jaww watani*). They didn't work with the French against the people of their country, but because they were the source of power in everyday affairs. They worked with the French for the community, for the sake of the quarter, as mediators for the people of the quarter, not for personal gain.

Non-Damasceneness re-emerged as a problem; but this time accusations of inexperience of the city were aimed not at director ʿAlaʾ al-Din Kawkash, who was born and raised in an Old Damascene quarter, or at screenwriter Sharbaji, a fellow Damascene, but at lead actor Asʿad Fidda, an ʿAlawi from the coastal region. According to a young translator, "Abu Kamil [Fidda] is not a Damascene; you can't give this role to someone who's not Damascene. He wasn't very good with the accent, he wasn't good with the way of speaking."

Despite their frequent protests about the base commercialism of television, and objections to my use of television material as an object of study, Syrian intellectuals and politicians do watch and take seriously the representations of the past shown in drama series, especially those shown during Ramadan, which they know are widely followed. The foremost haunt of the local intelligentsia, the Cham Palace Hotel's Café Bresil, wheels out a television set for the month, for their painter and writer patrons who claim otherwise never to watch television. The Damascene intellectuals came out in full force to condemn *Abu Kamil II* on television and in print. Anthropologists tend to look to so-called subversive cultural forms, such as pamphlets and cassette tapes, for expressions of cultural resistance; yet here is a case where sensitive issues such as formerly repressed local identities were being discussed and debated in state-controlled media. Najat Qassab Hasan and Colette Khuri appeared on the program *Television Magazine* to denounce *Abu Kamil II* as an attempt to belittle the Damascenes (20 March 1994). They warned the producers against any idea of a third part, which Qassab Hasan claimed would be scandalous. The Syrian television establishment was humbled. A letter from the editor published in the arts magazine *Funun* admitted:

Never before, in the entire history of Syrian Arab Television, has there been anything like the consensus on the rejection of a series—a condemnation of what was said in it, and a disapproval of what transpired in it—as occurred with part two of the series *Abu Kamil*, with agreement among critics, writers, viewers, and media figures. Declarations of rejection and condemnation were not restricted to people's living rooms during the month of Ramadan, but were also found on the pages of all the newspapers, and on radio and television programs. (J. al-Kisan 1994: 2)

In contrast, a series broadcast in the second Ramadan time slot, entitled *The End of a Brave Man* (*Nihayat Rajul Shujaʿ*), showed the people of Banias, a coastal town, struggling together against French forces. The religious affiliation of characters is never mentioned, but opening scenes take place in a village thought to be ʿAlawi. Beautifully filmed, with an infectious musical score, *The End of a Brave Man* was the work of a private production company, Sharikat al-Sham al-Duwaliyya (Damascus International), owned by the son of vice president ʿAbd al-Halim Khaddam, a Sunni Muslim from Banias. Its link to the regime was obvious. Based on a novel by acclaimed Syrian Christian author Hanna Mina, *The End of a Brave Man* won high praise in many circles for its tight plot and high production value, but also for its depiction of a valiant and noble past in which everyone was unified against French occupation. An ʿAlawi university professor argued that this depiction inverts historical fact, as the ʿAlawis are "well known for having collaborated with all foreign powers, from the Crusaders onwards."

Compounding the insult to the Damascenes was the fact that another series set in Old Damascus had vied for, and lost, the Ramadan prime time slot to *Abu Kamil II*. This was the dramatization of *Damascus, O Smile of Sadness* (*Dimashq Ya Basmat al-Huzn*), a novel by highly regarded Damascene author Ulfat al-Idlibi.[16] Like much of the literature written by Syrian women, this work involves a self-sacrificing female central character whose ambitions are squelched by a domineering patriarch. The book was hailed for rendering the rhythms of local idiom into classical Arabic, and for its loving descriptions of social life in the Old Damascus of the 1940s. The series, whose title was shortened to *Smile of Sadness* (*Basmat al-Huzn*), was aired shortly before Ramadan in early 1994, and therefore not widely viewed. Those Damascenes who saw it were disappointed with its treatment of a novel they hold dear, as "the novel was much better." Again, a non-Damascene director was castigated for daring to depict Damascus on the small screen. According to a Damascene television director:

It was very bad. I know the director, Lutfi Lutfi. He has no taste, he's not from Damascus, and he knows nothing about Damascus. It was a wonderful book, but it should never have been made into a series, because all the events surround a young woman's suicide. The screenwriter is a dirty, dirty man who now lives in Cairo.

Smile of Sadness was rebroadcast in 1996, this time during Ramadan, but on successive Friday afternoons rather than in one of the post-*iftar* periods. Hence it was overshadowed by two new Syrian productions shown in the more desirable time slots. The first, *Brothers of the Earth* (*Ukhwat al-Turab*), was the latest work of Najdat Isma'il Anzur, the American-trained director of *The End of a Brave Man*. This series, also riddled with historical inaccuracies, depicted the battles of the last days of Ottoman rule. It was the most expensive Syrian television drama ever produced. One Damascene director claimed that the series' skewed version of events is typical of Syrian treatment of history, and has a political aim: "they play with the facts, manipulate them, deform them. What is happening now is that Syria has no memory, and being without memory is without wisdom. And only cult regimes stress a total forgetfulness."

The other series was director Haytham Haqqi's *(The) Silk Bazaar* (*Khan al-Harir*). Sharikat Halab al-Duwaliyya, a production company established by wealthy Aleppines in answer to Sharikat al-Sham al-Duwaliyya, produced the series, the first in Aleppine dialect. Set in Aleppo during the 1950s, at the height of Arab nationalist sentiment, and filmed in the city's spectacular covered suq, this series depicts the merchant class debating the merits of unification with Egypt, and the loss of an elected parliament and domination by Damascus it would entail. Some characters argue for unification with Baghdad instead, a move which would have preserved Aleppo's position as the major Syrian commercial center. Here again we find a subject once considered divisive broached on prime-time television. Given the Syrian Ba'th Party's long-standing feud with its Iraqi sister, it is surprising that Syrian television censors would permit depiction of a period of more congenial relations. Yet politically sensitive historical subjects are now broached across the arts, but particularly in television dramas.[17]

A War of Images

Television dramas like those shown during Syrian Arab Television's Ramadan prime time provide a rich example of the local production and consumption of mass media. Ba'th Party censors may have hoped *Damascene Days*'s glowing portrait of an honorable and heroic past would incite feelings of national pride in all Syrian citizens. The structure of the Syrian state encourages such overinterpretation among Syrians and non-Syrians alike.[18] More likely, the series was simply allowed to "slip through the door." It intensified centrifugal tendencies instead of promoting national unity.

The battle continues over which group, whose history, dominates the small screen, arguably the most accessible and influential of media. Syrian television dramas and the debates they provoke are not mere celebrations of difference. At issue in these debates over televisual representations of past is the very question of who rules, or who ought to rule, in the present.

These expressions of dominance and resistance are central to the experience of Ramadan in Damascus. Contested understandings of the holy month, past and present, provide the cultural tools for boundary construction and maintenance. Ramadan is a period of heightened public identity assertion among Damascenes. It is also a time when criticisms of Damasceneness by those it excludes reach an annual peak. Yet this is a continual struggle in which Damascenes and their critics vie over both the physical space of the Old City and the symbolic space of its representation. As we will see in chapter 5, such contestation emerges as activists publicize the plight of endangered Old City architecture. Old Damascus advocates see their work as documentation, preservation, and celebration of local heritage. Their detractors see it as snobbery and exclusivism.

5

Conservation, Preservation, and Celebration

> A city is life in all its various permutations. It is places, people, trees, the smell of rain, the earth and time itself in a state of flux. A city is people's way of perceiving things: how they talk, how they dealt with events, how they faced and they transcended them. A city is the dreams and disappointments that filled people's minds and hearts, those dreams which came true and those which were frustrated, leaving in their wake wounds and scares. A city is the way in which it welcomed those it loved, and confronted those who were its enemies. A city is the tears with which it bade farewell to those who left it unwillingly for a time, or for ever, and it is the smiles with which those who return are greeted. A city is all of these things and more besides, both small and large, so how can it be recaptured?
> **—Abd al-Rahman Munif, *Story of a City***

Damascenes celebrate and commemorate Old Damascus through a variety of expressive cultural forms, commodified and otherwise. As I have demonstrated, links to an old urban elite culture form symbolic capital for those who can claim it. The prestige of connection to the Old City sometimes attracts non-Damascenes with aristocratic pretensions, as members of the "new class" often try to enhance their social position by association with the old aristocracy. Yet those most active in the movement to preserve and celebrate Old Damascus are not always among the wealthiest of Damascenes. It may be that wealthy Old Damascenes who have married their fortunes to new money do not need to promote their Old Damascus status in public forums. Whatever the reason, the very wealthy tend not to be at the forefront of a movement which contrasts the refined and cultivated taste of an old urban elite culture against the supposed crassness and vulgarity of new—and often big—money. Those at the margins of urban tradition dismiss this Old Damasceneness as snobbery and prejudice. The Old City itself, and representations of it, are pivotal points of Syrian political and social contestation. Old Damascus cultural forms criticize, often implicitly, sometimes explicitly, the growing veneration of wealth above all else. Yet these forms are themselves commodities in a growing public culture of leisure and lifestyle. Paradoxically, it is through consumption itself that critics of the new elites contest what they see as a new value system based largely on money.

This chapter takes a closer look at nostalgic cultural forms and their producers, key activists involved in the fight to save Old Damascus. Books, visual arts, and documentary films celebrating the Old City and promoting its preservation serve as expressions of resistance to the new social order, and as reassertions of social dominance. Created within the constraints of Ba'thist censorship, and sometimes with governmental support, these products often reflect the paradoxical relationship between old elites and new circumstances. Old City activists praise Old Damascus and associate it with cultural superiority; they also place it firmly within the cosmopolitanism of Syria's past and present.

Books and the Experience of a Lost Past

Books form an important component of a growing general interest in identity and heritage. Syrian bibliographer Amal Husayni describes a shift that has taken place in the Syrian Arabic book market:

> Books published in the forties were different from those published now in the nineties; those of the forties were intended to introduce a new culture to the ordinary citizen, rather than to defend their own heritage. Authors were trying to introduce new thinking, and to adapt themselves to new standards and criteria. But now, as I'm preparing a guide for the book fair,[1] I notice a huge proportion of books devoted to heritage and religion.[2]

Damascenes, mostly from well-known families, have been at the forefront of this trend, producing a series of books about the city. Approximately thirty of these are available—and often prominently displayed—in Damascus bookstores, a large number for the city's small book market. An early effort, Siham Tergeman's *Ya Mal al-Sham* (*O Wealth of Damascus*), was published in 1969. Others date from the mid-1980s onward. These books range from personal memoirs of social life in Old Damascus to the more folkloric and architectural. The differences among them are a matter of degree, as even the most personal are folkloric and documentary, and the most architectural include personal and nostalgic touches. Most of the more imagistic and sensory reminiscences are written by women, who are often the ones who reconstruct the past by recreating place through sense imagery (Slyomovics 1998: xx).

Unlike the traditional biographical and autobiographical form, the *tarjama*, these books do not merely recount the details and events of an individual's—usually a religious scholar's—life (Eickelman 1991). Rather, they construct fragmentary, imagistic, and highly emotive accounts of the past in a wider context. Part autobiography, part social history, these books are personal reminiscences which also evoke shared experience. A list of titles illustrates their nostalgic cultural pride: *Damascus in the Days of Old: Memories and Pictures of Old Damascus, Damascus of Secrets, Damascene Tales, Ramadan in the Damascus of Olden Days, Portraits of Damascene Society, The Story of the Grand Damascene House, Damascene Geniuses, In the Vastness of Damascus, Damascene Talk, Fire and Light in Maktab ʿAnbar,*[3] and *Generation of Courage.*[4]

In some ways, these authors are at the forefront of a movement marginal to Arab intellectual circles: many employ local vernacular language in documenting proverbs and folk songs.[5] Such appreciation for oral literature and popular culture is rare among Arab writers. Many express disdain for the colloquial, or "street" language, as they sometimes refer to it, and urge foreigners to study the updated classical language, or Modern Standard Arabic—al-Fusha—rather than the dialect which they themselves use in most conversation. This is particularly true of Syria, where there has been no "call for colloquial" as in turn-of-the-century Egypt (Armbrust 1996: 44–45). Such devaluing of the vernacular stems in part from lingering notions of Arab unity, which hold the presence of different dialects to be an obstacle to the creation of a united Arab state. It also reflects Islamic notions of Arabic as a sacred language which should only be rendered as it is in the Qurʾan. Beyond this, it reflects an intellectual tradition that continues to privilege the classical, and classical poetry in particular. In this context, folklorists are iconoclastic. In Syria, their work is often met with disdain from fellow Arab writers, who consider them unable to handle the intricacies of the formal language.

Most memoir authors are prominent professionals—doctors, lawyers, and journalists—who know each other well and form a literary circle. For instance, the introduction to the third edition of Najat Qassab Hasan's *Damascene Talk* (*Hadith Dimashqi*) includes acknowledgments of and letters of praise from many of the other memoir authors. Old Damascus reminiscences contain vivid, seemingly timeless descriptions of the Damascene-style house, methods of preparing and eating traditional foods, and customs and traditions related to holidays and rites of passage. All lament the passing of what is seen as a wholesome, integrated way of life.

Best known and perhaps best loved is Siham Tergeman's *Ya Mal al-Sham*. Here Tergeman lovingly recounts the sounds, smells, and tastes of her youth spent in various quarters of Old Damascus. Weddings, funerals, trips to the public bath, songs, tales, and proverbs are described in a glow of nostalgic yearning:

> When I go back to the old quarters where our ancient house sleeps or to the suqs with their smell of old age, I find that my attachment to things that are old is stronger than to modern ones. I discover that the only pure reality in my soul is the reality of childhood, as if childhood is a being, aware of what goes on around it, clinging to what is most genuine in order to keep it from changing. This reverence for the past reassures me that my knowing, attentive, pure childhood will reject anything false that tomorrow has to offer. (1994: 9)

What distinguishes these recent publications from earlier literary expressions of pride in and love for Damascus, notably Ibn Kinan's eighteenth-century *Damascus Diary* (*Yawmiyyat Shamiyya*) and Muhammad Kurd 'Ali's *Damascus: City of Enchantment and People* (*Dimashq: Madinat al-Sihr wal-Sha'b*), is precisely this sense of loss. A particularly poignant example is Nadia Khost's *Exile from Paradise* (*al-Hijra min al-Jinna*), a eulogy for an Old City quarter torn in half by the construction of Revolution Street:

> Much of what I feel today is sorrow because my daughter does not know what it is like to wake up in an Arab house, opening her eyes to its decorations. She does not know the joy of looking out from the ornaments of the parapet and jasmine down to the courtyard, and she does not know the alternations of light on the kabbad tree. Generations of lovers of civilization will not know what fell under the rubble in Damascus. (1989: 10)

Khost continues her memorializing of Old Damascus in *Damascus: Memory of People and Stone* (*Dimashq: Dhakirat al-Insan wal-Hajar*). Here she identifies the enemy as the West—primarily the French Mandate authorities—who designed the modernization of Damascus (1993: 26). She sounds a warning note for the future of the Old City: "Pardon me if there is a note of anger or sadness in what I write, for it is not fear of the past, but anxiety about the future" (ibid.: 17).

In his *Damascus of Secrets* (*Dimashq al-Asrar*), Damascene writer and former People's Assembly member Nasr al-Din al-Bahra also bemoans this loss of what he perceives as a prior and more authentic culture, as the concrete high-rises of the New City grow to engulf the two-story constructions of the Old: "Your Damascus is becoming two. The first, the authentic, is shrinking and declining. The second, having come into being like a small child, has come to grow like cancer, a blind growth, base and without identity" (1992: 14).

Yet no references to expulsion of foreigners or calls for separatism are to be found in these books. What is sought is something quite different: a recognition, by other Syrians and the world beyond, of the value, even the superiority, of Damascene culture. Parallels to the Old Damascus movement appear in the literature on heritage industries. The Damascenes have become a minority in "their" own country, and as David Lowenthal notes, minorities often "deploy heritage not to opt out of nation-states but to achieve gains within them" (1996: 81). Using a trope that James Fernandez refers to as "metonymic misrepresentation," memoir authors make Damascus and Damasceneness represent Syrian national culture (1986: 85–87). Once this was easier, as the more emotive term for Damascus, Sham, stood for both the city and for the Ottoman province of Syria, in the way that Misr signified both Cairo and all of Egypt. The construction of national identity involves the appropriation of detached cultural objects, which are then made to stand for national culture (Handler 1985: 207–208). In this case, Damascus itself and memories of it have become objects of Syrian nationhood. Siham Tergeman writes, "Damascus is the Syrian people and my people" (1994: 6). Likewise, Nadia Khost argues that the city's unique architectural style is "not just the attraction of visitors, not just the earth which brings together generations, or the house which wants next to it the rest; . . . rather, it is national memory" (1989: 11).

Because the Old City represents generations of civilization, Khost argues, its preservation is "a matter of major cultural and national significance" (1993: 5). Addressing a second-person Syrian

reader, she links her concern for Old Damascus to the loss of other
authenticities:

> The modernity around you leads you to believe the past is a disgrace, and
> that the historical Old City is an insult to you, until you distinguish be-
> tween the white and black thread in life, and the dryness and cement
> spreads around you.[6] You see others in the world, having left their par-
> adises for illusion and cold; they too gather fragments of memory and
> broken pieces of their abandoned gardens of the past. Before you, they un-
> derstood the value of what was demolished, of what they left behind.
> (1989: 26)

Memoir authors emphasize the value of personal experience in recounting Old Damascus; Damascenes can best represent Damasceneness. In his *Hadith Dimashqi*, which vies with *Ya Mal al-Sham* for
the most widely read Old City reminiscence, Najat Qassab Hasan argues his suitability as a source of Damascene social history:

> I am a witness of more than half a century, from the end of the Twenties to
> the year in which I wrote these memoirs, 1983. Therefore what I write
> about myself and my family are eyewitness accounts, and our descriptions
> of worthy authentic Damascene examples are accurate and true. If I speak
> about myself here and there, this is not because I am incapable of impar-
> tiality, but because I can describe myself as an example of my generation of
> Damascenes, raised in a popular environment. (1988: 13)

Memoirs, as representations of national memory, are among the cultural forms most readily accessible to the world beyond Syria. They
fit neatly into the growing global interest in other worlds, past
worlds, to which Khost alludes. Books recounting life in the Old City
have begun to attract translators. In 1994 the University of Texas
Press published an English translation of Tergeman's *Ya Mal al-Sham*,
under the title *Daughter of Damascus*. Authors like Tergeman are particularly attractive to a burgeoning global market for Third World
and women's literature.

In her nineteen-page introduction to her translation of *Ya Mal al-
Sham*, anthropologist Andrea Rugh promotes the book as exotic social history and folklore:

> The more the style and content appear alien, the more confidence we can
> place in its authenticity. This book was not dressed up for an American au-
> dience, nor was it written by someone who is familiar enough with Amer-
> ican culture to know what would "sound good." Remember, this is a book
> written for a younger generation of Syrians so they will not lose the feeling
> of what is "authentic" in their own culture. (1994: xxviii)

Rugh accepts the elision of the Damascene with the Syrian, and mentions only the adulatory reactions of other Damascene intellectuals to Tergeman's work. Yet Tergeman is a controversial figure; some Syrians are hostile to what they perceive as the elitism and exclusivity of the experience she recounts. Taken out of context, *Ya Mal al-Sham* loses its political force. Rugh removes *Daughter of Damascus* from the complex cultural conflicts within which it was conceived, and which render it richly illustrative of its milieu.

Also curious is Rugh's choice of material from the original. A chapter on Tergeman's efforts to preserve the Old City—which might have brought her cause international attention—was omitted, while a list of old family names is retained, although the reader is given no indication of the very different resonance these names have for various categories of Syrians (1994: 6).[7] With the authority of a Western anthropologist, Rugh legitimizes one group's cultural hegemony where one might instead situate *Ya Mal al-Sham* within the dynamic social and political context of contemporary Syria.

Another subset of books about Damascene culture is more straightforwardly folkloric. Among these, the works of Munir Kayyal deserve mention. In his 1984 *O Damascus: On Damascene Popular Cultural Heritage* (*Ya Sham: fil-Turath al-Sha‘bi al-Dimashqi*), Kayyal takes the reader through the life stages of a Damascene, with chapters on "Pregnancy and Birth," "Songs of the Cradle and Childhood," "Circumcision," "Games," "Schools," "Learning a Trade," "Engagements and Weddings," and ending with chapters on food and song. Yet no absolute distinction can be made between these and the more autobiographical works, and all have as their inspiration a deep nostalgia for the city:

> The book *Ya Sham* which I place in the readers' hands is nostalgia for Damascus. . . . Damascus is my great love, which took root in me from the time my eyes first saw light. I grew up in its popular quarters, began to read and write at the hand of a sheikh of one of its schools, and learned with a master of one of its trades that life is more than an olive and a piece of bread. . . . I took shade in its meadows and orchards, and drank from its schools, universities, and libraries. (Kayyal 1984: 17, ellipses in original)

In *Damascene Tales* (*Hikayat Dimashqiyya*) Kayyal, like Tergeman and Qassab Hasan, draws on familial sources:

> I took from my grandmother and her co-wives, from what was around me, from the mouths of the young and old, and from what circumstance brought me . . . material from their different environments, quarters, and social groups. The result was a large number of folktales. (1987: 16)

Kayyal's most recent work documents customs and traditions associated with the fasting month of Ramadan, a time at which Damasceneness—and reactions against it—are heightened (see chapter 4). Many Damascenes feel their local identity most keenly at this time of year. *Ramadan in the Damascus of Olden Days* (*Ramadan fil-Sham Ayyam Zaman*) continues the work Kayyal began with *Ramadan and Its Damascene Customs* (*Ramadan wa Taqaliduhu al-Dimashqiyya*).

Architecture can become a mnemonic symbol for an entire lost world (Slyomovics 1998: 143–144). The Damascene-style house, a central motif in Old City reminiscences, is often evoked to index a bygone way of life. Two books on the Old City are devoted entirely to houses: Dr. Kadhim al-Daghastani's *Story of the Great Damascene House* (*Hikayat al-Bayt al-Dimashqi al-Kabir*), and in English, Anghélos Keusseoglou's *The Disappearing Damascus* (*Damascus in the Therties* [*sic*]): *Scenes and "Cries" of the Street*, published with the support of the Ministry of Tourism. The cover blurb of the latter describes the author as belonging to an "old family of Byzantine [Turkish] culture."

The works of Damascene dentist Qutayba Shihabi also deserve mention: *Damascus: Pictures and History* (*Dimashq: Tarikh wa Suwar*), *Damascene Suqs and Their Historical Monuments* (*Aswaq Dimashq wa Mushayyadatiha al-Tarikhiyya*), *Damascene Minarets: History and Style* (*Maadhin Dimashq: Tarikh wa Taraz*), and with Ahmad Ibish, *Historical Monuments of Damascus* (*Ma'alim Dimashq al-Tarikhiyya*). Shihabi's well-researched and documented works are constructed as extended photo essays:

> I have found that the "picture" is a substantiation of reality free from influences of obligation, inclination, and fear, factors that silenced me in the past. In history writing, the obligations are many to recount realities from a truthful point of view. To this I say: history has been written in words; I shall write it in pictures. (1990: 5)

Some works deal with elite culture explicitly. 'Abd al-Ghani al-'Utari's *Damascene Geniuses* (*'Abqariyyat Shamiyya*) resembles a classical Arabic biographical dictionary, but also pays homage to prominent Damasceneness:

> From ancient times, Damascus has brought forth geniuses, distinguished persons and eminent figures in science, literature, poetry, art, politics, journalism, and all other fields. Books of Arab heritage teem with mention of these personages. (1986: 5)

Two books focus on Old Damascus's most elite school, Maktab ʿAnbar. In *Maktab ʿAnbar: Pictures and Memories of Our Cultural, Political, and Social Life* (*Maktab ʿAnbar: Suwar wa-Dhikrayat min Hayatina al-Thaqafiyya wal-Siyasiyya wal-Ijtimaʿiyya*), Zafir al-Qasimi describes the school's atmosphere as "pure Damascene (*jawwuhu kana dimash-qiyyan khalisan*), with all of what is Damascus in the way of features and characteristics" (1964: 38). Mutiʿ al-Murabit's *Fire and Light in Maktab ʿAnbar* (*al-Nur wal-Nar fi Maktab ʿAnbar*), presents an account of life in the school during the late Mandate and early post-independence periods. Many urban notable nationalists of the late-nineteenth and early-twentieth centuries were trained here.

Other books emerge from the experience of exile. Old Damascus nostalgia reaches beyond the borders of Syria, as prominent Damascenes living in the capitals of Europe add to the literary reminiscence of their former city. Novelist Rafik Schami's romance *Damascene Nights* and children's story *A Handful of Stars* were composed in Germany. Damascene-turned-Saudi financier Wafic Saïd recently sponsored a glossy pictorial history, written by former *Sunday Times* journalist and diplomat's wife Brigid Keenan. In the preface to this expensively and beautifully produced book, Saïd remembers his family home: "This house where I spent my childhood, which combined the inside and the outside, the hidden and the revealed, the warm and cozy with the cool and airy, inspired in me a lifelong passion for architecture. Nothing has ever seemed to me so beautiful again" (2000: 6).

First produced in English and later translated into Arabic, *Damascus: Hidden Treasures of the Old City* sells in the bookshops of the five-star hotels that are so central a part of the social life of local elites and Western expatriates in Damascus. It is also available through specialist art and antiquities booksellers in Europe and the United States. Shortly after its publication, author Keenan promoted her book with a series of slide lectures delivered to London's numerous Arab-British friendship societies. With the help of influential and sympathetic Westerners like Keenan, Damascenes now sidestep Syrian and Arab affiliations and present their case to a global audience of elite antiquity aficionados. Such cosmopolitan relationships reinforce a sense of cultural superiority. They also obscure the contested character of Damasceneness from those outside Syria, for whom the movement appears to be simply an expression of Syrian culture and heritage.

Whose Damascus?

Nostalgic books form part of a preservation movement under-pinned by serious activism. Dr. Nazih Kawakibi, architectural historian at Damascus University, dates the beginning of the interest in preserving Old Damascus to the 1960s, and particularly to 1968, with the implementation of the second master plan of Damascus, designed by French architect Michel Ecochard. They began in 1958 and worked until 1962, when the plan was approved by the governorate. The design emphasized access to modern modes of transport, calling for the widening of streets and the demolition of much old construction. Damascenes began to protest, but strongly organized opposition did not find a voice until 1984, when the first colloquium on the Old City was convened. By this time, large sections of Suq Saruja had already been torn down. The Syndicate of Engineers, the governorate, the Damascus University Faculty of Architecture, and the Society of Friends of Damascus gathered together for three days of consultation and produced a recommendation. A second colloquium resulted in the establishment of a government agency to oversee the preservation of the Old City and a law passed to protect old buildings within the Old City walls. Yet as activists are quick to point out, much of the most distinctive, beautiful, and historically significant architecture falls *outside* the walls. Campaigners continue to work to extend the law to include quarters such as al-Qanawat and what remains of Suq Saruja.

The fight to save Old Damascus reached a fever pitch in the late 1980s, with the government's "restoration" of its most important monument, the Umayyad Mosque. A plan was approved to "open" the area immediately surrounding the mosque, leveling approximately 300 shops. A car park now graces the main entrance to the mosque, and a wide dirt path circles its walls. Of the many changes to have occurred in Damascus between my study year in 1987 and my return in 1992, the area in front of the mosque was among the most striking. Dr. Afif Bahnasi, Department of Antiquities director, emphasized the archaeological discoveries resulting from the renovation, which shed light on centuries of history (Miller 1984). Yet most Old City activists oppose the changes. "The life of the city is its artisans and merchants," argued Siham Tergeman; "mosques have always been surrounded by shops and intricately connected to an Arab city's commercial life. Its walls have never been 'displayed' in Western-museum style" (ibid.).

At stake in such criticisms of the regime's changes to the Old City is which past, whose Damascus, matters more. Some Damascenes privately expressed what might be called a Foucauldian view of the renovations, arguing that what was sought was visibility, and beyond this accessibility, for now the president's motorcade, or more sinisterly, troop convoys, are able to reach the very heart of the Old City. There is nothing unique or far-fetched about such interpretations. Similar motives are often attributed to the modernization of medieval European cities. On the "Haussmannization" of nineteenth-century Paris, Walter Benjamin writes:

> The true purpose of Haussmann's work was to secure the city against civil war. He wanted to make the erection of barricades in Paris impossible for all time. . . . Haussmann seeks to prevent barricades in two ways. The breadth of the street is intended to make their erection impossible, and new thoroughfares are to open the shortest route between the barracks and the working-class districts. Contemporaries christened the enterprise "strategic embellishment." (1978: 160)

The Old City of Damascus, with its narrow, winding streets, unnumbered, inward-turned houses, and lockable gates enclosing quarters, contained a permanently erected series of barricades against military intrusion. As Nadia Khost argues, Old Damascene architecture of the Ayyubid period was "part of the resistance against crusader attack, and an embodiment of a civilization superior to that of the invaders" (1993: 26). The current regime has "opened" much of the Old City, destroying a safe haven for potential subversives.[8] However, the construction of a new city, with wide streets and numbered buildings, was begun decades before the current government's rise to power. It has continued modern construction, engulfing the Old City and leaving it a politically neutered museum piece, a playground for new middle-class money-spenders.

Activists or Chauvinists?

Over the past two decades a number of activists, following in the footsteps of local historian Khalid Moaz, have been working tirelessly to save what remains of Old Damascus. Expressive culture becomes a weapon against further destruction. "Writers play an important role in the Old Damascus cause" said one, "writers and artists, who exhibit work inspired by the Old City." According to another: "It's the writers and thinkers who are the ones protecting the Old City, not the government. We are against the leadership, against the governorate. The government is now afraid of the pens of writers."

Campaigners blame both the regime and the market for the threat to the Old City. While a two-story Arab-style residence spread over a plot of land houses a single family, a high-rise built on the same plot of land houses many, yielding several times the rent or sale value.

> There are people in the government who benefit, who will give [pieces of real estate] to businessmen, and make 10 million. It's terrible. . . . They're tearing down heritage and history to put up twelve-story buildings. Why? Ignorance, and money. We [the activists] have no money. But we defend the Old City with our humanity, to the extent we're able. But money is more powerful; money ruins.

Those at the forefront of the campaign to save the Old City met with me to share their views and talk about their work. Najat Qassab Hasan, prominent lawyer, media figure, and Old City folklorist, granted my first formal interview. We sat in his downtown office, above the Lanterna (al-Qandil), a restaurant partly owned by Qassab Hasan and a favorite haunt of Damascene artists and intellectuals.

The small room was decorated with many photographs, paintings, and drawings of Qassab Hasan. I began with a classic anthropological "naïve question": why was he interested in Old Damascus? He replied: "I want to describe Damascus before its features change. You are now a pretty girl, so it is necessary to photograph you before you become an old woman." Qassab Hasan sees Old City nostalgia as his generation's response to changing circumstances. His book *Damascene Talk* (*Hadith Dimashqi*) is intended to

> tie people to their roots, especially the old; it helps them to hold on, because the old feel that life casts them aside. Everything is new. The elderly person becomes overwhelmed with it all. Our children live a life impossible for us to imagine.

Qassab Hasan dismisses as mere novelty much of the current interest among the young in Old Damascus revivalism.

> There is also the fact that when the Western style becomes common and no longer amusing, people return to the old, because it then becomes the exception. It is true that modern weddings, for example, have begun to include Old Damascene-style elements, but only a few select ones. It used to be a Damascene way of life, but now it is all form. For instance, the way they used to sanction a wedding—which I described in my book. Would a bride agree to this now? Would she allow a midwife to attest to her virginity? Is this possible now? An English judge, a modern man, adjudicates wearing a powdered wig. This is what we're doing, putting the wig of the past on the head of the present.

He played down Damascene exclusivity, stressing that love for Damascus was not limited to Damascenes:

> There are people who feel passionately about Old Damascus and speak out for it who are not Damascenes. . . . The organization Friends of Damascus includes not only Damascenes but those living in Damascus. As the name indicates, it includes those who love Damascus, not just Damascenes. As for Damascene customs, we can't say they're exclusively Damascene. For example, our food is a mixture of Syrian, Turkish, and Aleppine cookery.

Such denial of Damascene exclusivism is rare among Old City aficionados, as is Qassab Hasan's somber representation of the past. Several women novelists, all of whom are considered to be Damascenes who love their city and campaign for its preservation, also contest the many rose-tinted constructs of the local past. Colette Khuri's *One Night* (*Layla Wahida*, 1961), Nadia al-Ghazzi's *A Very Private Matter* (*Qadiya Khassa Jiddan*, 1991), and Ulfat al-Idlibi's *Damascus: O Smile of Sadness* (*Dimashq: Ya Basmat al-Huzn*, 1980) all depict a life of hardship for young women in Old Damascus. The pressures, restrictions, and unabashed cruelty endured at the hands of fathers, brothers, husbands, sons, and mothers-in-law are described in graphic, if not melodramatic style. Yet such negative aspects of the past are more usually forgotten in Damascenes' nostalgic remembering. Details of the past may sit uncomfortably in the present, but in the idealized Old City of most Old Damascus aficionados, practices unattractive to modern Syrian sensibilities are sifted from an idealized essence. An Old Damascus of beautiful, fragrant courtyards and lavish, leisurely meals, of songs and proverbs, is the image which most frequently serves as the basis of Damascene identity.

A chief exponent of this aestheticized Old Damascus is Siham Tergeman, author of *O Wealth of Damascus* (*Ya Mal al-Sham*). She invited me to interview her in her spacious West Mezzeh apartment. I nearly arrived late for our appointment, having difficulty distinguishing her building among the many nearly identical concrete high-rises along the Mezzeh Autostrade. This gray monotony ended at Tergeman's door. Coming out of the elevator was like entering another world: her doorway is decorated with a wrought-iron floral gate, painted in white and with bronze flowers. Reminders of Old Damascus are scattered throughout Tergeman's flat: antiques and pieces of inlaid furniture, a mirror she hand painted with jasmine flowers. She served me rose-water-scented tamarind juice and homemade date pastry (*ma'mul*), noting that Damascenes are renowned

for their generosity. Speaking passionately about the Old City, Tergeman used its more emotive and evocative name, al-Sham.

> It's a great city. How can you be surprised that we defend it, and we long
> for it? It's my city. If someone told you, don't love your mother, would you
> stop loving her? She's your mother. Damascus is my mother. She's my
> mother, my flesh and blood.

Tergeman is at her most passionate in defense of the Arab-style
house, which, she argues,

> was grounded, clinging to the earth of Damascus. A building of many sto-
> ries lifts me up, puts me into the air, into emptiness. But our house below
> is what's authentic. Arabic architecture tied you to the earth, as a daughter
> of the earth.

For New Damascus, Tergeman had little but disdain. She echoes the
feeling of dislocation, even exile, common in Damascene discussions
of their modernized city:

> It appears that they want to build a modern Syria. But is this it, is this the
> new Syria, this cement? . . . Damascus was beautiful, but it's become the
> ugliest city in the world. Look, do you see a single tree? God save us, it's a
> block of cement; it's not Damascus. This whole area used to be filled with
> orchards. Now they are gone. . . . Is *this* the New Damascus, this block of
> cement?! . . . I'm not comfortable with this modern civilization. I've lost a
> lot. I've lost my identity. I walk down the street, and I don't recognize this
> as my city. I want my city to stay my city. . . . Why am I nostalgic? Because
> modernity has not brought me anything more beautiful.

Yet Tergeman does not reject development completely, and argues
that there are ways of combining past and present:

> They shouldn't continue to plan multi-story buildings. They should follow
> the design of Old Damascus, of the houses, streets, neighborhoods, and
> mosques, take patterns from Arab architecture, and build new buildings.
> Then it would become a city of harmony, harmony between the old and
> the new. . . . They built these cement buildings very quickly, without
> beauty, without taste, and without an Arab architectural identity.

Tergeman's folkloric and nostalgic work did not stop with *O Wealth
of Damascus;* she has continued to memorialize Damascus in two subsequent publications: *Ah . . . Ya Ana* and *Jabal al-Shaykh fi Bayti,* her
impassioned response as a Damascene to the 1973 war with Israel, in

which her husband, an 'Alawi pilot, was killed. She continues to combine writing with political action, and spoke proudly of her role in the campaign to save the quarter of Hamrawi:

> They wanted to tear down the quarter of Hamrawi, where [Caliph] Mu'awiya ibn Abi Sufyan lived![9] There are about four thousand houses in Hamrawi, the most beautiful houses in Damascus. I went to General Mustafa Tlas, taking with me Hamrawi merchants and homeowners, all of them. I was an employee of the Ministry of Defense at the time, and I said to him, "General, Sir, these houses are beautiful, they are not doing any harm, why tear them down?" Mustafa Tlas went to the president, and told him that these houses weren't dangerous, so why destroy them, they're beautiful houses. So the destruction stopped. I was the one who stopped it. Then three hundred people came from Hamrawi and Suq al-Bzuriyyeh—next to Hamrawi, near the Azm Palace—to the Political Section [of the Ministry of Defense] where I was working—these three hundred people came to the door and demonstrated, saying "We want to kiss the hand of this authentic daughter of Damascus, who enabled us to stay in our houses."

I first encountered Nadia Khost, author of *Exile from Paradise* (*al-Hijra min al-Jinna*) and *Damascus: Memory of People and Stone* (*Dimashq: Dhakirat al-Insan wal-Hajar*), at the opening of her Mezzeh art gallery, Arabesque. It was the very beginning of my fieldwork, and I did not yet know who she was. But the gallery itself was striking; instead of the usual gilded mirrors and chandeliers were geometric carpets and other local handicrafts. Waiters circulated with large flat baskets filled with dried apricots, dates, and nuts, and trays of apricot and tamarind juice. Such a self-consciously "traditional" atmosphere is uncommon in a Syrian art gallery, where Francophilia usually predominates. Much later, I visited Dr. Khost in her Villat Gharbiyyeh garden flat. A doctor of Arabic literature, Khost's approach to Old Damascus is scholarly, her language elevated. She had recently sparked controversy in intellectual circles by lobbying for the expulsion of the poet Adonis—Syria's most prominent contemporary cultural figure—from the Syrian Writers Union for having engaged in "normalization" with Israel.[10] She had also just published a lengthy first novel, *Love in the Lands of Damascus* (*Hubb fi Bilad al-Sham*).

We sat in a study filled with books and inlaid furniture, facing each other across a small table laden with Turkish coffee and raisins. Khost is adamant in blaming the real estate merchants (*al-'aqariyyin*) for the threat to Old Damascus. She tells the following story of one such businessman's self-justification:

A private Arabic television station was making a film about Arab cities. I went with the filmmakers to film some examples of historic buildings in Suq Saruja—in what's left of it—buildings of a type not found in any of the other quarters. Along came a very well dressed man, screaming "What are you filming. You're filming ruins! There's nothing in Suq Saruja but ruins! Go film that building over there." He indicated a building next to the Madrasa Shamiyya, a very ugly building which degrades the Madrasa's environment. There's a story to this building; we [activists] had tried to get a limit placed on its height. He pointed to this building and said, "Look, *this* is civilization, *this* is beauty, *this* is modernity." I had no idea who this person was. I said to him, "You're not speaking for us. We are for the Old City, you're against it, we didn't ask for your opinion." Later I spoke to some residents of the quarter, who said to me, "Don't you know who he is? He's the one who bought a large section of Suq Saruja." Somehow he had discovered that a television production company was filming Suq Saruja. . . . The *'aqariyyin* (real estate merchants) are at war with the intellectuals, academics, and engineers. I believe that the *'aqariyyin* are against human civilization, not just heritage.

Yet both Khost and Tergeman own expensive New City flats, which they rent—at exorbitant market prices—to foreign diplomats and oil company employees. Perhaps unwittingly, perhaps unavoidably, they operate within a market with little regard for old-style architecture.

I met another Damascus advocate, Nasr al-Din al-Bahra, at a dinner party given by mutual friends. When he learned of my research, he readily offered an interview, and soon showed up at my door bearing a huge bouquet. Noticing my shocked expression—I feared what the neighbors might think—he immediately reassured me: "We Damascenes have a custom: when we visit someone's home for the first time, we bring flowers." Bahra argues that there are many reasons for the interest in Old Damascus, some of which are psychological:

Psychologically, new houses built in the Western style do not engender psychological comfort. Walls block the view, and the low ceilings—Arab houses had high ceilings—limit the sense of space. A person feels he can't breathe. The old house had wide-open spaces, with trees and greenery. In the middle was a fountain with water from the Barada River. New houses are nothing like this; they're like matchboxes, with narrow spaces.

Other reasons are historical:

The style of the Arab house embodied the people's collective consciousness. The architect who designed them was Arab. Their fathers and grandfathers lived in this style. Some houses—the large ones—had sophisticated decorations: paintings, trimmings on walls and ceilings, painted wood panels, calligraphic lines from the Qurʾan or poetry. It had a clear relation to history, to national history.

Lastly, Bahra provided social and cultural causes for the interest in Old Damascus, linking local concerns to global movements:

> There is now a cultural awakening in our country, the result of the spread of education. It is also connected to currents in international culture. We notice that the return to the old is happening all over the world, even in Europe. This is probably the result of the crisis that Western society is going through, with mechanization, automation, and computerization.

I interviewed Damascene Christian author Colette Khuri in her Qassaʿ flat, shortly after her election to the Syrian People's Assembly (Majlis al-Shaʿb). She expressed a much more sanguine view of development:

> Contrast is the most interesting thing about this city. You'll find people living life in old ways in the Old City, and you will also find people living in a very modern style; you'll find fully equipped modern apartments, and very old houses. For me, this is the continuity of life—given that Damascus is the oldest inhabited city in the world. . . . Damascus is always renewing itself. . . . I am sorry that some buildings have been lost. But there must be progress, and sometimes the flow of evolution takes with it in its path that which it shouldn't take. I am always with evolution.

However, later in the interview, elegantly and formally dressed in black velvet to receive colleagues from the (Syrian) Arab Writers Union, Khuri added: "The historical role of Damascus is to bring civilization to everything that surrounds it. It is the heart of Syria. When Damascus says 'no,' even if the rest of the Syria says 'yes,' then the answer is 'no.'"

In these sketches I have profiled some of the key players in the Old Damascus preservation movement, who combine lobbying the government with promoting the Old City through artistic expression. They reflect many of the paradoxes of the Damascene elite: a sense of displacement and marginalization within the city but identification with the cosmopolitan West; and relative success in the very marketplace and political system which they blame for the Old City's demise. In their lives and work, these activists reflect the uneasy ways in which the Damascene elite has had to change to accommodate new circumstances in order to try to maintain both their social position and their city's unique heritage.

Another prominent Damascene questions the rosy nostalgia for Old Damascus among its most ardent proponents. A Yale-educated philosopher of international reputation, and member of one of the city's leading notable families, Sadik Jalal al-Azm tells his own tale of patriarchal oppression:

> When my grandfather's old house in al-Jisr al-Abyad was torn down, I felt no sense of loss. I was a young man then, but reflecting on it later, I wondered why, since when other buildings are destroyed or defaced, I feel sad. Then I realized that I got it from my mother—she hated the place. For her, it was a symbol of oppression, of everyone interfering in her life, of the fact that she was not able to continue her education. It was run by my grandfather, who was a despotic patriarch. In the end my mother married my father and got out, because basically she just wanted to be rid of the place. This attitude was conveyed to us, her children, in a variety of imperceptible ways. So when the house went, I felt nothing at all. There was a saying about the old Azm Palace, "from the outside the stones are red, but inside life is short."

al-Azm points to an aestheticization of everyday objects and practices which he sees as a sign of modernity, rather than "authentic" tradition:

> I was invited to an *iftar*, at the Cham Hotel, organized by the Society of Friends of Damascus. They had the Mawlawi Sufis come, and the first thought that came to my mind, which I told the friends that were with me, is that when the Mawlawis are put on show like that, it means that they are becoming an antique, a collector's item. They are no longer part of the functioning order of religious life, or are on their way out. There is a return to the Old City in a sense, but it is pretty much in the way that Europeans or Westerners come and collect Bedouin jewelry or brocade, which now have become collectors' items for us, too. But in the past, they were functioning aspects of life.

al-Azm would agree with Appadurai that authenticity becomes significant only in the presence of doubt (1986: 25). Authenticity, Appadurai tells us, is an outsider's concern (ibid.). Damascenes are so removed from their past that they are in a sense outside it, and are thus able to contrast what and who is authentic, *asil*, with the inauthenticity of the new. Being modern means being able to mark off "the traditional" as such. Showing me around his home, al-Azm points to his own self-conscious use of once ordinary utilitarian objects as decorative or artistic identity markers:

> This is our salon, and do you know what this is? It is [a mortar and pestle] for making kibbeh. Now it sits on exhibit in my salon. The original place

for it was in the kitchen. You would never show it to your guests, because it was just part of the kitchen like the spoons and dishes. But now that it is no longer functional, it is on exhibit. My mother would never have done this. . . . If my wife and I were not Western educated, we would never think of putting *jurn al-kibbeh* there. When more traditional cousins of mine come to visit, they can't understand the logic. In a way I am returning, but returning under extremely different circumstances.

al-Azm argues that modern, global processes of travel and tourism have contributed to a reevaluation of the local, as imitation of the metropolis necessitates treating indigenous cultural products with the reverence afforded works of art:

> We are also imitating the Westerners; they are our model, unconsciously. People here learned to value things that they had, that they lived with, when they saw that Westerners were coming, buying them, and making them collectors' items, adornments, and decorations. Now we tend to use these things to decorate, as they do. In a house like mine, for example, which is not set up like an Arabic house, with tables and chairs and sofas, some of my friends will have what they call an "Arabic room." Now when you start enclosing a space in the house and calling it the "Arabic room," it means the "Arabic room" is not really a functioning part of your life. . . . In an Arabic house, you don't have an "Arabic room."

Here individual social actors folkloricize aspects of the local, setting them up as self-conscious expressions and representations of identity which are nevertheless cordoned off from the "modern" parts of a house. The Damascene elite exoticize their own past, treating its material vestiges as curios from another country. As in much of Old Damascus revivalism, old objects are also put to new uses. al-Azm describes such reworking in his own house:

> This bar, the mother-of-pearl part, is the top of my mother's old cupboard, and on it would sit the [family] crown. In my grandfather's house this would have fit perfectly well because the ceiling would have been five or six meters high. As we started moving into more modern houses, first we had to remove the crown. My father cut down the base on which the crown sits, because ceilings were becoming lower. He was going to throw this part away, and when my wife and I came from the States we said, "this would make a wonderful bar." Only a Westernized person would come up with something like that. . . . All these things that people are returning to are being recycled for the purposes of modern living. They give you some satisfaction of not losing touch with the past. There is an emulation aspect of it, because we think that what Europeans do is implicitly always better, superior, more sensible and rational. We see that Europeans come and take care of these things, put them in museums, so we tend to do that too. . . . My feeling about all these things that are being recuperated or recycled for

modern life is that they are on their way out. I think the logic of life imposes this. But to think of it as going back to some sort of authenticity is nonsense.

Old Damascus Filmed

While nostalgic literature attempts to recreate an Old Damascus of the past, documentary film is the only cultural form to tackle the problems facing Old City residents in the present. Syrian rent-control laws have prevented landlords from raising rents beyond a nominal increment each year. They make almost no money on Old City properties and either cannot afford, or are disinclined to spend, the considerable sums required to keep up Old City houses—susceptible as they are to damp rot. Compounding this problem are the laws designed to "preserve" the architectural character of the Old City, which often make ordinary repairs or improvements a lengthy bureaucratic process. Old City tenants cannot afford to rent or buy modern flats in newer neighborhoods at current rates. Life is difficult in the contemporary Old City; one woman is now burdened with the work that several women in an extended family once shared, in a house literally crumbling around her. Often several families are crowded into a house built for one.

Hind Midani's 1987 documentary, *Damascus: A Point of View* (*Dimashq: Masafat al-Nazar*), depicts dilemmas facing the current residents of Old Damascus. The film explores the tensions between the aesthetic concerns of Old City activists and the material needs of Old City dwellers, focusing on the quarter of Hamrawi, site of a devastating fire in 1958. Hamrawi residents were turned out of their damaged houses by state renovators and placed in dilapidated accommodation elsewhere in the Old City, with the understanding that their houses would be restored and returned to them. Twenty years later, they found themselves caught in a bureaucratic black hole, neither returned to their houses nor appropriately recompensed. Discovering a Governorate of Damascus plan to demolish the quarter and build in its place a modern commercial center, the people of Hamrawi rose to action. With the help of Friends of Damascus activists, they submitted over 500 petitions and appealed to thirty important figures (*shakhsiyat*) and tens of officials over a span of ten years. They succeeded in halting the destruction, but the future of Hamrawi and the entire Old City remains precarious. Midani conveys a sense of hopelessness and frustration, interviewing residents and following them as they walk in and out of government offices, armed with briefcases crammed full of forms and documents.

The aims of those involved in the campaign differ, and although Midani tends to underplay these distinctions, it is clear that the first priority of some Hamrawi residents is some form of financial compensation, while Old City activists who themselves live in modern New City flats seek to preserve Old City buildings as monuments of local and national heritage. Discussions appear purposely blurred; it is difficult to distinguish between those who have retained Hamrawi houses but fear future demolition, and those from other quarters brought in to attest to the deplorable living conditions found in much of the Old City. The film moves back and forth from the Hamrawi story to the Old City in general.

Interview segments are interspersed with scenes of children playing in the contemporary Old City and stills of photographs and paintings of Damascus at different historical periods, set to a specially commissioned score by Syrian National symphony conductor Sulhi al-Wadi. Old City activist Nazih Kawakibi, University of Damascus professor of architecture, Nadia Khost, and venerable historian Khalid Moaz speak of the need to restore and save from annihilation what remains of Damascene architecture. Images of bulldozers tearing down the once grand quarter of Suq Saruja, and those of ugly concrete high-rises that dominate much of Damascus, warn of what may come. A local merchant whose clientele consists of foreign tourists and expatriates argues that when he goes abroad people may not know about Syria, but they all know Damascus. The film ends with the ominous words of a longtime Old City resident: "These walls could live another 350 years. But will they let them live that long? God knows."

Other documentaries take a more folkloric or archival approach. One example is Lutfi Lutfi's *Story of the Neighborhood of al-Qanawat* (*Qissat Hayy al-Qanawat*). Screened in March 1996 as part of a Friends of Damascus-sponsored colloquium on al-Qanawat, the film traces the history of this neighborhood, underscoring its political importance. Home to politically active notables of the late Ottoman and Mandate periods, such as Fakhri al-Barudi, Qanawat's importance is both architectural and social historical. Falling outside the Old City walls, Qanawat is among the quarters threatened with destruction.

Jews of Damascus (*Yahud Dimashq*), produced by Syrian Arab Television, is a documentary of a very different sort. Directed by Damascene Sunni Ghassan Jabri, and narrated in English by Dr. Yahya al-Aridi, director of Syrian Channel Two—who, like all high-ranking media officials, maintains close ties to the regime—*Jews of Damascus* is intended primarily to disprove claims that Syrian Jews are victims of government or social harassment. Aridi interviews prominent members of the Jewish community in English and Arabic, asking questions which elicit testimonies of their freedom of worship, foreign travel, and economic well-being. Jews are depicted as an integral part of the Damascene "mosaic," and many scenes take place in the Old City. The film's portrayal of Damascene social integration conforms to Ba'th Party socialist ideology; over and over again, interviewees claim that they are Syrian citizens first and Jews second. All stress their cordial relations with the city's other religious groups. The film was aired on Syrian television, perhaps with a view to promoting social harmony.

Here the Old City, with its diverse, multi-denominational composition, serves the government's purpose: the erasure—or at least disregard—of sub-national identities. This is one of many instances where the regime appropriates Old Damascus and the Damascenes for political purposes. Yet in his comments to me, director Jabri stressed not the Syrian but the Damascene, reappropriating the film's subjects for the city. Pointing to one particular figure—an Old City gold merchant—as quintessentially Damascene, Jabri said: "he is responsible and honorable."

Public culture nostalgia, I argue, lies at the heart of social and political contestation in contemporary Damascus. Prominent Damascenes both produce and consume books and films evoking and eulogizing the Old City and its former inhabitants. These works promote efforts to preserve remaining sections of the Old City endangered by both property developers and, some believe, state security concerns. They also reassert an elite urban social identity, an exclusive "authenticity" that forms the basis of both implicit and explicit criticism of the regime, the new ruling elite, and the conspicuously consuming "new class" of those—including some Old Damascenes— who have benefited from the Asad era. This exclusivity and resistance is often tempered with references to Damascus as part of a larger Syrian Arab nation, reflecting the conflicting tensions and necessary co-optations that operating in contemporary Syria necessitates. The Damascene elite often must capitulate to the new power structure, but they do not do so without protest.

Old Damascus still serves as cultural capital for the aspiring; upwardly mobile non-Damascenes sometimes tap into the prestige of Old City advocacy. The state itself occasionally adopts Old Damascus as part of Syrian national heritage. Other non-Damascenes object to what they see as the chauvinism and self-aggrandizement of Damasceneness. The claims and counterclaims of social value and moral worth embodied in artistic representations of the Old City, and in different approaches to urban development, are articulated in the agonistic idiom, the poetics of accusation, that I maintain is a central mode of Syrian sociability. Argumentation serves as a means of identity construction. For both activists and opponents, the Old City is central to memory of the past, evaluation of the present, and contests over the future.

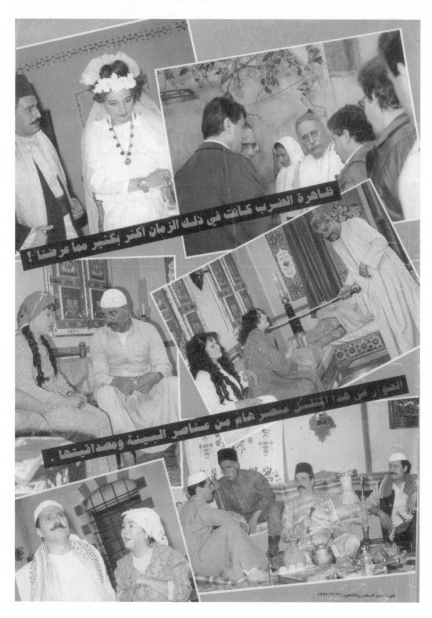

Scenes from *Damascene Days*

(above) Restoring
Old Damascus

(left) Bayt Jabri,
exterior

Bayt Jabri, foyer

Bayt Jabri, interior

Bayt Jabri, Internet room

al-Barjees Café, exterior

al-Barjees Café, interior

Conclusion
Weapons of the Not-So-Weak

Old Damascenes find themselves increasingly sidelined by new groups. By local standards the old elite live comfortably, sometimes luxuriously; yet many feel a sense of marginalization after the social and economic transformation of the last several decades. They are relatively successful in a world they no longer dominate, and one they do not much like. As modes of political and economic dominance are no longer available, elite Damascenes increasingly assert identity through public cultural production and consumption. Commodified forms of Old Damascus itself, in restaurants, bars, and cafés, and its representation in books, art exhibits, social clubs, and television programs, offer politically permitted avenues of social and political critique. Old Damascus and Damasceneness are commodified; paradoxically, they are also expressions of resistance to what many Damascenes see as the shift toward entirely consumption-based criteria for elite status. Consumption of Damascus is a medium through which the consumptive practices of others are criticized, either implicitly or explicitly. Such contestation shapes the social lives of urban Syrians; Old Damascus, like the bodies of women, forms a focal point around which status competitions pivot.

Shifting Identities?

To my suggestion that the interest in Old Damascus was an expression of a society in which social identities are in flux, Damascene philosopher Sadik al-Azm replied:

> There is no identity crisis here, certainly not in the sense in which Americans understand it. In Damascus, still, everyone knows exactly who he is, who his father is, who his mother is, his social position, his situation. The

merchants know this too, know that they have been merchants and project this into the future. The identity crisis is *very* marginal. The idea that
you must define yourself, find yourself, and make decisions about your life
in the way that Americans do doesn't apply here. On the contrary, what
we have here is too much identity! Identities here are solid, strong, and,
from my point of view, almost overly ossified.

Yet Syrian class and social identities show little evidence of ossifica-
tion. Or perhaps elites are changing to remain the same, as many of
the older modes of social distinction are fading. Higher education is
no longer seen as an important mark of social status for the elite, or
as a reliable means to upward mobility for the humble. A university
degree now weighs less on the marriageability scale. Likewise, the
professions of law, medicine, and religious leadership carry less prestige than they once did. The title *doktur* no longer has the same deep
resonance.

This devaluing of education is related to the absence of a shared
sense of a local high culture. Instead, wealth is displayed in elite hotels, expensive restaurants, and at engagement parties, weddings,
funerals, and other rite of passage events. Some of these events involve references to Old Damascus, or at least allusions to older forms
of social life—Old Damascus theme cafés, old-fashioned horse-drawn
wedding carriages, Ramadan meals *iftar* and *suhur* in posh restaurants. The most talked about wedding of the 1995 season, staged by
Najdat Isma'il Anzur, director of *The End of a Brave Man*, featured the
bride riding into the Sheraton hotel on camelback.

The trappings of Western elite culture—familiarity with current
movements in the performing and visual arts; theater-, opera-, and
cinema-going; museum and gallery visiting, highbrow fiction reading—do not constitute symbolic capital in the upper reaches of Damascene society. Foreigners—diplomats and oil company employees—are virtually the only art patrons. Often the more impoverished
part of the artistic community itself makes up the audience and
readership for local high cultural production. The same faces can be
seen at all highbrow art events: concerts, plays, films, and exhibit
openings.

Given this situation, there appears to be some justification for
the claim, popular among Old Damascus proponents, that the quality of social life, and particularly of elite culture, has deteriorated under the dominance of wealthy peasants who hold money as the
measure of all good. Yet this supposed deterioration is at least in part
a figment of the nostalgic imagination. Non-Damascenes, for their
part, are quick to retort that the Damascenes have always had a mer-

cantile mentality, that they have never been great artistic patrons, and that both the artistic community and its audience are largely non-Damascene. Damascenes are rarely found among vocal opposition figures, and Damascenes tend not to prioritize freedom of expression. As a prominent industrialist answered when asked if economic liberalization would bring about increased political freedom: "Not only do I not think so, I do not really wish it. All we want is economic freedom and political stability; for us, democracy often means a coup d'état every two years" (Bahout 1994: 80). For a Damascene writer, superficial collaboration is the quintessence of Damascene success:

> We keep silent, but we stay alive. This silence is a weapon. Perhaps this is why Damascus is the oldest continuously inhabited city in the world. Many leaders, invaders, and criminals have come and ruled her, but they have all gone. There is genius in this art of politics: today we keep quiet, tomorrow we'll speak, and the day after that, we'll return.

Individuals and groups are struggling either to hold on to dissolving forms of social prestige, or lay claim to new ones. Elite social statuses are being redefined through new consumptive practices, as ways of life are transformed into lifestyles of the modern sort. Such processes are rarely discussed in literature on the Middle East, where it is assumed, despite evidence of rapid and profound social transformation, that the old urban notables still know who they are—and are known by everyone else—and have nothing to prove.

As sub-national social identities become discussed and debated in public culture, Damascus and Damasceneness is feted by those who claim links to it. Through the media and in new consumption sites, Damascenes are re-emerging into public prominence. So many Damascene businessmen were chosen in the 1994 parliamentary elections that jokes circulated about the new People's Assembly resembling the Damascus Chamber of Commerce.

I have attempted here to explore the ways in which various Syrian elites are appropriating global cultural forms and transforming them for their own purposes. I have also tried to show how their efforts do not proceed uncontested. The indigenization of television, restaurants, nostalgic literature, and other global cultural forms is in fact producing prolific diversity; yet as Appadurai (1990: 5–6) and Lila Abu-Lughod (1993: 510) point out, this in turn creates and reinforces local hegemonies, as dominant groups control access to modes of representation. As Appadurai puts it, "one man's imagined community is another man's political prison" (1990: 6). In Syria, local cultural hegemonies never rule supreme; elite groups have become increasingly vocal critics of media and other representations, and use them in agonistic competitions occurring in a burgeoning public culture arena.

Syrian cultural producers and consumers participate in the creation of sub-national imagined communities. Television programs like *Damascene Days* and organizations such as Friends of Damascus allow Damascenes to imagine themselves distinct from the rest of Syria. The Old Damascus debate reminds us not to assume that the presence of a state implies a strong sense of nationhood. As an 'Alawi painter asserted: "Syria is not a nation, and has never been one; it's a mélange of people who happen to live here."

Newly adopted cultural forms—television programs, restaurants, books—reflect the self-conscious construction and commodification of ideas about and ideals of the past. Objects, sights, sounds, tastes, and smells once a part of kin- and religious-based relations and identities have become experiences enjoyed as part of a "spectacle of modernity," in which social relations are increasingly mediated through imagery and atmosphere (Debord 1994). New leisure practices are transforming ways of life into lifestyles. Authentic culture has become an event organized by Friends of Damascus or packaged by an enterprising restaurateur. The "authentic" Old Damascus of *Damascene Days* represents true mass consumption, available to all, rejected by some. But those who produce authenticity for the masses may themselves frequent exclusive venues like Le Piano Bar, where drinks cost five dollars each and the decor is an ironic hodgepodge of past and present, local and foreign.

An exploration of the return to an "authentic culture" of Old Damascus is a journey into the urban, Middle Eastern experience of modernity: from the Old City itself (whose mostly lower-middle-class inhabitants would leave if they could), to intellectuals and media figures who claim to represent local tradition and complain of apathy and frustration; from exhibits and dinner parties, bookshops and television shows, to that favorite haunt of the Old Damascenes, the Sheraton Hotel; and finally, to the ultimate decenteredness of Le Piano Bar, which, in the words of one Syrian,

> has absolutely no identity. It has something from Damascus. But what about that riding equipment? The one who did the décor has assimilated too many cultures. We have a saying which fits: "from every orchard one flower." Those dishes on the wall are Dutch, but they are not arranged in a Dutch way. It's for younger people. You can never place it anywhere. They offer a very limited menu—*shish tawuq*, which is Turkish, and spaghetti,

which is Italian. They have an old piece behind the bar that was part of the
Umayyad Palace. Such a combination is unbelievable. And the curtains! I
have never seen this fabric, which used to be used for cushions, used for
drapes. Yes, it is Damascene, but it is used in a totally different way. Next
I'm afraid I'll find part of my mother's underwear hanging as a curtain!
They are arranging old things in a rather modern art way. We have this desire to live in a modern way, because at least in furniture we can do it. In
our thoughts we are often tied to old ideas.

The final paradox is that "old ideas" is itself a concept distinctive
of modernity, and the pursuit of the Old City is a contemporary phenomenon. Old Damascus as historic space and imagined ideal forms
the basis of what I have called a "poetics of accusation," through
which the different groups living in Damascus deal with the complexities of modern life, its ruptures and reversals, its global flows
and local specificities. Real and perceived successes and failures of
Baʿth socialist nationalism and its modernist project are debated
through identity contests over what Lefebvre has called "the right to
the city" (1996), and in the Syrian case might be expanded to "the
right to the nation."

Epilogue
Of Hubble Bubbles and Cell Phones

A decade has passed since I began fieldwork in Damascus, and many of the phenomena I wrote about have since proliferated. Visits to Syria from my new base in Beirut in the years 2002–2004 reveal an intensification of the cleavages and tensions I examined in the early 1990s. Issues of social distinctions have become more salient, but they remain sensitive. So it was with great apprehension that I shared my published work on these topics with informants in Damascus. Yet my two articles pleased those in the restaurant and television industry, who now see my early interest in their work as justified, both by their own subsequent success and by seeing their words printed in an academic medium.

While Syrians had hoped the new regime would loosen the restraints on freedom of expression, the expectations raised during the final days of Hafiz al-Asad's leadership, and Bashar al-Asad's presidential honeymoon, have largely been disappointed. From the relaxations granted in 1999 and 2000 emerged the beginnings of a legal opposition. For nearly a year, social and political life was enlivened. Calls for democratization were featured in a weekly lecture held by the Organization for Economic Sciences (Jam'iat al-'Ulum al-Iqtisadiyya), with the state's approval. The first series, held in 1999 at the Damascus Arab Cultural Center, bore the title "Reform and Change." My informants, now cynical, point to the posturing these gatherings elicited: "It was a great opportunity for all those seeking new positions to show off their reformist ideas."

Numerous other intellectual forums (*muntadayat*) sprang up in houses all over Damascus, and people attended these once forbidden gatherings ostensibly to discuss art and culture, but inevitably to debate politics and reform. Among the sensitive topics openly debated was the role of sectarian groups in the Syrian polity. The infamous Mezzeh political prison was closed, and hundreds of long-imprisoned dissidents released. An opposition press sprouted, and eminent political cartoonist Ali Farzat won the Dutch Prince Claus Award for achievement in culture and development for his satirical weekly *The Lamp Lighter* (*al-Dumari*). Intended, as Farzat put it, to "bring light to the economic, political, and social situation" in contemporary Syria, *The Lamp Lighter* sold out in the morning of its first day of publication (Whitaker 2001). The tabloid criticized official corruption, naming high-ranking targets.

But like Syria's other new expressive cultural forms, *al-Dumari* has had to endure peaks and troughs of official favor. A backlash in 2001 again silenced numerous opposition voices. Many dissidents were rearrested after demanding democratic reform too stridently for the regime's comfort. As Farzat told a foreign reporter, "We are like someone in the bathroom who finds the water is hot one minute and cold the next" (Hammond 2002).

While Damascus does enjoy a more relaxed atmosphere and greater access to the outside world than it did in the 1990s, for many Syrians, impatient to leave behind decades of repression, these modest changes do not go as far as they would like. The slow pace of political reform and the backlash against criticism of the regime have left many despondent. As one Damascene intellectual commented:

> Change is there, but it has been overshadowed by what remains the same. In 2000 a new attitude emerged: respect for individuality, creativity, and innovation. This was promoted in many different ways and means. People thought there would be freedom of expression. Then all of a sudden, it was changed, just like that. Now life in Damascus is very dull, compared to the expectations we had.

Global trends also seem not to have spurred the transformations many predicted. Satellite political debate shows like those Syrians now watch on al-Jazeera TV at first seemed revolutionary, but have failed to engender political reform (Salamandra 2003). And while satellite television stations now reach a growing number of Syrian homes, local television continues to flourish. The spread of pan-Arab television has enhanced Syria's local industry, whose products sell to numerous Arabic satellite stations, and even attract the interest of the American press (Lancaster 1998; Peterson 1997). Television seems to go where other cultural forms cannot, and many programs retain their satirical edge. Comedian Yasir al-ʿAzma's *Mirrors* (*Maraya*), continues to amuse audiences around the Arab world with gentle gibes at Arab politics and society. *Mirrors* targets both official corruption and private foibles. Old Damascus is a favorite subject, and in one episode the Damascene al-ʿAzma depicts two Old City quarters embroiled in a feud so old none of the combatants can remember its cause. A newer satirical program, *Spot Light* (*Buqaʿt al-Dawʾ*), wows Ramadan audiences with biting criticisms of the intelligence services' (*mukhabarat*) ubiquitous informants and ruthless detention practices. Top officials complain that corrupt characters always speak in distinct ʿAlawi dialect, but state censors have yet to silence the program.

Musalsalat, serial dramas, remain the strongest format, with over forty produced in 2002. Damascus has again starred in Ramadan *musalsalat,* in Hani Rummani's multi-part *Hammam al-Qishani,* broadcast in alternate years, and in Bassam al-Malla's *al-Khawali* (*Bygone Days*) of 2001. *The Middle Room* (*Nusiyya*), filmed in three magnificent old Damascene houses, Bayt Nizam, Bayt Sbaiʿi, and Bayt Sawan, was aired in 1998. In this multi-layered mystery, a dying man hides the name of his murderer in a young girl's favorite room. According to director Ghassan Jabri, the eponymous *nusiyya,* a middle space between the upper (winter) and lower (summer) floors of an Old City house, serves as a metaphor for an endangered middle class. "If you break the middle class," he argued, "you break the whole of society." My informants make increasingly overt reference to social distinctions. As one of those involved in the production admitted, "it is really about what happened to the people of Damascus with the invasion of a new culture."

While political reform has been a bumpy road, economic liberalization has advanced unabated and private industry has boomed. Bashar al-Asad's government has promoted economic liberalization, bringing many new commodities and creating new venues for displaying them. Expensive new private schools have opened in the wealthy neighborhoods of Damascus, charging tuition fees many times higher than their long-established counterparts. These institutions train a new generation in the arts of elite distinction; they also create competitive consumption events for their students' mothers. An informant notes of one school's opening celebration, "I went just as I was, after a long day at work, but everyone else was there dressed as if they were going to a wedding."

A significant number of new private businesses have women at the helm. The Committee of Commercial Businesswomen (Lajnat Sayidat al-ʾAʿmal al-Tijariyya), affiliated with the Damascus Chamber of Commerce, was established in 2002. A lavish opening party was held at Nadi al-Sharq, and members arrived clad in the latest expensive fashions. Critics point to a preference for style over substance. "It was women acting as women," noted one member. "They spent a lot of time planning the opening—what kind of food would be served, where it would be held—but when I asked them the logic behind the organization, what special services it offers, and how our needs might differ from those of businessmen, no one could answer my questions." Time pressures create shifts in the form but not the degree of competitive consumption. For working elite women, the long, leisurely afternoon *istiqbal* has been replaced with the *subhiyyeh*, morning coffee.

Locally produced goods of all sorts now line Damascus store shelves, including trendy European brand-name clothing, such as Stefanel and Dolce & Gabbana, made under license. New advertising practices market these products, as huge billboards now line once bare desert highways. Communications too have expanded, with more households gaining access to satellite dishes. Internet connections have spread more slowly, but there are a few connected cafés in the upscale areas of Abu Rummaneh and Malki. Newly introduced cellular phones are all the rage.

Cell phone users are among the most frequent patrons of Old City night spots, the latest offering from Nokia clamped to one ear as they puff on hubble bubbles (water pipes) in the courtyards of old merchant houses. Restaurants have mushroomed in Old Damascus. More are expected, as a new and "very Damascene" deputy minister of tourism, dubbed the "king of licenses," now maintains jurisdiction over restaurant licenses in the Old City. These establishments represent a confluence of well-connected entrepreneurs and interested officials, and they enjoy enormous success. In the most popular, reservations are de rigueur, and the less fashionable benefit from the overflow. "I'm in the restaurant and hotel industry myself, and I should know what is going on, but even I am surprised how often I wake up to find a new restaurant here," notes Sami Farah. "Next year you'll see even more." Farah left the Sheraton in early 2003 to open his own Old City nightspot, al-Mayasa. Old Damascus now boasts over thirty flourishing restaurants and cafés. Many have sprung up around, and largely superceded, Le Piano Bar in the Christian neighborhoods near Bab Sharqi, and serve alcohol along with a variety of cuisines. A disco, Hannibal, has now joined these Old City nightspots.

Yet the most frequented establishments are also the most "traditional": cafés such as Bayt Jabri and al-Barjees, located in Muslim neighborhoods, serve traditional homey foods such as *fatteh* and *sahlab* (a warm custard thickened with the powder of dried tubers), along with the usual restaurant fare of grilled meats and mezzeh. Tea, coffee, and the hubble bubble (*nargileh*) replace the alcohol served in Bab Sharqi establishments, and patrons spend long evenings puffing and chatting. Bayt Jabri combines old-fashioned homeyness with an Internet room. Al-Barjees is named for a game played with shells on an embroidered cloth. Rarely played now, this Old Damascene women's equivalent of backgammon can be seen in the historic tableaux of the Azm Palace folklore museum; it occasionally appears at the tables of al-Barjees's older patrons.

In the late 1990s, hubble bubbles spread beyond their usual habitat of working-class cafés to a new generation of aficionados in recently established nightspots in the Old City and beyond. It is a trend Damascus shares with neighboring capitals, as elite youth of Beirut and Cairo also enjoy this expensive but licit treat in posh cafés decorated with a touch of the folkloric. In the elite neighborhoods of new Damascus, some thirty recently opened establishments with open-air spaces designed for smoking bridge a generation gap that once characterized Damascene nightspots. The smoking ritual marks the threshold of adulthood for Damascus youth. Health concerns raised in the press, and by anxious parents, do little to halt the trend. "You find a table of middle-aged women right next to one full of loud kids," an informant noted. The sweet scent of *tufahtayn* ("double apple") smoke wafts through cafés and restaurants large and small, foreign and local. A specialist waiter, dressed in traditional costume of baggy trousers and embroidered vests, often sporting the all but extinct fez, swings a brazier and searches among the patrons for those in need of fresh charcoal. One glance brings him scurrying to your table, scraping the dead coals off the foil-lined top of your pipe, and replacing them with glowing red chunks held gingerly in tapered tongs. Young women number among habitual smokers, but it is young men who have "mastered the art," as one Damascene mother put it:

> Our young men enjoy being pampered by these hubble bubble waiters. I was amazed to watch my sixteen-year-old son at it. He made eye contact with the waiter, who rushed over, and said to him—gruffly—"*tufahtayn, mu'allim*" ("double apple, waiter"). Then he sat back, puffed on the pipe stuck in the corner of his mouth, and watched all the girls go by.

Old City hubble-bubble spots like Bayt Jabri have become favorites for *suhur:* an expansive courtyard makes an ideal setting for
the social interactions so central to Ramadan in Damascus. Damascenes and others vie for tables around the fountain; once there,
they play backgammon and cards, and exchange greetings with
friends and relatives into the small hours. In, of, and about the Old
City, Bayt Jabri and its like exemplify the contradictions and complexities of modernity in Damascus. Old elites have had to change to
stay the same, and these accommodations do not always sit comfortably. According to one *bint ʿaʾileh:*

> The phenomenon of restaurants in Old Damascus is the clear expression of
> the new order. An ordinary Damascene could never get a license to open a
> restaurant. An Old Damascene will give the place his name, but he'll have
> to go into partnership with a son of the regime to get permission to open.

Old Damascus restaurants are popular among some Damascenes, who see them as a way to preserve old houses without for-
feiting the comforts of modernity. While many Syrians enjoy leisure
hours in the Old City, and some are profiting from the restaurant
trade, few show any interest in reviving old houses for other purposes. It is foreigners who have begun to revitalize old houses with
new ventures. In 2000, the Danish government established a research institute in the renovated Bayt Akkad, providing an Old City-
steeped environment for students and researchers. Nora Jumblatt,
the wife of Lebanese politician Walid Jumblatt, and Kuwaiti art con-
noisseur and collector Sheikh Hussah Al-Sabah have both restored
Old City houses, and a Japanese corporation is sponsoring the con-
version of the eighteenth-century Khan Asʿad Basha in al-Bzuriyyeh
into a natural history museum. These projects may add a new dimension to the experience of Old Damascus modernity, and supple-
ment restaurants and cafés with new sights, sounds, and associa-
tions. But for some of its sons and daughters, Old Damascus is a
memory of a life, a pattern of social relations, that is impossible to
capture in the modern culture of consumption:

> I become upset when I find yet another Damascene house turned into a
> restaurant. It shows a lack of respect for the life of the city. They are trying
> to create a picture postcard Damascus, but this image is superficial. If you
> sit in an Old Damascene house, drinking whiskey, surrounded by disco
> lights, video screens, and half-naked people dancing, is this Damascus? No,
> it isn't! But sitting by the courtyard fountain in the morning, sipping cof-
> fee, with the perfume of jasmine around you, listening to the elders talk

after they return from prayers, all about who was working at what, who is getting married, who is fighting with whom, *this* is how you find the spirit of Damascus. This place I personally do not want to see turned into a disco. It's like someone seeing a saint, noticing only that she is pretty, and stripping her clothes off.

Yet one might argue that while the aesthetics have changed, the social relations long central to the lives of Damascenes remain paramount, and are recreated, reworked, and put to new uses. In places like Syria, relationships are as political as they are social, and an ethnography of consumption practices and expressive cultural forms adds a perspective missing from analyses of conventional politics. The lives of contemporary Damascus elites still revolve around commercial ventures, marriage patterns and their prestige, and social rivalries. Contests, political and social, take place through new modes of consumption, and in recently introduced leisure sites, but much of what is competed over—prestige, position, power—was not unknown among their grandparents.

Notes

1. A strong local liquor distilled from grapes and flavored with anise.

2. I define elite groups, broadly, as those with control of or access to material and/or intellectual resources (Pina-Cabral 2000: 2).

3. The return to "tradition" is widespread in the Middle East. See, for example, Montigny (1998) on Qatar, Stokes (2000) on Istanbul, and Khalaf (2001) on Dubai.

4. For more on the importance of marriage ceremonies among the upper strata of Damascene society, see Tapper (1998/99).

5. All quotations, except where noted, are from fieldwork interviews and personal communication. The translations, except where noted, are my own.

6. For a detailed discussion of this problem, see Dresch 2000.

7. For example, Nabati poetry in the Gulf, and the use of colloquial dialogue in Egyptian fiction.

8. One asked how my advisor had approved my topic, lacking as it was in "deep structure"; another dismissed television as "mere diversion."

9. Writing of an Andean community, Rudi Colloredo-Mansfield puts it succinctly: "In 1994, the most commonly used object in an Ariasucu home was a loom; the second most common thing was a television" (1999: xi).

10. Interviews were conducted primarily in Arabic, sometimes in English, and sometimes in a mixture of Arabic, English, and French.

11. For historical treatments of Damascene notables, see Schilcher 1985 and Khoury 1983.

12. For a concise treatment of 'Alawi belief and religious hierarchy, see F. Khuri 1991.

13. Following the demise of the Ottoman Empire, the League of Nations granted France a mandate to govern Syria. French occupation forces ruled Syria from 1920 to 1946.

14. Rabo describes a similar tension between the native inhabitants of the northeastern Syrian town of Raqqa and the rural migrants who have politically and economically displaced them (1999).

15. See, for instance, Rabinovich 1972; Van Dusen 1972, 1975; Devlin 1976; Batatu 1978, 1981, 1999; Picard 1980; Drysdale 1981; Roberts 1987; Hinnebusch 1989, 1990, 1991; Sadowski 1988; Van Dam 1996.

16. Some analysts stress 'Alawi domination. Batatu notes that all of Asad's chief advisors and heads of the all-powerful security forces are not only 'Alawi, but also members of the Asads' tribal group, the al-Matawira

(1981: 331–332). More recently, Wedeen argues that the Ba'th Party created a new political elite drawn "especially from the 'Alawi sect" (1999: 8). Al-Khalil sees "a combination of constrained universalism and sectarianism in practice" as the hallmark of Ba'th pan-Arabism (1989: 189). In contrast, Hinnebusch emphasizes the Ba'th Party's popular base, demonstrating how it has mobilized a coalition of peasants, educated villagers, small rural landowners, urban lower middle classes, and trade unionists, expanding the regime's initially narrow base to "outflank its rivals in the old urban center" (1991: 35). Likewise, Waldner stresses the salience of class over sect in the allocation of state resources (1999: 75). For Sadowski, a system of patronage in which all groups engage is the key mechanism of the Syrian polity (1988).

17. Lailat al-Qadr, the twenty-seventh of Ramadan, the night the Qur'an descended.

18. A similar situation has arisen in Crete, where virtually all of the families who formed the commercial elite of Rethemnos at the turn of the century have since left the town. Those who remain bemoan the loss of "aristocratic values," even though they themselves can rarely claim aristocratic status (Herzfeld 1991: 66).

19. Handler's problematic assumption that anthropologists are all Westerners who study the non-West exclusively also warrants challenge.

20. Walter Armbrust, personal communication.

21. For work on agonism among rural men, see Campbell 1964; Herzfeld 1985; Gilsenan 1996. Meneley (1996) looks at contestation among Yemeni townswomen.

22. See, for instance, Pitt-Rivers 1963, 1977; Péristiany 1966, 1976; Davis 1977; Gilmore 1987.

23. Gilmore's (1982) review of the anthropology of the Mediterranean depicts a budding field and suggests interesting areas for further research. Unfortunately, comparative work on Mediterranean societies virtually ceased in the 1990s, with the notable exception of Péristiany and Pitt-Rivers 1992.

24. For a contemporary Muslim philosophical exploration of linkages between Mediterranean cultures, see Arkoun 1994.

25. There is very little anthropological or other material available on Middle Eastern elite classes. For Saudi Arabian elites, see Altorki 1986 and Yamani 1987.

1. "His Family Had a House in Malki, So We Thought He Was All Right"

1. The political turmoil in 1950s Damascus is depicted, through the eyes of a child, in Malas's 1984 feature film *Dreams of the City* (*Ahlam al-Madina*). In one amusing refrain, a shopkeeper periodically changes the portrait of the leader hanging in his store.

2. For critiques of the Islamic City concept, see D. Eickelman 1974; Brown 1986; AlSayyad 1992; J. Abu-Lughod 1987.

3. Most recent studies of Middle Eastern cities move away from the Islamic City concept and toward ethnographic specificity (Singerman 1995; Hoodfar 1997).

4. I use the term "quarter" to connote the Damascene *hayy* and *hara,* although I am aware that there is some disagreement over its precision (Khoury 1984).

5. My use of the phrase "Old Damascus" (Dimashq al-Qadimeh) reflects Damascene colloquial usage in that it includes pre-twentieth-century neighborhoods lying outside the Old City walls.

6. Exchange rate: 50 SP = 1 USD.

7. Bookstores selling inexpensive Arabic-language and religious books are located south of Bawabat Salhiyyeh Square.

8. Prickly pears, genus *Opuntia,* are a New World import. I was unable to date their introduction into Syria.

9. Foreign-language classes are a major social activity for well-heeled youths, who pass many evenings in the several institutes dotting Malki and Abu Rummaneh.

10. The Society of Friends of Damascus (Jam'iat Asdiqa' Dimashq).

2. "That Color Looks Great on You"

1. Wealthy women of the 1920s and 1930s were among the city's first cinema-goers, an activity that required both disposable income and familiarity with French or English (Thompson 2001).

2. Wolf's theory of a specifically post-feminist "beauty myth" is not entirely persuasive; her own use of nineteenth-century literature reflects the importance of appearance for women long before their twentieth-century emancipation.

3. These are Intermarkets, Publigraphics, TMI, and Saatchi and Saatchi.

4. The social significance of serial dramas cannot be overstressed. Lila Abu-Lughod presents the compelling theory that among Egyptian women television serial melodramas are engendering new notions of personhood, as individuals increasingly see themselves in terms of the characters whose lives they watch unfold on the screen (1996).

5. To ensure the appearance of virginity on the wedding night, some women undergo a surgical procedure in which the hymen is restitched. For analyses of this practice in the Middle East, see Khair-Badawi 1986 and Dialmy 2002/2003.

6. Ossman points to this problem in urban Morocco, where, as in Damascus, young adults have difficulty finding legitimate spaces in which to form opposite-sex relationships. The park and street serve as meeting places, and the gaze is paramount (1994: 46–47). The same is true in Cairo, where "there is no socially sanctioned custom of single males and females socializing in an unchaperoned setting" (Armbrust 1998: 418).

7. Rana Kabbani (1998) refers to a form of depilation using *halaweh,* a mixture of sugar and water (sometimes with lemon juice). The Body Shop

cosmetics chain has introduced this method, labeled "sugaring," to Western markets.

8. An Old City neighborhood in southern Damascus.

9. A woman's gold forms a means of insurance.

10. A type of silk fabric.

11. The phrase "the problem of what to wear" is borrowed from Tarlo's (1996) study of fashion among Indian elites.

12. As a Syrian woman quoted in Lindisfarne-Tapper and Ingham's all-too-brief description of Damascene wedding fashions puts it: "There is no place in Damascus now for classic simplicity" (1997a: 32).

13. Here Damascus contrasts with Cairo, where an industry in elaborate, ornate *hijab* clothing offers an alternative to the plainer styles worn in Syria.

14. For instance, one young woman was a victim of incest, another of spousal abuse.

15. See El-Guindi 1981, 1999; Rugh 1986; Zuhur 1992; Macleod 1991.

16. See, for instance, Rosenfeld 1974; Makhlouf 1979; Altorki 1986; Watson 1992; Early 1993; Hoodfar 1997.

17. In her study of childrearing in a Syrian village, Rugh finds that children have little time or opportunity to develop friendships outside the home, and that relationships with non-relatives were perceived as dangerous for the young and inexperienced (1997: 225–226). This practice would more greatly affect females, whose restriction to the home continues well into adulthood.

18. In her study of visiting practices in Yemen, Meneley describes a similarly agonistic form of sociability, an "inclination for invidious distinction" (1996: 33) among the women of Zabid.

19. Cowan hints at this in discussing Greek women's conversation over coffee; yet here the competition is referred to as "gossip" (1991: 185).

20. Wikan's second book on Cairo, *Tomorrow, God Willing* (1996), is more in keeping with the general trend to romanticize Middle Eastern women.

21. The difficulty of building friendships with Syrian women, in sharp contrast to the ease of our male counterparts' relationships with Syrian men, was a continual lament among Western women researchers in Damascus. I first encountered this discrepancy as a student of Arabic living in a Damascus University dormitory. My American colleague and I made no friends in the women's section—despite much effort—and moved out as soon as possible, while our fellow students in the men's section stayed the entire year, forming intensely close friendships among their housemates that have lasted to this day.

22. I restrict my own use of the term "friend" to the few women with whom I have managed to maintain close relationships of sentiment.

23. A notable exception is al-Rasheed's study of Iraqi Christians in London, in which she describes her fieldwork experience as a journey "From Rejection to Acquaintance" (1998: 20–23).

24. Hoodfar's fieldwork provides an instance of cultural compromise: living alone in an impoverished quarter of Cairo, she became a role model as a young unmarried woman who was both a proper Muslim and an independent professional. Her example inspired informant families to allow their daughters to work abroad (1997: 32).

3. Old Damascus Commodified

1. With the 1995 opening of the elaborate Versailles-style Qasr al-Nubala (Nobles' Palace), the Sheraton has been somewhat eclipsed as prime site for elite weddings and other celebrations.

2. McGuinness notes a similar phenomenon in Tunis, where "a return to the medina" touted in the local press involved restoration of old houses for use as art galleries, restaurants, and performance spaces rather than as residences (2001).

3. The caravan route of the pilgrimage to Mecca.

4. A similar conflict occurs in Crete, where bureaucrats, working with a concept of "monumental time," seek to preserve the architecture of Old Rethemnos from its current residents' attempts at modernization (Herzfeld 1991).

5. The Night of Power (Laylat al-Qadr), the twenty-seventh of Ramadan, the night the Qur'an was revealed. A *dhikr* is a Sufi ceremony of remembrance, in which the names or qualities of God are intoned.

6. A French architect and urban planner who designed plans for the modernization of Damascus that were partially implemented, first by French Mandate authorities and later by the Ba'thist government.

7. Aleppines refer to an insincere invitation as an "*'azimeh shamiyyeh*," a "Damascene invitation." I am grateful to Jonathan Shannon for pointing this out.

4. Ramadan Lived and Consumed

1. Some non-Damascenes living in Damascus—including 'Alawis—do in fact fast during Ramadan. Yet public displays of fast-related activities are generally associated with Damasceneness.

2. Literally "upside down," a rich dish of layered lamb pieces, rice, fried eggplant, and nuts, which is turned out onto a plate after cooking and resembles a layer cake.

3. Vegetable availability in Syria remains seasonal.

4. An Arab lute.

5. A special prayer said during Ramadan, which involves the bending of the torso and then prostration (Yamani 1987: 89).

6. This was very much true in 1993, but by the end of the following year middle-class households were gaining access to satellite dishes.

7. For more on Shaykh al-Buti, see Christmann 1998, 2000.

8. The term *musalsal* (pl. *musalsalat*) is sometimes translated as "soap opera." Yet *musalsalat* are closer to short dramatic miniseries like *Roots* or

North and South than they are to the long-running daytime dramas of American television. The word *musalsal* literally means "chained" or "continuous." I have rendered it as "series." For material on Egyptian *musalsalat,* see Armbrust (1996) and L. Abu-Lughod (1993, 1995).

9. For a discussion of *Hilmiyya Nights,* see L. Abu-Lughod 1995.

10. This practice is mentioned in Daoud's entertaining autobiographical treatment of mustaches in Arab culture (2000: 275).

11. Refers to the hunger and hardship Syrians endured during the last days of the Ottoman Empire, when many were conscripted into the Ottoman army to fight in the Balkan wars.

12. This concern with positive representation is not limited to Damascenes. Members of Syria's Druze population were angered over a recent Syrian film's "negative" depiction of a Druze woman leaving her husband for another man. This film, *al-Lajat,* won second prize at the Damascus International Film Festival of 1995. Yet it was not shown outside the festival because Druze sheikhs threatened to attack any cinema that dared run it. In addition, some Aleppines objected to negative aspects of *The Silk Bazaar* (*Khan al-Harir*), a 1996 Ramadan television series set in Aleppo considered by many to be Syria's finest television production to date. The director of *Brothers of the Earth* (*Ukhwat al-Turab*), another 1996 Ramadan drama, was physically attacked while filming the series in Suweida, southern Syria, by local people who suspected he would portray their region in an unflattering light.

13. Depictions of Christians in Middle Eastern mass media are rare, despite their frequent involvement in media production.

14. An abridged version of *O Wealth of Damascus* has been published in English as *Daughter of Damascus,* translated by Andrea Rugh.

15. A Christian quarter of Damascus.

16. This novel has been published in English as *Sabriya: Damascus Bitter Sweet.*

17. See Kawakibi 1997 on depictions of Syrian history in *musalsalat* of the mid-1990s.

18. Questions about government intentions dominated the discussion of my *Damascene Days* presentation at the conference "Anthropology and Television," University of Kent (a section of the 1996 Ethnographic Film Festival).

5. Conservation, Preservation, and Celebration

1. The Asad Library book fair, held annually in September.

2. *Al-turath* (heritage) often refers to religious heritage, but Husayni is using the term in its broadest sense.

3. Maktab 'Anbar was an elite boys' school, Old Damascus's equivalent of Britain's Eton, or Egypt's Victoria College.

4. Written by Najat Qassab Hasan in response to a more critical work, Bashir al-Azma's *Generation of Defeat* (*Jil al-Hazima*).

5. For more on the ambiguous position of the vernacular in Arabic language and culture, see Armbrust 1996: 37–62 and Ferguson 1971 (1959).

6. A reference to a saying (*hadith*) of the prophet Muhammad regarding the appropriate time to break fast during Ramadan, when it is so dark that a black thread can no longer be distinguished from a white thread, and more generally, when to say the dawn prayer.

7. Tergeman told me that Rugh made these editorial decisions (interview, 18 February 1996).

8. The al-Asad regime demolished the Old City of Hama, which provided a sanctuary and staging point for Sunni Islamist groups during the 1982 uprising.

9. Mu'awiya founded the Umayyad caliphate, with Damascus as its capital, in A.D. 661.

10. Adonis had gone to a conference also attended by an Israeli.

References

Abu-Lughod, Janet L. 1961. "Migrant Adjustment to Urban Life: The Egyptian Case." *American Journal of Sociology* 76: 22–32.

— 1971. *Cairo: 1001 Years of the City Victorious.* Princeton, N.J.: Princeton University Press.

— 1980. *Rabat: Urban Apartheid in Morocco.* Princeton, N.J.: Princeton University Press.

— 1987. "The Islamic City—Historic Myth, Islamic Essence, and Contemporary Relevance." *International Journal of Middle East Studies* 19 (2): 155–176.

Abu-Lughod, Lila. 1986. *Veiled Sentiments: Honor and Poetry in a Bedouin Society.* Berkeley and Los Angeles: University of California Press.

— 1990. "Anthropology's Orient: The Boundaries of Theory in the Arab World." In *Theory, Politics, and the Arab World: Critical Responses,* edited by Hisham Sharabi, 81–131. New York: Routledge.

— 1991. "Writing against Culture." In *Recapturing Anthropology,* edited by Richard Fox, 137–162. Santa Fe, N.Mex.: School of American Research Press.

— 1993. "Finding a Place for Islam: Egyptian Television Serials and the National Interest." *Public Culture* 5 (3): 493–513.

— 1995. "The Objects of Soap Opera: Egyptian Television and the Cultural Politics of Modernity." In *Worlds Apart: Modernity through the Prism of the Local,* edited by Daniel Miller, 190–210. London: Routledge.

— 1996. "Language and the Politics of Emotion." Twenty-first George Antonius Memorial Lecture, Middle East Center, St. Antony's College, Oxford, 13 June.

Abu Shanab, 'Adil. 1988. *Dimashq Ayyam Zaman* (Damascus in the days of old). Damascus: al-Sham li-l-Dirasat wal-Nashr.

— 1994. "*Abu Kamil* Yartadi Taqiyyat al-Ikhfa': al-Mu'allif Khalata al-Habil bil-Nabil wa Saqata fi Dars al-Tarikh" (*Abu Kamil* hides his head: The writer creates confusion, and fails a history test). *Funun,* 23 March, 24–25.

Adelkhah, Fariba. 1999. *Being Modern in Iran.* Translated by Jonathan Derrick. London: Hurst and Company.

al-'Allaf, Ahmad Hilmi. 1976. *Dimashq fi Matla' al-Qarn al-'Ishrin* (Damascus at the rise of the twentieth century). Damascus: Dar Dimashq.

AlSayyad, Nezar. 1991. *Cities and Caliphs: On the Genesis of Arab Muslim Cities.* Westport, Conn.: Greenwood Press.

— 1992. "The Islamic City as a Colonial Enterprise." In *Forms of Dominance: On the Architecture of the Colonial Enterprise,* edited by Nezar AlSayyad, 27–43. Aldershot: Avebury.

Altorki, Soraya. 1986. *Women in Saudi Arabia: Ideology and Behavior among the Elite.* New York: Columbia University Press.

———. 1988. "At Home in the Field." In *Arab Women in the Field: Studying Your Own Society,* edited by Soraya Altorki and Camillia Fawzi El-Sohl, 49–68. Syracuse, N.Y.: Syracuse University Press.

Altorki, Soraya, and Camillia Fawzi El-Solh, eds. 1988. *Arab Women in the Field: Studying Your Own Society.* Syracuse, N.Y.: Syracuse University Press.

Anderson, Benedict. 1983. *Imagined Communities: Reflections on the Origin and Spread of Nationalism.* London: Verso.

Antoun, Richard T. 1968. "The Social Significance of Ramadan in an Arab Village." *Muslim World* 58 (1, 2): 36–42, 95–104.

Appadurai, Arjun. 1986. "On Culinary Authenticity" (letter to the editor). *Anthropology Today* 2 (4): 25.

———. 1988. "How to Make a National Cuisine: Cookbooks in Contemporary India." *Comparative Studies in Society and History* 30 (1): 3–24.

———. 1990. "Disjuncture and Difference in the Global Cultural Ecumene." *Public Culture* 2 (2): 1–24.

Arkoun, Muhammad. 1994. *Rethinking Islam: Common Questions, Uncommon Answers.* Translated by Robert D. Lee. Boulder, Colo.: Westview Press.

Armbrust, Walter Tice. 1996. *Mass Consumption and Modernism in Egypt.* Cambridge: Cambridge University Press.

———. 1998. "When the Lights Go Down in Cairo: Cinema as Secular Ritual." *Visual Anthropology* 10 (2–4): 413–442.

———. 2001. "Colonizing Popular Culture or Creating Modernity? Architectural Metaphors and Egyptian Media." In *Middle Eastern Cities 1900–1950: Public Spaces and Public Spheres in Transformation,* edited by Hans Chr. Korsholm Nielsen and Jakob Skovgaard-Petersen, 20–43. Aarhus: Aarhus University Press.

al-Aswad, Nizar. 1990. *al-Hikayat al-Sha‘biyya al-Dimashqiyya* (Damscene folk tales). Damascus.

‘Ayadah, Lou‘i. 1994. "Mulahazat Hawla al-Musalsal al-Mahalli *Abu Kamil* fi Juz’ihi al-Thani" (Observations on the local series *Abu Kamil* in its second part). *Funun,* 18 April, 12.

Bahout, Joseph. 1994. "The Syrian Business Community, Its Politics and Prospects." In *Contemporary Syria: Liberalization between Cold War and Peace,* edited by Eberhard Kienle, 42–80. London: British Academic Press.

al-Bahra, Nasr al-Din. 1992. *Dimashq al-Asrar* (Damascus of secrets). Damascus: Al-Jumhuriyya.

Barth, Fredrik. 1969. *Ethnic Groups and Boundaries: The Social Organization of Cultural Difference.* Oslo: Universitetsforlaget.

Batatu, Hanna 1978. *The Old Social Classes and the Revolutionary Movements of Iraq.* Princeton, N.J.: Princeton University Press.

———. 1981. "Some Observations on the Social Roots of Syria's Ruling Military Group and the Causes for Its Dominance." *Middle East Journal* 35 (3): 331–344.

1999. *Syria's Peasantry, the Descendants of Its Lesser Rural Notables, and Their Politics.* Princeton, N.J.: Princeton University Press.

Benjamin, Walter. 1978. "Paris, Capital of the Nineteenth Century." In Benjamin, *Reflections: Essays, Aphorisms, Autobiographical Writings,* edited by Peter Demetz, translated by Edmund Jephcott, 146–162. New York: Schocken Books.

Bianco, Stefano. 2000. *Urban Form in the Arab World: Past and Present.* London: Thames and Hudson.

Bourdieu, Pierre. 1977. *Outline of a Theory of Practice.* Translated by Richard Nice. Cambridge: Cambridge University Press.

1979. "The Disenchantment of the World." In *Algeria 1960,* translated by Richard Nice, 1–94. Cambridge: Cambridge University Press.

1984. *Distinction: A Social Critique of the Judgment of Taste.* London: Routledge and Kegan Paul.

Breckenridge, Carol, and Arjun Appadurai. 1988. "Editor's Comments." *Public Culture* 1 (1): 1–4.

Brown, Kenneth L. 1986. "The Use of a Concept: The Muslim City." In *Middle Eastern Cities in Comparative Perspective,* edited by Kenneth L. Brown, Michele Jole, Peter Sluglett, and Sami Zubaida, 73–82. London: Ithaca Press.

Buitelaar, Marjo. 1993. *Fasting and Feasting in Morocco: Women's Participation in Ramadan.* Oxford: Berg.

Calvino, Italo. 1969. *Time and the Hunter.* Translated by William Weaver. London: Harcourt, Brace and World.

Campbell, John K. 1964. *Honour, Family, and Patronage: A Study of Institutions and Moral Values in a Greek Mountain Community.* Oxford: Clarendon Press.

Çelik, Zeynep. 1986. *The Remaking of Istanbul: Portrait of an Ottoman City in the Nineteenth Century.* Seattle: University of Washington Press.

1997. *Urban Forms and Colonial Confrontations: Algiers under French Rule.* Berkeley and Los Angeles: University of California Press.

Christmann, Andreas. 1998. "Islamic Scholar and Religious Leader: A Portrait of Shaykh Muhammad Saʿid Ramadan al-Buti." *Islam and Christian-Muslim Relations* 9 (2): 149–169.

2000. "Islamic Scholar and Religious Leader: Shaikh Muhammad Said Ramadan al-Buti." In *Islam and Modernity: Muslim Intellectuals Respond,* edited by John Cooper, Ronald Nettler, and Mohamed Mahmoud, 57–81. London: I. B. Tauris.

Clifford, James. 1988. *The Predicament of Culture: Twentieth-Century Ethnography, Literature, and Art.* Cambridge, Mass.: Harvard University Press.

Colloredo-Mansfield, Rudi. 1999. *The Native Leisure Class: Consumption and Cultural Creativity in the Andes.* Chicago: University of Chicago Press.

Coon, Carleton S. 1951. *Caravan: The Story of the Middle East.* New York: Holt, Rinehart and Winston.

Cowan, Jane K. 1991. "Going Out for Coffee? Contesting the Grounds of Gendered Pleasures in Everyday Sociability." In *Contested Identities: Gen-*

der and Kinship in Modern Greece, edited by Peter Loizos and Evthymios Papataxiarchis, 180–202. Princeton, N.J.: Princeton University Press.

Daoud, Hassan. 2000. "Those Two Heavy Wings of Manhood: On Moustaches." In *Imagined Masculinities: Male Identity and Culture in the Modern Middle East,* edited by Mai Ghoussoub and Emma Sinclair-Webb, 273–280. London: Saqi Books.

Das, Veena. 1995. "On Soap Opera: What Kind of Object Is It?" In *Worlds Apart: Modernity through the Prism of the Local,* edited by Daniel Miller, 169–189. London: Routledge.

Davis, John. 1977. *People of the Mediterranean: An Essay in Comparative Anthropology.* London: Routledge and Kegan Paul.

Debord, Guy. 1994 (1967). *The Society of the Spectacle.* New York: Zone Books.

Devlin, John F. 1976. *The Ba'th Party: A History from Its Origins to 1966.* Stanford, Calif.: Hoover Institution Press.

Dialmy, Abdessamad. 2002/2003. "Premarital Sexuality in Morocco." *Al-Raida* 20 (99): 75–83.

Douglas, Mary. 1966. *Purity and Danger: An Analysis of the Concepts of Pollution and Taboo.* London: Routledge and Kegan Paul.

Dresch, Paul. 2000. "Wilderness of Mirrors: Truth and Vulnerability in Middle Eastern Fieldwork." In *Anthropologists in a Wider World,* edited by Paul Dresch, Wendy James, and David Parkin, 109–127. New York: Berghahn Books.

Drysdale, Alasdair. 1981. "The Syrian Political Elite: A Spatial and Social Analysis." *Middle Eastern Studies* 17 (1): 3–30.

Early, Evelyn A. 1993. *Baladi Women of Cairo: Playing with an Egg and a Stone.* Boulder, Colo.: Lynne Rienner.

Edgeworth, Maria. 1992 (1800). *Castle Rackrent and Ennui.* Edited by Marilyn Butler. London: Penguin.

Eickelman, Christine. 1984. *Women and Community in Oman.* New York: New York University Press.

Eickelman, Dale F. 1974. "Is There an Islamic City? The Making of a Quarter in a Moroccan Town." *International Journal of Middle Eastern Studies* 5 (3): 274–278.

    1991. "Traditional Islamic Learning and Ideas of the Person in the Twentieth Century." In *Middle Eastern Lives: The Practice of Biography and Self-Narrative,* edited by Martin Kramer, 35–59. Syracuse, N.Y.: Syracuse University Press.

    1998. *The Middle East and Central Asia: An Anthropological Approach.* 3d ed. Upper Saddle River, N.J.: Prentice Hall

Elias, Norbert, and John L. Scotson. 1994 (1965). *The Established and the Outsiders.* London: Sage.

Erman, Tahire. 1998. "Becoming 'Urban' or Remaining 'Rural': The Views of Turkish Rural-to- Urban Migrants on the 'Integration' Question." *International Journal of Middle East Studies* 30 (4): 541–561.

Errington, Shelly. 1998. *The Death of Primitive Art and Other Tales of Progress.* Berkeley and Los Angeles: University of California Press.

Fallers, L. A. 1974. "Notes on an Advent Ramadan." *Journal of the American Academy of Religion* 42 (1): 35–52.

Ferguson, Charles. 1971 (1959). "Diglossia." In *Language, Structure, and Language Use: Essays by Charles Ferguson,* selected and introduced by Anwar S. Dil. Stanford, Calif.: Stanford University Press.

Fernandez, James W. 1986. *Persuasions and Performances: The Play of Tropes in Culture.* Bloomington: Indiana University Press.

Finkelstein, Joanne. 1989. *Dining Out: A Sociology of Modern Manners.* New York: New York University Press.

Fiske, John. 1987. *Television Culture.* London: Methuen.

Gans, Herbert J. 1962. *The Urban Villagers: Group and Class in the Life of Italian-Americans.* New York: Free Press of Glencoe.

Geertz, Clifford. 1976. "From the Native's Point of View: On the Nature of Anthropological Understanding." In *Meaning in Anthropology,* edited by Keith A. Basso and Harry A. Selby, 221–238. Albuquerque, N.Mex.: School of American Research Press.

—— 1995. *After the Fact: Two Countries, Four Decades, One Anthropologist.* Cambridge: Harvard University Press.

Gelvin, James. 1998. *Divided Loyalties: Nationalism and Mass Politics at the Close of Empire.* Berkeley and Los Angeles: University of California Press.

Ghannam, Farha. 1997. "Re-imagining the Global: Relocation and Local Identities in Cairo." In *Space, Culture, and Power: New Identities in Globalizing Cities,* edited by Ayşe Öncü and Petra Weyland, 119–139. London: Zed Books.

al-Ghazzi, Nadia. 1991. *Qadiya Khassa Jiddan* (A very private matter). Damascus: Dar Tlas.

Giddens, Anthony. 1979. *Central Problems in Social Theory: Action, Structure, and Contradiction in Social Analysis.* Berkeley and Los Angeles: University of California Press.

Gilmore, David. 1982. "Anthropology of the Mediterranean Area." *Annual Review of Anthropology* 11: 175–205.

——, ed. 1987. *Honour, Shame, and the Unity of the Mediterranean.* Washington, D.C.: American Anthropological Association.

Gilsenan, Michael. 1996. *Lords of the Lebanese Marches: Violence and Narrative in an Arab Society.* London: I. B. Tauris.

Ginsburg, Faye D. 1989. *Contested Lives: The Abortion Debate in an American Community.* Berkeley and Los Angeles: University of California Press.

Glass, Charles. 1990. *Tribes with Flags: A Journey Curtailed.* London: Secker and Warburg.

Golde, Peggy, ed. 1986 (1970). *Women in the Field: Anthropological Experiences.* 2d ed. Berkeley and Los Angeles: University of California Press.

Grundy, Isobel. 1999. *Lady Mary Wortley Montagu: Comet of the Enlightenment.* Oxford: Oxford University Press.

El-Guindi, Fadwa. 1981. "Veiling *Infitah* with Muslim Ethic: Egypt's Contemporary Islamic Movement." *Social Problems* 28 (4): 465–487.

1999. *Veil: Modesty, Privacy, and Resistance.* Oxford: Berg.

Haim, Sylvia, ed. 1962. *Arab Nationalism: An Anthology.* Berkeley and Los Angeles: University of California Press.

Hamadeh, Shirine. 1992. "Creating the Traditional City: A French Project." In *Forms of Dominance: On the Architecture and Urbanism of Colonial Enterprise,* edited by Nezar AlSayyad, 241–257. Aldershot: Avebury.

Hammond, Andrew. 2002. "The State of Syria's Media: 'Damascus Spring' or Indian Summer?" *World Press Review,* 3 January. http://www.worldpress.org/Mideast/886.cfm.

Handler, Richard. 1985. "On Having a National Culture: Nationalism and the Preservation of Quebec's Partimoine." In *Objects and Others: Essays in Museums and Material Culture,* edited by George W. Stocking Jr. Madison: University of Wisconsin Press.

1986. "Authenticity." *Anthropology Today* 2 (2): 2–4.

Herzfeld, Michael. 1985. *The Poetics of Manhood: Contest and Identity in a Greek Mountain Village.* Princeton, N.J.: Princeton University Press.

1987. "As in Your Own House: Hospitality, Ethnography, and the Stereotypes of Mediterranean Society." In *Honour, Shame, and the Unity of the Mediterranean,* edited by David Gilmore, 75–89. Washington, D.C.: American Anthropological Association.

1991. *A Place in History: Social and Monumental Time in a Cretan Town.* Princeton, N.J.: Princeton University Press.

1997. *Cultural Intimacy: Social Poetics in the Nation-State.* New York: Routledge.

Hinnebusch, Raymond A. 1989. *Peasant and Bureaucracy in Baʿthist Syria: The Political Economy of Rural Development.* Boulder, Colo.: Westview Press.

1990. *Authoritarian Power and State Formation in Baʿthist Syria.* Boulder, Colo.: Westview Press.

1991. "Class and State in Baʿthist Syria." In *Syria: Society, Culture, and Polity,* edited by Richard T. Antoun and Donald Quataert, 29–47. Albany: State University of New York Press.

Hobsbawm, Eric, and Terence Ranger, eds. 1983. *The Invention of Tradition.* Cambridge: Cambridge University Press.

Hoodfar, Homa. 1997. *Between Marriage and the Market: Intimate Politics and Survival in Cairo.* Berkeley and Los Angeles: University of California Press.

Hopwood, Derek. 1988. *Syria 1945–1986: Politics and Society.* London: Unwin Hyman.

Hourani, Albert, and S. M. Stern. 1970. *The Islamic City.* Philadelphia: University of Pennsylvania Press.

Ibish, Ahmad, and Qutayba Shihabi. 1996. *Maʿalim Dimashq al-Tarikhiyya: Dirasa Tarikhiyya wa-Lughawiyya ʿan Ahyaʾiha wa-Mawaʿqiha al-Qadima, Turathiha wa ʿUsuliha wa Ishtiqaq Asmaʾiha* (Historical monuments of Damascus). Damascus: Ministry of Culture.

Ibn Kinan, Muhammad. 1994. *Yawmiyyat Shamiyya: 1111/1699–1153/1740.* Edited by Akram Hasan ʿUlabi. Damascus: Dar al-Tabbah.

al-Idlibi, Ulfat. 1980. *Dimashq: Ya Basmat al-Huzn* (Damascus: O smile of sadness). Damascus: Dar Tlas.

1995. *Sabriya: Damascus Bitter Sweet.* Translated by Peter Clark. London: Quartet.

Jabbur, Diana. 1993. *"Ayyam Shamiyya:* al-Sham fi Ruh al-Nas wal-Ikhraj" (*Damascene Days*: Damascus in the spirit of text and moving picture). *Fann,* 17 May, 26–27.

Jansen, Willy. 1987. *Women without Men: Gender and Marginality in an Algerian Town.* Leiden, Netherlands: Brill.

Kabbani, Rana. 1998. "Global Beauty: Damascus." *Vogue* (UK) 164 (2394) (January): 134–135.

Karpat, Kemal H. 1976. *The Gecekondu: Rural Migration and Urbanization.* Cambridge: Cambridge University Press.

Kawakibi, Salam. 1997. "Le rôle de la télévision dans la relecture de l'histoire." *Maghreb-Machrek* 158: 47–55.

Kayyal, Munir. n.d. *Ramadan wa Taqaliduhu al-Dimashqiyya* (Ramadan and its Damascene traditions). Damascus: Author.

1984. *Ya Sham: fil-Turath al-Shaʿbi al-Dimashqi* (O Damascus: On Damascene popular cultural heritage). Damascus: Ittihad al-Kuttab al-ʿArab.

1986. *al-Hammamat al-Dimashqiyya* (Damascene bath houses). Damascus: Ibn Khaldun Press.

1987. *Hikayat Dimashqiyya* (Damascene tales). Damascus: Dar al-Katib al-ʿArabi.

1992. *Ramadan fil-Sham Ayyam Zaman* (Ramadan in the Damascus of olden days). Damascus: Muʾassasat al-Nuri.

Keenan, Brigid. 2000. *Damascus: Hidden Treasures of the Old City.* Tim Beddow, photographer. London: Thames and Hudson.

Kepel, Gilles. 1987. *Les banlieues de l'Islam.* Paris: Éditions du Seuil.

Khair-Badawi, Marie-Thérèse. 1986. *Le désir amputé; vécu sexuel des femmes libanaises.* Paris: L'Harmattan.

Khalaf, Sulayman N. 2001. "Globalisation and Heritage Revival in the Gulf: An Anthropological Look at Dubai Heritage Village." Paper delivered at the "Globalisation and the Gulf" conference, Institute of Arab and Islamic Studies, University of Exeter, 2–4 July.

al-Khalil, Samir. 1989. *Republic of Fear.* Berkeley and Los Angeles: University of California Press.

1992. *The Monument: Art, Vulgarity, and Responsibility in Iraq.* London: André Deutsch.

Khost, Nadia. 1989. *al-Hijra min al-Jinna* (Exile from paradise). Damascus: al-Ahli Press.

1991. "Genuineness of Damascus." In *Dimashq esh-Sham: Texts and Pictures about the Oldest Inhabited City in the World,* edited by Ayoub Saadieh, translated by Walid Shehadeh, 21–24. Damascus: Ministry of Tourism.

1993. *Dimashq: Dhakirat al-Insan wal-Hajar* (Damascus: Memory of people and stone). Damascus: Nadwat al-Thaqafa al-Nisaʾiyya.

1995. *Hubb fi Bilad al-Sham* (Love in the lands of Damascus). Damascus: Ittihad al-Kuttab al-ʿArab.

Khoury, Philip S. 1983. *Urban Notables and Arab Nationalism: The Politics of Damascus 1860–1920.* Cambridge: Cambridge University Press.

1984. "Syrian Urban Politics in Transition: The Quarters of Damascus during the French Mandate." *International Journal of Middle East Studies* 16 (4): 507–540.

Khuri, Fuad I. 1991. "The Alawis of Syria: Religious Ideology and Organization." In *Syria: Society, Culture, and Polity,* edited by Richard T. Antoun and Donald Quataert. Albany: State University of New York Press.

Khuri, Colette. 1961. *Layla Wahida* (One night). Beirut: al-Maktab al-Tijari

al-Kisan, Jan. 1994. "Awwal Kalima" (First word). Editor's comments, *Funun,* 11 April, 2.

al-Kisan, Randa. 1993. "al-Fannan Rafiq Sbaiʿi: Zgurti *Ayyam Shamiyya* Jassada Qiyam al-Shakhsiyya al-Shaʿbiyya" (The actor Rafiq Sbaiʿi, the Zgurti of *Damascene Days,* embodies the values of the folk character). *Funun,* 22 March, 20–21.

Kurd ʿAli, Muhammad. 1944. *Dimashq: Madinat al-Sihr wa al-Shiʿr* (Damascus: City of poetry and enchantment). Damascus: Dar al-Fikr.

Lampedusa, Giuseppe di. 1960. *The Leopard.* Translated by Archibald Colquhoun. New York: Pantheon Books.

Lancaster, John. 1998. "Syria: The Hollywood of the Middle East?" *Washington Post,* 2 February, S-9.

Lee, Robert D. 1997. *Overcoming Tradition and Modernity: The Search for an Islamic Authenticity.* Boulder, Colo.: Westview Press.

Lefebvre, Henri, 1996. "The Right to the City." In *Writings on Cities,* edited and translated by Eleonore Kofman and Elizabeth Lebas, 147–159. Oxford: Blackwell.

LeVine, Mark. 2001. "The 'New-Old Jaffa': Tourism, Gentrification, and the Battle for Tel Aviv's Arab Neighbourhood." In *Consuming Tradition, Manufacturing Heritage: Global Norms and Urban Forms in the Age of Tourism,* edited by Nezar AlSayyad, 240–272. London: Routledge.

Lindisfarne-Tapper, Nancy, and Bruce Ingham. 1997a. "Approaches to the Study of Dress in the Middle East." In *Languages of Dress in the Middle East,* edited by Nancy Lindisfarne-Tapper and Bruce Ingham, 1–39. London: Curzon.

———, eds. 1997b. *Languages of Dress in the Middle East.* London: Curzon.

Longueness, Elizabeth. 1979. "The Class Nature of the State in Syria." *MERIP Reports* 9 (4): 3–4.

1985. "The Syrian Working Class Today." *MERIP Reports* 15 (6): 17–24.

Lowenthal, David. 1989. "Nostalgia Tells It Like It Wasn't." In *The Imagined Past: History and Nostalgia,* edited by Christopher Shaw and Malcolm Chase, 18–32. Manchester: Manchester University Press.

1996. *The Heritage Crusade and the Spoils of History.* London: Viking.

Lull, James. 1991. *China Turned On: Television, Reform, and Resistance.* London: Routledge.

Lutgendorf, Philip. 1995. "All in the (Ragu) Family: A Video Epic in Cultural Context." In *To Be Continued . . . Soap Operas around the World,* edited by Robert C. Allen, 321–353. London: Routledge.

Macleod, Arlene Elowe. 1991. *Accommodating Protest: Working Women, the New Veiling, and Change in Cairo.* New York: Columbia University Press.

Makhlouf, Carla. 1979. *Changing Veils: Women and Modernisation in North Yemen.* London: Croom Helm.

Mankekar, Purnima. 1993. "Television Tales and a Woman's Rage: A Nationalist Recasting of Draupadi's 'Disrobing.'" *Public Culture* 5 (3): 469–492.

1999. *Screening Culture, Viewing Politics: An Ethnography of Television, Womanhood, and National Postcolonial India.* Durham, N.C.: Duke University Press.

Mansur, Muhammad. 1994. "al-Hara al-Dimashqiyya: Khazzan Kabir lil-Qiyam al-ʿArabiyya" (The Damascene Quarter: A treasurehouse of Arab values). *Fann* 171: 60–63.

Massey, Doreen. 1994. "Double Articulation: A Place in the World." In *Displacements: Cultural Identities in Question,* edited by Angelika Bammer, 111–121. Bloomington: Indiana University Press.

McGuinness, Justin. 2001. "Neighbourhood Notes: Texture, Space, and Streetscape in the Médina of Tunis." In *The Walled Arab City in Literature, Architecture, and History: The Living Medina in the Maghrib,* edited by Susan Slyomovics, 97–120. London: Frank Cass.

Meijer, Roel. 1989. *History, Authenticity, and Politics: Tariq al-Bishri's Interpretation of Modern Egyptian History.* Occasional Paper 4. Amsterdam: Middle East Research Associates.

———, ed. 1999. *Cosmopolitanism, Identity, and Authenticity in the Middle East.* London: Curzon.

Melman, Billie. 1992. *Women's Orients: English Women and the Middle East, 1718–1918: Sexuality, Work, and Religion.* Basingstoke, U.K.: Macmillan.

Meneley, Anne. 1996. *Tournaments of Value: Sociability and Hierarchy in a Yemeni Town.* Toronto: University of Toronto Press.

Mennell, Stephen. 1994. "The Formation of We-Images: A Process Theory." In *Social Theory and the Politics of Identity,* edited by Craig Calhoun, 175–197. Oxford: Blackwell.

El-Messiri, Sawsan. 1978. *Ibn al-Balad: A Concept of Egyptian Identity.* Leiden, Netherlands: Brill.

Miller, Judith. 1984. "Tempers Rise as Shops Fall in Damascus Restoration." *New York Times,* 15 April, Sec. 1: 18.

Mina, Hanna. 1993. *Fragments of Memory: A Story of a Syrian Family.* Translated by Olive Kenny and Lorne Kenny. Austin: University of Texas Press.

Mitchell, Timothy. 1988. *Colonising Egypt*. Cambridge: Cambridge University Press.

2001. "Making the Nation: The Politics of Heritage in Egypt." In *Consuming Tradition, Manufacturing Heritage: Global Norms and Urban Forms in the Age of Tourism*, edited by Nezar AlSayyad, 212–238. London: Routledge.

Montigny, Annie. 1998. "Retour à la tradition au mois du Ramadan." *Techniques et culture* 31–32: 89–104.

Munif, Abd al-Rahman. 1996. *Story of a City: A Childhood in Amman*. Translated by Samira Kawar. London: Quartet Books.

Murabit, Muti'. 1961. *al-Nur wal-Nar fi Maktab 'Anbar* (Fire and light in Maktab 'Anbar). Damascus: Dar al-Fikr.

Nieuwenhuijze, C. A. O. van. 1997. *Paradise Lost: Reflections on the Struggle for Authenticity in the Middle East*. Leiden, Netherlands: E. J. Brill.

Öncü, Ayşe. 1997. "The Myth of the 'Ideal Home' Travels across Cultural Borders to Istanbul." In *Space, Culture, and Power*, edited by Ayşe Öncü and Petra Weyland, 56–72. London: Zed Books.

Ossman, Susan. 1994. *Picturing Casablanca: Portraits of Power in a Moroccan City*. Berkeley and Los Angeles: University of California Press.

Park, Robert E., Ernest W. Burgess, and Roderick D. McKenzie. 1925. *The City*. Chicago: University of Chicago Press.

Péristiany, J. G., ed. 1966. *Honour and Shame: The Values of Mediterranean Society*. Chicago: University of Chicago Press.

1976. *Mediterranean Family Structures*. Cambridge: Cambridge University Press.

Péristiany, J. G., and Julian Pitt-Rivers, eds. 1992. *Honor and Grace in Anthropology*. Cambridge: Cambridge University Press.

Perthes, Volker. 1991. "A Look at Syria's Upper Class: The Bourgeoisie and the Ba'th." *Middle East Report* 21 (3): 31–37.

1995. *The Political Economy of Syria under Asad*. London: I. B. Tauris.

Peterson, Scott. 1997. "Syrian Soaps Grab Arabs' Prime Time." *Christian Science Monitor*, 2 October. http://search.csmonitor.com/durable/1997/10/02/intl/intl.4.html.

Petonnet, Colette. 1972. "Espace, distance et dimension dans une société musulmane: À propos du bidonville marocain de Douar Doum à Rabat." *L'Homme* 12: 47–84.

Picard, Elizabeth. 1980. "Y a-t-il un probléme communautaire en Syrie?" *Maghreb-Machrek* 87: 7–21.

Pina-Cabral, João de. 2000. Introduction to *Elites: Choice, Leadership, and Succession*, edited by João de Pina-Cabral and Antónia Pedroso de Lima, 1–5. London: Berg.

Pitt-Rivers, Julian. 1977. *The Fate of Shechem: or, The Politics of Sex: Essays in the Anthropology of the Mediterranean*. Cambridge: Cambridge University Press.

————, ed. 1963. *Mediterranean Countrymen: Essays in the Social Anthropology of the Mediterranean.* Paris: Mouton.

Porter, Josias Leslie. 1870. *Five Years in Damascus: With Travels and Researches in Palmyra, Lebanon, and the Giant Cities of Bashan, and the Hauran.* 2d rev. ed. London: John Murray.

al-Qasimi, Zafir. *Maktab ʿAnbar: Suwar wa Dhikrayat min Hayatina al-Thaqafiyya wal-Siyasiyya wal-Ijtimaʿiyya* (Maktab ʿAnbar: Pictures and memories of our social, political, and cultural life). Beirut: al-Matbaʿa al-Kathulikiyya.

Qassab Hasan, Najat. 1988. *Hadith Dimashqi* (Damascene talk). Damascus: Dar Tlas.

————. 1993. *Jil al-Shajaʿa: Hatta ʿAmm 1945* (Generation of courage: Up to 1945). Damascus: Alif Baʾ al-Adib.

Rabinovich, Itamar. 1972. *Syria under the Baʿth, 1963–1966: The Army Party Symbiosis.* Jerusalem: Israel Universities Press.

Rabo, Annika. 1999. "Faith and Identity in Northeast Syria." In *Muslim Diversity: Local Islam in Global Contexts,* edited by Leif Manger, 173–199. Surrey, U.K.: Curzon and the Nordic Institute of Asian Studies.

al-Rasheed, Madawi. 1998. *Iraqi Assyrian Christians in London: The Construction of Ethnicity.* Lampeter: Edwin Mellen Press.

Redfield, Robert. 1941. *The Folk Culture of Yucatan.* Chicago: University of Chicago Press.

Reilly, James A. 1995. "Women in the Economic Life of Late-Ottoman Damascus." *Arabica* 42: 79–106.

————. 1996. "Inter-Confessional Relations in Nineteenth-Century Syria: Damascus, Homs, and Hama Compared." *Islam and Christian-Muslim Relations* 7 (2): 213–224.

Roberts, David. 1987. *The Baʿth and the Creation of Modern Syria.* London: Croom Helm.

Robins, Kevin. 1995. "Collective Emotion and Urban Culture." In *Managing Cities: The New Urban Context,* edited by Patsy Healey, Stuart Cameron, Simon Davoudi, Stephen Graham, and Ali Madani-Pour, 45–61. Chichester, U.K.: John Wiley and Sons.

Roden, Claudia. 1988. "Middle Eastern Cooking: The Legacy." *Aramco World* 39 (2): 2–3.

Rofel, Lisa. 1995. "The Melodrama of National Identity in Post-Tiananmen China." In *To Be Continued . . . Soap Operas around the World,* edited by Robert C. Allen, 301–320. London: Routledge.

Rojek, Chris. 1995. *Decentring Leisure: Rethinking Leisure Theory.* London: Sage.

Rosenfeld, Henry. 1974. "Non-Hierarchical, Hierarchical, and Masked Reciprocity in an Arab Village." *Anthropological Quarterly* 47 (1): 139–166.

Rugh, Andrea. 1986. *Reveal and Conceal: Dress in Contemporary Egypt.* Syracuse, N.Y.: Syracuse University Press.

————. 1994. Foreword to *Daughter of Damascus,* by Siham Tergeman, xiii–xxxi. Austin: University of Texas Press.

1997. *Within the Circle: Parents and Children in an Arab Village.* New York: Columbia University Press.

Saad, Reem Mikhail. 1994. "Peasants' Perceptions of Recent Egyptian History." Ph.D. diss., Institute of Social and Cultural Anthropology, University of Oxford.

Saadieh, Ayoub, ed. 1991. *Dimashq esh-Sham: Texts and Pictures about the Oldest Inhabited City in the World.* Translated by Walid Shehadeh. Damascus: Ministry of Tourism.

Sa'ar, Amalia. 2001. "Lonely in Your Firm Grip: Women in Israeli-Palestinian Families." *Journal of the Royal Anthropological Institute* 7 (4): 723–739.

Sadowski, Yahya. 1988. "Ba'thist Ethics and the Spirit of State Capitalism: Patronage and the Party in Contemporary Syria." In *Ideology and Power in the Middle East: Essays in Honor of George Lenczowski,* edited by Peter J. Chelkowski and Robert J. Pranger, 160–184. Durham, N.C.: Duke University Press.

Said, Edward. 1978. *Orientalism.* New York: Pantheon.

Saïd, Wafic, 2000. Preface to *Damascus: Hidden Treasures of the Old City,* by Brigid Keenan. London: Thames and Hudson.

Salamandra, Christa. 2003. "London's Arab Media and the Construction of Arabness." *Transnational Broadcasting Journal* 10 (spring/summer). http://www.tbsjournal.com/Archives/Spring03/salamandra.html.

Schami, Rafik. 1989. *A Handful of Stars.* London: Puffin Books.

1994. *Damascus Nights.* Translated by Philip Boehm. New York: Scribner.

Scheherezade. 1999. "My Sister Isabelle." In *Intimate Selving in Arab Families: Gender, Self, Identity,* edited by Suad Joseph, 92–105. Syracuse, N.Y.: Syracuse University Press.

Schilcher, Linda Schatkowski. 1985. *Families in Politics: Damascene Factions and Estates of the Eighteenth and Nineteenth Centuries.* Wiesbaden, Germany: F. Steiner.

Scott, James C. 1985. *Weapons of the Weak: Everyday Forms of Peasant Resistance.* New Haven, Conn.: Yale University Press.

1990. *Domination and the Art of Resistance: Hidden Transcripts.* New Haven, Conn.: Yale University Press.

Sharim, Akram. 1993. "Awwal Liqa' ma'a Katib Musalsal *Ayyam Shamiyya*" (First encounter with the writer of the series *Damascene Days*). *Funun,* 22 March, 18–19.

Shihabi Qutayba. 1986. *Dimashq: Tarikh wa Suwar* (Damascus: Pictures and history). Damascus: Ministry of Culture.

1990. *Aswaq Dimashq wa Mushayyadatiha al-Tarikhiyya* (Damascene suqs and their historical monuments). Damascus: Ministry of Culture.

1993. *Maadhin Dimashq: Tarikh wa Taraz* (Damascene minarets: History and style). Damascus: Ministry of Culture.

Shryock, Andrew. 1997. *Nationalism and the Genealogical Imagination: Oral History and Textual Authority in Tribal Jordan.* Berkeley and Los Angeles: University of California Press.

Shryock, Andrew, and Sally Howell. 2001. "'Ever a Guest in Our House': The Emir Abdullah, Shaykh Majid al-ʿAdwan, and the Practice of Jordanian House Politics, as Remembered by Umm Sultan, the Widow of Majid." *International Journal of Middle Eastern Studies* 33 (2): 247–269.

Simmel, Georg. 1955 (1908). "Conflict." Translated by Kurt H. Wolf. In *Conflict and the Web of Group Affiliations,* 11–123. New York: Free Press of Glencoe.

Singerman, Diane. 1995. *Avenues of Participation: Family Politics and Networks in Urban Quarters of Cairo.* Princeton, N.J.: Princeton University Press.

Singerman, Diane, and Hoda Hoodfar, eds. 1996. *Development, Change, and Gender in Cairo: A View from the Household.* Bloomington: Indiana University Press.

Slyomovics, Susan. 1998. *The Object of Memory: Arab and Jew Narrate the Palestinian Village.* Philadelphia: University of Pennsylvania Press.

Sollors, Werner, ed. 1989. *The Invention of Ethnicity.* Oxford: Oxford University Press.

Stokes, Martin. 2000. "'Beloved Istanbul': Realism and the Transnational Imaginary in Turkish Popular Culture." In *Mass Mediations: New Approaches to Popular Culture in the Middle East and Beyond,* edited by Walter Armbrust, 224–242. Berkeley: University of California Press.

Tapper, Nancy. 1998/99. "Changing Ceremonial and Gender Roles in the Arab World: An Anthropological Perspective." *Arab Affairs* 8: 117–133.

Tarlo, Emma. 1996. *Clothing Matters: Dress and Identity in India.* London: Hurst and Company.

Tergeman, Siham. 1990 (1969). *Ya Mal al-Sham.* Damascus: Alif Baʾ al-Adib.

1985. *Ah . . . Ya Ana.* Damascus: Dar Tlas.

1986. *Jabal al-Shaykh fi Bayti.* Damascus: al-Idara al-Siyasiyya lil-Jaysh wal-Quwwat al-Musallaha.

1994. *Daughter of Damascus.* Translated by Andrea Rugh. Austin: University of Texas Press.

Thompson, Elizabeth. 2000. *Colonial Citizens: Republican Rights, Paternal Privilege, and Gender in French Syria and Lebanon.* New York: Columbia University Press.

2001. "Sex and Cinema in Damascus: The Gendered Politics of Public Space in a Colonial City." In *Middle Eastern Cities 1900–1950: Public Spaces and Public Spheres in Transformation,* edited by Hans Chr. Korsholm Nielsen and Jakob Skovgaard-Petersen, 89–110. Aarhus, Denmark: Aarhus University Press.

Tibi, Bassam. 1997. *Arab Nationalism: Between Islam and the Nation-State.* 3d ed. London: Macmillan.

Twain, Mark. 1996 (1869). *The Innocents Abroad.* New York: Oxford University Press.

al-ʿUtari, ʿAbd al Ghani. 1986. *ʿAbqariyyat Shamiyya* (Damascene geniuses). Damascus: al-Hindi Press.

Van Dam, Nikolaos. 1996. *The Struggle for Power in Syria: Politics and Society under Asad and the Baʿth Party.* London: I. B. Tauris.

Van Dusen, Michael H. 1972. "Political Integration and Regionalism in Syria." *Middle East Journal* 26 (2): 123–136.

——— 1975. "Downfall of a Traditional Elite." In *Political Elites and Political Development in the Middle East,* edited by Frank Tachau, 115–155. Cambridge, Mass.: Schenkman/Wiley.

Waldner, David. 1999. *State Building and Late Development.* Ithaca, N.Y.: Cornell University Press.

Waltz, Susan E. 1990. "Another View of Feminine Networks: Tunisian Women and the Development of Political Efficacy." *International Journal of Middle East Studies* 22: 21–36.

Watson, Helen. 1992. *Women in the City of the Dead.* London: Hurst and Company.

Wedeen, Lisa. 1999. *Ambiguities of Domination: Politics, Rhetoric, and Symbols in Contemporary Syria.* Chicago: University of Chicago Press.

Weidman, Hazel Hitson. 1986. "On Ambivalence in the Field." In *Women in the Field: Anthropological Experiences,* 2d ed., edited by Peggy Golde, 239–263. Berkeley: University of California Press.

Weulersse, Jacques. 1946. *Paysans de Syrie et du Proche-Orient.* Paris: Gallimard.

Whitaker, Brian. 2001. "Cartoonist Gives Syria a New Line in Freedom." *Guardian Unlimited,* 3 April. http://www.guardian.co.uk/international/story/0,3604,467467,00.html.

Wiener, Margaret. 1999. "'Pay No Attention to the Man behind the Curtain': Irreverent Notes on Gender and Ethnography." *Anthropology and Humanism* 24 (2): 95–108.

Wikan, Unni. 1980. *Life among the Poor in Cairo.* Translated by Ann Henning. London: Tavistock.

——— 1982. *Behind the Veil in Arabia: Women in Oman.* Baltimore, Md.: Johns Hopkins University Press.

——— 1996. *Tomorrow, God Willing: Self-Made Destinies in Cairo.* Chicago: University of Chicago Press.

Wolf, Naomi. 1991. *The Beauty Myth: How Images of Beauty Are Used against Women.* London: Vintage.

Yamani, Mai Ahmed Zaki. 1987. "Fasting and Feasting: Some Social Aspects of the Observance of Ramadan in Saudi Arabia." In *The Diversity of the Muslim Community: Anthropological Essays in Memory of Peter Lienhardt,* edited by Ahmed al-Shahi. London: Ithaca, 1987.

——— 1997. "Changing the Habits of a Lifetime: The Adaptation of Hejazi Dress to the New Social Order." In *Languages of Dress in the Middle East,* edited by Nancy Lindisfarne-Tapper and Bruce Ingham, 55–66. London: Curzon.

Zubaida, Sami. 1989. *Islam, the People and the State: Essays on Political Ideas and Movements in the Middle East.* London: Routledge.

Zuhur, Sherifa. 1992. *Revealing Reveiling: Islamist Gender Ideology in Contemporary Egypt.* Albany: State University of New York Press.

Filmography

Anzur, Najdat Isma'il. 1994. *Nihayat Rajul Shuja*ᶜ (The end of a brave man). Thirty-episode serial. Damascus: Sharikat Sham al-Duwaliyya.
1996. *Ukhwat al-Turab* (Brothers of the earth). Thirty-episode serial. Damascus: Sharikat al-Sham al-Duwaliyya.

Haqqi, Haytham. 1996. *Khan al-Harir* (The silk bazaar). Thirty-episode serial. Aleppo: Sharikat Halab al-Duwaliyya.

Jabri, Ghassan. 1987. *La-ki. . . .Ya Sham* (To you . . . Damascus). Fifteen-episode serial. Damascus: Syrian Arab Television.
1986. *Yahud Dimashq* (Jews of Damascus). Documentary. Damascus: Syrian Arab Television.

Kawkash, 'Ala' al-Din. 1994. *Abu Kamil, Part II.* Thirty-episode serial. Damascus: Syrian Arab Television.

Lutfi, Lutfi. 1993. *Basmat al-Huzn* (Smile of sadness). Fifteen-episode serial. Damascus: Syrian Arab Television.
1995. *Qissat Hayy al-Qanawat* (Story of the neighborhood of al-Qanawat). Documentary.

Mahshawi, Ramiz. 1993–94. *Dhakiratuna Sha'biyya* (Our popular memory). Series. Damascus: Syrian Arab Television.

Malas, Muhammad. 1984. *Ahlam al-Madina* (Dreams of the city). Feature film. Damascus: National Film Organization.

al-Malla, Bassam. 1993. *Ayyam Shamiyya* (Damascene days). Fifteen-episode serial. Damascus: Syrian Arab Television.

al-Malla, Mu'min. 1994. *Min Nashwat al-Madi* (Intoxication with the past). Series. Damascus: Syrian Arab Television.

Midani, Hind. 1987. *Dimashq: Masafat al-Nazar* (Damascus: A point of view). Documentary.

Syrian Arab Television. 1993–1994. *Dirasat al-Qur'an* (Qur'anic studies). Series with Shaykh Muhammad Sa'id Ramadan al-Buti. Damascus: Syrian Arab Television.

Tutunji, Mamduh. 1993–1994. *Ayyam Ramadaniyya* (Ramadan days). Series. Damascus: Syrian Arab Television.

Zarzuri, Haytham Muhammad. 1992. "Sahra ma'a Usrat *Ayyam Shamiyya*" (An evening with the *Damascene Days* cast). Damascus: Syrian Arab Television.

Index

Page numbers in italics indicate illustrations.

Christa Salamandra holds a D.Phil. in anthropology from the Institute of Social and Cultural Anthropology, University of Oxford. She is Assistant Professor of Anthropology, Lehman College, The City University of New York, and has been a visiting lecturer in the Department of Anthropology, The School of Oriental and African Studies, University of London, and a visiting professor at Lebanese American University in Beirut.